Regicide and republic

England 1603–1

Graham E. Seel

CAMBRIDGE
UNIVERSITY PRESS

For all Stuart historians at The Manchester Grammar School

CAMBRIDGE UNIVERSITY PRESS
Cambridge, New York, Melbourne, Madrid, Cape Town, Singapore, São Paulo, Delhi

Cambridge University Press
The Edinburgh Building, Cambridge CB2 8RU, UK

www.cambridge.org
Information on this title: www.cambridge.org/9780521589888

© Cambridge University Press 2001

First published 2001
6th printing 2009

Printed in the United Kingdom at the University Press, Cambridge

A catalogue record for this publication is available from the British Library

ISBN 978-0-521-58988-8 paperback

Map artwork by Kathy Baxendale

The cover shows a painting of Cromwell after the Battle of Marston Moor (oil on canvas) by Ernest Crofts (1847–1911). Reproduced courtesy of Towneley Hall Art Gallery and Museum, Burnley, Lancashire/Bridgeman Art Library.

ACKNOWLEDGEMENTS

Barnaby's Picture Library/Fotomas Index: p.39; *Laud's dream* (engraving) by English School (17th century), Ashmolean Museum, Oxford, UK/Bridgeman Art Library (BAL): p.62; *The execution of the earl of Strafford (1593–1641) on Tower Hill, 22 May 1641* (engraving) by German School (17th century), Ashmolean Museum/BAL: p.77; *England's ark secured and the enemies to the parliament and kingdom overwhelmed (1645–46)* (engraving, b/w photo) by English School (17th century), Ashmolean Museum/BAL: p.103; *An allegory of the events surrounding King Charles I in 1649* (engraving) by English School (17th century), Ashmolean/BAL: p.116; *Coronation procession of Charles II to Westminster from the Tower of London, 1661*, by Dirck Stoop (c.1614–c.1683), Museum of London, UK/BAL: p.161; by permission of the British Library: p.29; Corsham Court Collection /photograph: Photographic Survey, Courtauld Institute of Art: p.3; Mary Evans Picture Library: pp.82, 91, 109, 180; The Fotomas Index: pp.23, 66, 69, 74, 80, 100, 114, 129, 140, 143, 146, 176, 177, 183, 193, 196; Hulton/Archive: p.43; *detail of Thomas Wentworth, 1st earl of Strafford*, by an unknown artist, by courtesy of the National Portrait Gallery, London: p.52; *detail of William Laud* by an unknown artist, by courtesy of the National Portrait Gallery: p.57; The Royal Collection ©2000, Her Majesty Queen Elizabeth II: pp.12, 33.

Picture Research by Sandie Huskinson-Rolfe of PHOTOSEEKERS

Contents

Politics and religion, 1603–29

1

England in 1603

Introduction

It is extraordinary that the death of Elizabeth I in 1603 did not result in a political crisis, perhaps even civil war. The virgin queen had failed to produce an heir and there were a number of contenders for the English throne and the Tudor inheritance. Nevertheless, shortly after the queen's death, James VI, the Stuart king of Scotland, was successfully proclaimed as her successor and henceforth took the dual title of King James VI of Scotland and King James I of England. Yet, within 40 years of James's accession, England was divided by civil war. To find an explanation for this has proved to be one of the most intractable historical problems in English history.

Before considering the key events and developments of early and mid seventeenth-century England, we need to consider an outline view of the condition of this country in the latter period of the reign of Elizabeth I. The actions and words of individuals as important as Sir Thomas Wentworth, William Laud, John Pym and Oliver Cromwell, all of whom were born in the Elizabethan period, cannot be explained without some knowledge of England before the arrival of James Stuart.

A decade of crises, 1593–1603

In 1598 Elizabeth celebrated her 40th year as queen, four decades in which, for the large part, she had ruled with care, caution and with no little skill. At a time when other countries were being divided by religious conflict between Catholic and Protestant, Elizabeth had managed to avoid driving either group to rebellion, mainly by desiring not to make 'windows into men's souls'. Instead, she deliberately steered a **middle way** between the two extremes. Moreover, at a time when royal marriages often caused political division and sometimes even civil war, Elizabeth had refused to marry. Another cause of potential political division was **faction** at **court** but, in this respect also, the queen, at least until the very end of her reign, had managed to balance different factions.

The **middle way** became a term used to describe the religious settlement fashioned by Elizabeth in 1559, which was a compromise between Catholicism and Protestantism. Notably, although celebration of the mass was henceforth forbidden, bishops remained.

A **faction** is a small group of courtiers, usually based on support for the leading figure, or figures, of the group, for example the Howards, though the identity was often based on policy as well, for example war with Spain. Monarchs usually listened to different factions at the same time. If they listened to one only then an excluded faction might out of frustration resort to violence, as was the case with Essex and his followers in 1601.

The royal **court** was both a physical and a political entity, and although usually based in the palace at Whitehall it would also accompany the monarch on any royal progress into the country. By 1585 it was

Elizabeth I with figures representing Time and Death in an allegorical portrait, painted after her death, by an unknown artist. Her appearance is in vivid contrast to the glorious representations of the queen from the earlier part of the reign.

War with Spain

Yet, in the last ten years of Elizabeth's reign, England was beset by no less than four major crises: a foreign war, a rebellion in Ireland, a court revolt and an economic depression. Each on its own represented a challenge to Elizabeth's government but, combined, they proved a severe test.

The foreign war was against Spain, the wealthiest and most powerful of all European states. As the leading Catholic state, Spain had, for some time, been attempting to put down a rebellion against its authority in the Netherlands (also known as the United Provinces or Holland). In 1585 England had gone to war in support of the Netherlands, a fellow Protestant state. This was the immediate background to the Spanish Armada campaign in 1588. Even though the Armada was defeated, the Spanish did not give up and the war dragged on until 1604.

Essex and the revolt in Ireland

By the late 1590s it had been clear that the earl of Tyrone represented a challenge to English authority in Ireland which had to be put down, not least because the Irish were for the large part Catholic and thus represented what

also firmly established as a centre of artistic performance and patronage, an aspect which flourished during the reign of Charles I. The court was composed of hundreds of servants known as the household who were attendant upon the needs of the monarch.

Ulster is the most northern of the four Irish provinces, comprising the counties of Fermanagh, Tyrone, Londonderry, Antrim, Armagh, Down, Donegal, Cavan and Monaghan.

The **Poor Laws** were medieval in origin. Drawn up by parliament, they enshrined the principle of compulsory giving. Amongst other things they included provision for the relief of those genuinely unable to work and measures to restrain vagrants. By the early seventeenth century it is possible to speak of a national Poor Law system in England.

Identify four problems that Elizabeth bequeathed to her successor, James VI and I.

Monopolies, which gave to the purchaser the sole right either to make or to distribute a particular commodity, were sold by the crown. They became a grievance of the political nation and featured in the parliaments of 1621 and 1624 (see pp. 13 and 14).

many in England believed were the 'enemy within'. In 1599 the earl of Essex, the queen's favourite, led a force to crush a rebellion in **Ulster** headed by Tyrone. Having failed in his objective, however, and believing that his position at court was under threat, Essex returned to London and launched a revolt against royal authority – an action for which he was executed in 1601. In the same year, the Irish Rebellion, briefly supported by a Spanish force, was ultimately defeated.

Economic depression

The economic depression was caused by a series of bad harvests, an effect of which was the doubling of the price of wheat in the three years from 1594 to 1597. There is evidence of starvation, or near starvation, in parts of northern England and it is certain that the number of able-bodied beggars and vagabonds increased. The **Poor Laws** had to be revised in 1598 and 1601 in order to help deal with the problem.

Parliamentary opposition

There were other problems that resulted from these crises. In particular, Elizabeth had to meet with parliament in 1589, 1593, 1597–98 and 1601 in order to request money. Consequently, to the higher prices of the 1590s was added the extra burden of higher taxes. Even as they agreed to more taxes, MPs grumbled about financial devices such as **monopolies** and complained about what they saw as the abuse of royal power. Alarmingly for the crown, as more was asked of parliament, MPs began to demand more in privileges and freedoms.

What was the nature of the government that had to deal with the consequences of these several crises?

The government of England

At the head of the government was the crown. It enjoyed extensive powers collectively known as the royal prerogative and ruled by means of the main formal institution of government, the privy council, supplemented from time to time by a parliament (see page 5). The privy council had its origins in the medieval royal council. It varied in size from no more than 11 in 1590 to 13 in 1603. It grew steadily to over 30 during the reign of James VI and I and was about 40 strong under Charles I. It was composed of men chosen directly by the monarch. They were expected to discuss matters of state and present advice to the monarch. According to a contemporary of Elizabeth, the council acted as 'the wheels that hold the chariot of England upright'. It discharged a wide range of political, administrative and judicial functions.

Crown
- ruled by divine right
- advised by ministers
- called, suspended and dissolved parliament
- appointed archbishops and bishops
- issued proclamations (orders which had the force of law but could not be used to take away life or property)
- appointed judges
- ruled with the advice of the privy council, which consisted of the chief officers of state – lord chancellor, lord treasurer, chancellor of the exchequer, lord high admiral, secretaries of state, archbishop of Canterbury, some lords lieutenant and officers of the royal household. Its size varied over time

Parliament sat infrequently: during James I's reign parliament sat for a total of about 33 months; from 1625 to 1640 it sat for about 11 months

The crown depended upon the voluntary support of the local lords and gentry in order to ensure that its will was implemented

Parliament

Composed of:

House of Lords
- 24–26 archbishops and bishops
- 50–60 temporal lords: hereditary peers and great officers of state

House of Commons
- consisted of two members for every county and two from each borough (a town granted special privileges by royal charter)
- in 1603 there were 462 members

Its functions included:
- creating laws (called statutes)
- granting taxation to the crown (subsidies)
- acting as a court
- offering advice to the monarch

Since justices of the peace were usually MPs the crown could not afford to offend them in either capacity

Local government

Carried out principally by:

justices of the peace
- appointed annually from among the leading landowners
- responsible for law and order
- answerable to the assize judges (12 judges from Westminster who travelled around the country to judge cases in courts of assize)

lords and deputy lieutenants
- responsible for recruiting, equipping, training and commanding the local militia

The machinery of state in early seventeenth-century England. Members of the political nation served the crown and their local communities. Justices of the peace, for example, were usually MPs. In certain circumstances, this dual allegiance could lead to dangerous stresses within the system. This, in turn, could result in a 'functional breakdown' of government.

In an age when there was no civil service, efficient royal government was largely dependent upon the monarch obtaining and maintaining the goodwill of members of the political nation – composed of those members of society who, as a consequence of their wealth (usually measured in terms of property, family connections and education) enjoyed power and influence in the political process. Indeed, MPs would also often act in their localities as **justices of the peace**, a dual role that sometimes resulted in tension. However, this was generally avoided through the distribution of royal **patronage**. In turn, councillors could use patronage to manipulate parliament and control local government.

The monarch was powerful but not all-powerful. The crown had to live within the law of the land. Judges, even though appointed by the crown, did not always make the legal judgements the crown wanted and were obliged to uphold the law in the form of **common law** and **statute law**. England was, therefore, a mixed monarchy rather than an absolute monarchy and the Magna Carta of 1215 remained an important constitutional document. Nevertheless, at a time when many European monarchs were trying to establish some kind of royal absolutism, many English people feared that England might go the same way.

The church in England

The government of early modern England also included the church. Religious beliefs and practices were central to people's lives. They believed that Heaven and Hell really existed. They went to church at least once a week. There was only one religion, Christianity, as was the case throughout Europe. There was only one Christian church, the Church of England. The head of the Church of England was the crown, not the archbishop of Canterbury. England had what was known as an established or Erastian church, one attached to and subordinate to the government. This had been so since the reign of Henry VIII. Until then, the church in England had been part of the Catholic Church, with the pope in Rome as its head. Everyone in England was a member of the church, at least in theory. It was an age of religious uniformity. The idea of religious toleration did not exist in the sixteenth century. There were still some who believed in the Catholic faith, who saw the pope as their spiritual leader, but they were a persecuted minority. They had to practise their Catholic faith in secret. Most Englishmen believed that the pope was the Antichrist. Because people's religion followed the monarch's, because religious uniformity was the norm, religious identity became tied up with national identity. A defining feature of late sixteenth-century England was its Protestant faith. This helped to bring it into conflict with Catholic states such as Spain, as was the case from 1585 onwards.

Catholicism was not the only challenge to the established church. Many Protestants wanted to make it more Protestant. They disliked Elizabeth's middle way. These reformers, the 'hotter sort of Protestant', became known as Puritans. They wanted to purify the church of any form of Catholic influence. Some Puritans wanted to simplify the church service and little more. Others wanted to reform the whole structure of the church, to replace the **episcopalian** church with a **Presbyterian** version. As long as Elizabeth was queen, English Puritans would not get very far. They looked with hope to her successor.

The royal succession

Unmarried, Elizabeth had no children to succeed her. The closest royal claimant was a descendant of her aunt, Margaret Tudor, sister of Henry VIII, who had married the king of Scotland. Their great-grandson was James VI. There was no one else with as strong a claim. Cecil, the dominant figure at Elizabeth's court in the last few years of her reign, made secret contact with James VI in order to ensure that, on Elizabeth's death, authority was passed quickly and peacefully to the Stuart king. 'The queen is dead. Long live the king.'

An **episcopalian** church was governed by the episcopacy. This was a hierarchy of bishops and archbishops, appointed by the head of the church.

Presbyterian churches were governed by presbyteries. A presbytery was a hierarchy of church elders, often appointed by the church congregation.

What were the two main challenges to the established church?

2

The reign of James I, 1603–25

Focus questions

◆ What was the relationship between James I and parliament?

◆ How were relations between James I and parliament affected by financial matters?

◆ How serious were religious divisions in England?

◆ How were relations between James I and parliament affected by foreign affairs?

Significant dates

1603	James VI of Scotland becomes James I of England.
1604	The Treaty of London is signed with Spain. James I holds the Hampton Court Conference. James I calls his first parliament, which lasts until 1611.
1605	The Gunpowder Plot is uncovered.
1606	Bate's Case occurred.
1610	The Great Contract between king and parliament is drawn up.
1614	James calls his second parliament (known as the Addled Parliament).
1615	George Villiers (earl of Buckingham from 1617) becomes James's favourite.
1618	The Thirty Years' War breaks out in the Holy Roman Empire.
1621	James calls his third parliament.
1623	Prince Charles and Villiers (to be made duke of Buckingham upon his return) travel to Madrid.
1624	James calls his fourth parliament.
1625	War breaks out against Spain. James I dies.

Overview

In March 1603 James Stuart, James VI of Scotland, also became James I of England. His 22-year rule of England has been the cause of great historical debate, mainly in the context of the civil war that broke out within 18 years of his death. Some historians have argued that James I was a key factor in bringing war about as his method and policies of government made relations between crown and parliament, between king and country very strained. His son, Charles I, certainly did not help improve relations, so this school of thought argues, but the root of the problem lay with James I. Other historians view James I more sympathetically. They believe that his government of England was, in the circumstances, quite successful and that he managed the problems of governing England with some skill. This school does not hold James I as being significantly responsible for causing the English Civil Wars.

So, what was the reality? How well did James I govern England? What problems did he face? How did he deal with them? If the key political relationship in early modern England was, moreover, that between crown and parliament, how well did the new Stuart king get on with English bishops, Lords and Commons? We need first to examine the nature of that relationship.

Crown and parliament

Introduction

The powers and privileges possessed by the crown are collectively known as the royal prerogative. A key aspect of the royal prerogative concerned parliament. The monarch could summon and dissolve parliament at will. The crown also had the ability to prorogue parliament, in other words to adjourn a session and thus leave open the prospect of calling it to a sitting at a later date. This was an important weapon in the management of parliament. It meant that the crown could prevent the development of any sustained opposition. The sovereign also had the right to veto any legislation passed by parliament. (Elizabeth rejected a total of seventy bills during her entire reign. James I was to veto seven bills, Charles I one.) The prerogative also gave monarchs the right to appoint and dismiss ministers, judges and bishops and to declare peace and war.

Though the prerogative gave monarchs great power, it did not allow them absolute power. England was often called a 'mixed monarchy', in which political power is shared, and the key body with which English monarchs had to work was parliament.

Parliament is usually seen as including the House of Lords and the **House of Commons**, though strictly it involves the crown as well. This is best illustrated by the need for all three branches of government to approve legislation before it becomes the law of the land. The House of Lords included the Lords Spiritual and **Lords Temporal**. The former consisted of 24 bishops as well as the archbishops of York and Canterbury, all appointed by the monarch.

The **House of Commons** was far larger numerically than the Lords, totalling 462 in 1586 and 507 by the meeting of the Long Parliament in 1640. This growth was the result of new boroughs, or towns, being enfranchised.

The **Lords Temporal** were hereditary peers, who were non-churchmen. By 1628 they were to have grown in number to 126 from 81 in 1615, as many peerages were sold by the crown.

The Lords Temporal were hereditary peers, either dukes, marquises, earls, viscounts or barons (in descending order of rank). An appointment to a title was often a reward for service to king and country, which could take the form of paying money into the royal accounts. Elizabeth had been reluctant to create peerages. James I was not. This expansion of the peerage was soon to become a political issue. English monarchs could usually rely on the support of the House of Lords, which saw itself as trying to keep the peace between the crown and the more argumentative House of Commons.

The House of Commons consisted of MPs who represented a certain territorial area, or constituency. There were two types of constituency, county and borough or country and town. The MPs were chosen by election but only men who owned land with a rateable value of 40 shillings a year or more had the franchise, the right to choose MPs. In other words, the franchise was restricted to property owners. It has been estimated that, during this period, the total electorate numbered some 300,000, which amounted to more than a quarter of the adult male population of England. Contested elections were rare. The victor was normally a nominee of the greater landowners.

Why would the monarch call a parliament? There were three main reasons. Firstly, it was a useful way of obtaining advice from and the support of the political nation. Secondly, parliament was needed to pass legislation. Although the crown did have the right to rule by issuing proclamations, a form of royal decree, these were limited in scope and often difficult to enforce. Statute law, as the laws passed by parliament were known, was more effective. The proposal for a new law, known as a bill, had to go through a number of stages in both Houses before being sent to the monarch for final approval, after which, if given, it became an act of parliament. In Elizabeth's parliaments, there was an average of 126 bills per session, of which around a quarter normally became acts. Few of these acts would have come from the king's government, unlike today. Thirdly, parliament could provide the crown with a form of income known as subsidies. Subsidies were a property tax, levied on goods and land. The rate of tax on goods was 2 shillings in the pound (10 per cent), on land 4 shillings in the pound (20 per cent). In 1603 one subsidy was worth about £70,000. Parliament would normally grant a number of subsidies at the same time. Only the House of Commons could introduce proposals to raise subsidies, which in this respect made it more important than the House of Lords.

If the crown had the royal prerogative, peers and MPs had parliamentary privilege as a counter balance. They claimed the right not to be arrested when parliament was sitting – except if accused of treason, felony or breach of the peace. Both Elizabeth and James had refrained from arresting any member while a parliament was sitting. Charles I was to be less cautious. Both Houses also claimed the right to free speech. Yet, Elizabeth, James and Charles all believed that parliament could debate only those issues that they put before it. They resisted parliament's attempts to discuss what they considered to be part of the royal prerogative, matters such as religion and foreign policy. The boundaries between what the Houses could and could not discuss remained necessarily vague. They were often breached, sometimes with disastrous consequences. A third privilege claimed by the Houses was the right to determine their own membership. They were particularly sensitive to government attempts to pack the Commons by ensuring the election of its nominees. This issue was to arise as early as 1604.

Identify the three component parts of parliament and list its main functions.

The new king

James I was 36 years old when he became the king of England. He had been king of Scotland for 35 years; during his adult life he had governed Scotland with considerable skill. He was married with three young children, two of them boys. Thus, the royal succession was secure. He was something of an intellectual, enjoying theological argument and debate and writing a number of pamphlets.

The most significant of these was *The trew law of free monarchies* (1598) in which he expounded on the theory of the divine right of kings. This was the belief that 'kings are not only God's lieutenants upon earth, and sit upon God's throne, but even by God himself they are called gods', as he told parliament in a speech on 21 March 1610. James has often been criticised for the forthright manner in which he reminded parliaments that his authority was his by divine right. It is alleged that this resulted in difficulties between this king and his parliaments, for MPs feared that divine right could be used to justify an absolute rather than a mixed monarchy. Yet, in this same speech, James made it clear that he saw himself as obliged to observe the fundamental laws of the kingdom. He said that 'the king *with his parliament* here are absolute . . . in making or forming any sort of laws'.

What, therefore, were James I's aims as king of England? His main ones seem to have been:
- a political union of the kingdoms of England and Scotland;
- peace abroad;
- religious stability and greater conformity at home.

We need to reconsider these aims once we have studied the reign of James I.

The first parliament, 1604–11

Within a year of his becoming king, James met his first English parliament. Relations soon became strained over several issues. One of these was interference by the king's courts in an election result. One of the high courts

The sharp intelligence of King James VI and I is clear to the viewer in this portrait.

overturned the election of an MP who had defeated a government councillor, Sir John Fortescue. MPs angrily disputed the outcome, ordering the elected candidate, Sir Francis Goodwin, to take his seat. At this point James intervened, stating that the Commons 'derived all matters of privilege from him and by his grant' and ordered them 'as an absolute king' to attend a conference with the judges. In the end, the issue was resolved amicably: a fresh election was held and a parliamentary committee was established to resolve election disputes.

Historical opinion has divided over the significance of this event. The traditional school argued that James's actions provoked the Commons into drawing up the **Form of Apology and Satisfaction**. Revisionists conclude that James, in finally agreeing to another election, accepted a tactful compromise. They assert that there is no real evidence that the affair, in itself, unduly soured relations between the king and the Commons.

The second issue causing strain came about as a result of James I's attempts to create a political union between England and Scotland. These came to nothing, despite James's best efforts over several years. Many of his subjects thought that a 'community of commerce' would cause English prosperity to be

The **Form of Apology and Satisfaction**, 1604, was a document drawn up by a committee of MPs in which they rehearsed their privileges and liberties at length. The document was not passed by the Commons and never presented to the king.

undermined by Scottish poverty. They also feared an influx of Scots. Finally, James's desire to secure union under one law alarmed many. Rather than trying to merge the two legal systems, English MPs would consider a union with Scotland only on the basis that Scottish laws were subordinate to English.

It has been argued that the failure of the union project produced a dangerous distrust between king and Commons, particularly when James made himself 'king of Great Britain' and adopted a single 'Union Flag' for England and Scotland by royal proclamation. However, there was resistance to James's scheme in Scotland as well as England. Moreover, disaffection between the king and the Commons can be seen as a consequence of MPs being encouraged by the House of Lords to resist the scheme.

In 1605–6 the Gunpowder Plot caused further tension (see page 22). MPs were so relieved that the plot was stillborn that they voted James a financial grant of £400,000. It was soon spent. By the time of the fourth session of the parliament, in 1610, the most pressing matter was that of royal finances. Many MPs were resentful of the king's use of wardship and purveyance (see page 15). They were particularly fearful of impositions (see page 16), against which the lawyer MPs raised constitutional objections. They argued that a fourteenth-century law prohibited the king from receiving monies from custom duties that had not been sanctioned by parliament. This was the background to the Great Contract (see page 19) which collapsed in the fifth session. As a result of this, James I dissolved the parliament. It had lasted for almost seven years, an unusually long period.

What were the main reasons for relations between James and his first parliament becoming strained?

The second parliament, 1614

If James's first parliament was longer than most, his second was very short. It lasted for just three months. It had been called to provide finances to help meet increasing royal expenditure. This parliament had such a short life because the Commons refused to grant **subsidies** unless impositions were abolished. The latter James considered as part of his prerogative. He called the House of Commons 'a body without a head . . . At their meetings nothing is heard but cries, shouts and confusion. I am surprised that my ancestors should ever have permitted such an institution to come into existence.' He did add, 'I am obliged to put up with what I cannot get rid of.'

Subsidies were a form of parliamentary taxation. They were a tax on land and other forms of property.

He meant parliament as an institution. The 1614 parliament he soon dissolved. It passed no legislation at all and thus became known as the Addled Parliament.

The third parliament, 1621

After the final session of the 1604–11 parliament followed by the Addled Parliament, James seems to have tried to manage without parliaments and to

The Thirty Years' War
(1618–48) was a long,
complex and bloody series
of wars involving most of
the continental great
powers. It began with a
dispute between the
Habsburgs and a German
ruler, the elector Palatine;
James I's daughter was
married to the elector.

Impeachment is a legal
process by which MPs can
bring government ministers
and officials to account. In
England, it involved the
Commons putting charges
to the Lords. The process
died out in Britain but has
survived in the USA.

As a means to resolving
the Palatinate Crisis (see
p. 28) James was pursuing
complex negotiations
which would have resulted
in **Charles's marriage** to
the daughter of the king of
Spain, the infanta.
However, MPs were deeply
unhappy at the prospect of
the heir to the throne
marrying a Spanish
Catholic.

**George Villiers, duke of
Buckingham,**
(1592–1628) had in
1614, at the age of 22,
been introduced at court
and quickly proved himself
able to supply the
emotional requirements of
the king. He consequently
experienced a meteoric
rise from gentleman of the
bedchamber in 1615 to
earl of Buckingham in
1617, marquis of
Buckingham in 1618 and

try and finance future expenditure by resorting to various feudal devices. For seven years, he ruled without parliament. By 1621, however, he had no choice but to call parliament again. His continued extravagance and the outbreak of the **Thirty Years' War** meant that he had to summon another parliament. This happened just as the country was experiencing one of the most severe economic depressions of the seventeenth century.

The first session, in which James was quickly granted two subsidies, was a success. Parliament seems to have forgotten its grievance over impositions. More probable is the argument that MPs realised that to raise the issue would jeopardise their continued sitting. Instead, MPs concentrated their resentment against monopolists and, in order to remove them from their positions of influence, revived the medieval device of **impeachment**. It was successfully used for the first time since 1459 in order to try Sir Giles Mompesson, who had been granted a patent for the licensing of inns, and Sir Francis Michell, a monopolist of gold and silver thread. In the process, the lord chancellor, Francis Bacon, was impeached on a charge of corruption. However, the second session was less successful and lasted less than a month. The Commons drew up and approved the Protestation, in which MPs insisted that freedom of speech was part of their 'ancient and undoubted birthright'. On the next day, James I ripped the Protestation from the Journals of the House and then arrested several of the more outspoken MPs. Apart from the subsidy bill, the parliament had achieved nothing.

Yet, one week later, James said that he wanted 'to govern our people in the same manner as our . . . predecessors'. The disagreement was the result of a misunderstanding. It was unclear whether the king wanted MPs to discuss foreign policy and the subject of Prince **Charles's marriage**. The end of the 1621 parliament did not mark a breakdown in crown–parliament relations.

The fourth parliament, 1624–25

There is evidence that James did not intend to call another parliament but, in 1624, he had to. The situation of the Palatinate was worse than ever (see page 28). When he met the parliament James assured MPs that 'ye may freely advise me'. His son Charles and his favourite, **George Villiers, duke of Buckingham**, had recently returned from their disastrous trip to **Madrid** determined upon war with Spain. They worked with leaders of the Commons to ensure the new parliament was a success. Although James was voted three subsidies, they were insufficient for the needs of government.

The main issue now dividing king and Commons was over what type of war should be fought. If he wanted to fight at all, James wanted to fight a land war for the Palatinate. MPs, remembering the exploits of Elizabethan privateers, wanted to fight a war at sea against Spain. In order to try and ensure that the money that they granted was spent on the war they wanted, the Commons specified the ways in which the subsidies should be spent. To the subsidy bill, they attached four appropriation clauses, which stated among other things that a navy should set sail as soon as possible.

Despite imposing on the king's prerogative by these appropriation clauses and by impeaching Cranfield, the lord treasurer and an opponent of Buckingham's quest for war with Spain, MPs were on good terms with the crown. In part, this was because James I accepted the Monopolies Act, which declared grants of monopolies to individuals illegal. More significantly, England was going to war against an old enemy of England. Thus ended 21 years of peace.

What is the main reason that James called parliaments in 1621 and 1624?

Royal finances

Introduction

It was understood by all concerned that the crown would ask for subsidies only during times of emergency, which usually meant war. As long as the country remained at peace, the crown was expected to rely upon its own resources, perpetuating the medieval notion that the sovereign should 'live of his own'. Asking for parliamentary subsidies was meant to be a last resort – a form of extraordinary income. The crown was therefore obliged to raise revenue from other sources, from ordinary income. So, from where did the crown normally raise its income?

Ordinary sources of crown revenue

The main source was rents from crown lands. The monarch was the largest landowner in the country – though, by 1603, many lands had been sold off to raise extra revenue, a short-term move that created long-term problems. In addition, the crown obtained revenue from certain sources because it was head of church and state. Most were based on ancient feudal rights. They included:

- Purveyance. This was the crown's right to buy and transport provisions at less than half the market price. Though purveyance provided the monarch with an obvious source of income, it annoyed the person who sold the goods.
- Wardship. When a minor – under the age of 21 if male, under 14 if female – inherited property, he or she became a ward of the crown. The revenue of the minor's estate went to the crown. When the heir came of age, he was often forced to make a payment to the crown in order to regain control of his estate.
- Monopolies. The crown sold the sole right to make or distribute a particular product or commodity, usually for a number of years.

then duke of Buckingham in 1623 – the first non-royal duke to be created since 1551. The nature of the hatred that Buckingham induced in the Commons was so intense that it suggests that he was more than an empty-headed courtier or an attractive figure at court.

Charles and Buckingham set off for **Madrid** on horseback in February 1623, because they were impatient with the slow pace of the marriage negotiations. They donned false beards and called themselves Thomas and John Smith. Poorly treated, they were prevented from meeting with the infanta.

In 1606 John Bate refused to pay impositions on currants. When **Bate's case** was taken to court, the judges upheld the crown's right to levy impositions. A series of revised Books of Rates, the first of which was in 1608, made impositions ever more lucrative. They were worth £250,000 per annum by 1640.

What is meant by ordinary and extraordinary income? Give examples.

- Impositions. These were duties on goods entering or leaving the country, which were additional to those normally charged. After **Bate's case**, income from this source amounted to about £70,000 per annum, which was more than one subsidy was worth by the late 1620s.
- Forced loans. In special circumstances, the crown could also compel people to pay money to the state, even without the approval of parliament. The payment was a loan in name only.

In peacetime, the monarch would spend this money on the royal family, if the monarch had one (Elizabeth I did not), the royal household, royal palaces and the court. The attitude of the monarch towards royal expenditure was very significant. A frugal monarch could help maintain a balance between income and expenditure. An extravagant one would not. Elizabeth I had been so frugal as to be almost a miser. It soon became clear to which school James I belonged.

What was the state of royal finances in 1603? Reference has already been made to the extraordinary cost of the war with Spain. Thus, it is no surprise that Elizabeth had died leaving a public debt of £420,000. However, subsidies granted by parliament in 1601, totalling £300,000, were still to be collected. In addition, about £120,000 had been raised in the form of forced loans. In other words, James I inherited a kingdom with the books balanced, which is rather surprising. He saw himself 'like a poor man wandering about forty years in a wilderness and barren soil and now arrived at the land of promise'. After the poverty of the Scottish court, he was looking forward to the riches of England.

Royal expenditure

Robert Carr, earl of Somerset (d. 1645), fell from grace as a consequence of one of the greatest scandals of the age. In 1615 he was found guilty of poisoning Sir Thomas Overbury in the Tower. Overbury, an attendant of Carr's, probably had evidence that would have prevented his master's marriage to Frances Howard. Carr and his wife were condemned to be executed, although they were pardoned by James in 1622.

James, as the archbishop of York observed, was 'too much inclined to giving'. The numbers receiving pensions increased, one page of the chamber being awarded £300 per annum. Above all, James showered gifts on royal favourites, individuals who received special favours from the king simply because he liked them. James gave a Scottish favourite whose motto was 'Spend and God will send' more than £400,000. Sir **Robert Carr**, earl of Somerset, was James's favourite from 1607 until 1615. The countess of Somerset – the wife of Carr – received £10,000 on her marriage. Carr was replaced in the king's affections by George Villiers, who was soon to be created duke of Buckingham. During the course of the next 13 years, Buckingham was to become a significant political figure. James was infatuated with him and showered him with countless gifts.

The problem of extravagance was compounded by the fact that James appears to have been incapable of appreciating the value of money. Once,

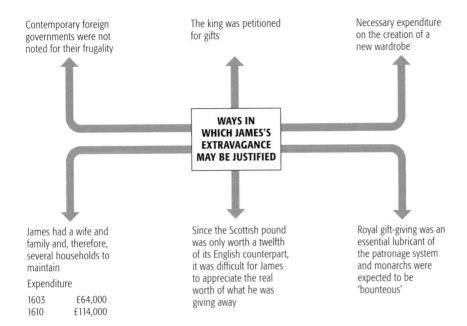

Contemporary foreign governments were not noted for their frugality

The king was petitioned for gifts

Necessary expenditure on the creation of a new wardrobe

WAYS IN WHICH JAMES'S EXTRAVAGANCE MAY BE JUSTIFIED

James had a wife and family and, therefore, several households to maintain

Expenditure

| 1603 | £64,000 |
| 1610 | £114,000 |

Since the Scottish pound was only worth a twelfth of its English counterpart, it was difficult for James to appreciate the real worth of what he was giving away

Royal gift-giving was an essential lubricant of the patronage system and monarchs were expected to be 'bounteous'

when he declared his intention to give £20,000 to his favourite Robert Carr, an exasperated lord treasurer, **Robert Cecil**

> 'left the money upon the ground in a room through which His Majesty was to pass: who, amazed at the quantity, as a sight not unpossibly his eyes never saw before, asked the treasurer whose money it was, who answered, "Yours, before you gave it away"; whereupon the king fell into a passion, protesting he was abused, never intending such gift: and casting himself upon the heap, scrabbled out the quantity of two or three hundred pounds, and swore he [Carr] should have no more.'

With the additional expenses of a young family and of court entertainment on a scale never allowed by Elizabeth, royal finances soon went into the red. The royal debt accumulated steadily for very nearly the whole of James's reign. In 1606 it was more than £700,000. Although reduced to £300,000 by 1610, it had risen to £500,000 by 1613. In 1618 it had grown to £900,000. This deterioration could not be linked with the costs of war because James ended the long-running war with Spain within a year of becoming king. There was the expense of the campaigns to control Ireland in the early 1600s but that was not a long-term commitment. The royal finances had become an urgent problem. What was to be done?

Expenditure could be curbed. Various lord treasurers tried to do so, especially Salisbury (1608–12) and Cranfield (1621–24). They had some success. However, James was hard to control. Courtiers disliked attempts to curb

Robert Cecil, earl of Salisbury (1563–1612), was an important figure in Elizabeth's government; he found his position strengthened after the execution of his rival, Essex, in 1601. He successfully straddled the reigns of Elizabeth and James and was lord treasurer from 1608.

James's extravagance meant that he had to use methods of taxation that depended on his use of the royal prerogative, especially since the monarch was expected to 'live of his own'
Insufficient subsidies from parliament meant that James was forced to exploit his prerogative taxation devices even more

HOW THE ROYAL DEBT DAMAGED RELATIONS BETWEEN CROWN AND PARLIAMENT

When James called parliament in the expectation of gaining subsidies, MPs criticised his use of prerogative taxation devices because:
- they provided the crown with money whose levy had not been sanctioned by parliament
- these devices – especially impositions – provided the crown with the potential to rule independently of parliament. MPs, therefore, granted insufficient subsidies or none at all

expenditure. Their opposition helps explain the downfall of Cranfield at the hands of the 1624 parliament.

Income could be increased. Salisbury was particularly active in doing so and in a variety of ways: revising rents, expanding the scope of impositions in the aftermath of the Bate's case and granting more monopolies. His efforts explain why the royal debt was reduced during his time as lord treasurer. New sources of income were also developed. Some were successful, others not. They included:

- The sale of honours. A new title, baronet, was created in 1611. Those who owned land worth £1,000 per annum or more could buy one for £1,095; by 1614, £90,000 had been raised in this way. In 1615 peerages were put up for sale, each costing £10,000. One historian has estimated that the crown gained at least £620,000 from the sale of honours during the period 1603–29, although at a political cost. Selling titles created disaffection amongst the long-established nobility.

- The Cockayne project of 1614. William Cockayne planned to export cloth in its finished, or dyed, state, rather than in its unfinished 'white' form. He promised to enrich James by £300,000 a year and was granted a monopoly. In fact, the whole scheme was a disaster. Cockayne was poorly funded and it damaged the interests of others, including the Dutch, who resented losing the privilege of importing English cloth. The main importers of English cloth went elsewhere for the product. His monopoly was ended in 1617. Such revenue-raising schemes could not be endlessly exploited and MPs were reluctant to provide subsidies on the scale that was needed to balance the books. The financial system was breaking down. More fundamental reform was needed.

The Great Contract, 1610

Only once was fundamental reform attempted. In 1610 Salisbury proposed that parliament should grant James a single payment of £600,000, and £200,000 each year, in return for which James would abolish the prerogative revenues of wardship and purveyance. It became known as the Great Contract. After initially agreeing to the idea, MPs had second thoughts. They were concerned that an annual grant of £200,000, the equivalent of roughly three subsidies, might weaken the position of parliament. On the other hand, the king came to believe that a grant of £200,000 was probably insufficient to meet the needs of government. The opportunity for such a radical reform did not occur again during the reign of either James I or his son. After 1610 the royal finances once more began to deteriorate. By 1625, when the war with Spain had hardly started, the debt totalled almost £1 million.

Religious policy

Introduction

Religious beliefs caused great disputes in early modern Europe. In the sixteenth century, the monopoly of the Catholic (or universal) Church in western Europe had been broken. Protestant churches gained support in many areas, most importantly from state governments. Religious wars – which were never just wars about religion – broke out in many countries. Under Henry VIII, England had rejected the authority of the Catholic Church, which it replaced with the Church of England. Under Elizabeth I, the Church of England developed as a kind of middle way in religious form and practice in order to make itself acceptable to both moderate Catholics and moderate Protestants. The more extreme Protestants, known as **Puritans**, became dissatisfied with this halfway house. They expected James I to support their plans, as Scotland was a more Protestant country than England. It had a **Presbyterian** Church – even though there was some form of episcopacy. The English Puritans saw James I as a hotter sort of Protestant and likely to reform the Church of England.

There were two features of the Anglican Church, already well established by 1603, which no English monarch could allow to be challenged. They were:
- the monarch was the head of the church, as laid down in the **Act of Supremacy**;
- the church was governed by bishops appointed by the crown.

Why was James so deeply in debt?

The term '**Puritans**' covered all those who wanted to purify the church, to remedy its faults and to reach new standards of godliness. They are often defined as 'the hotter sort of Protestants'.

A **Presbyterian** was a Puritan who wanted to reform the church organisation in a particular way. Presbyterians disliked the church being run by bishops (the episcopacy), who were wealthy and often corrupt. They disliked the church being controlled by the state (i.e. an Erastian church). Instead they wanted an independent church led by presbyters or elders, who were appointed by the members of the church to run church affairs.

According to the terms of the 1534 **Act of Supremacy**, the monarch was also the head of the church.

In addition, as in all states at the time, religious uniformity was an essential feature of religious – and social – order. All subjects were expected to follow the monarch's religious beliefs. Formal and open religious toleration was just not possible. This made the position of Catholics in England very difficult. Since their loyalty was first and foremost to the pope, they were open to the charge of treason. This was especially so from 1570, when Elizabeth I was **excommunicated** by the papacy. English Catholics were enemies of the state, the enemy within. As a result, they suffered harsh penal legislation. Between 1590 and 1603, 88 Catholics were executed, 53 of them priests.

The accession of a new king in 1603 meant that Catholics as well as Puritans petitioned James I for an improvement in their circumstances. These pressures suggested the need to create a new *via media*, or middle way, a Jacobean modification of the Elizabethan church settlement. It aimed to permit the majority of Puritans to remain within the existing national church but without jeopardising royal authority and the episcopal structure. The position of the Catholics in 1603 remained unclear. The initial issue was the Puritan challenge.

Puritans and the Hampton Court Conference

The English Puritans lost no time in making James aware of their hopes and expectations. As the king was riding south in April 1603, they presented him with the Millenary Petition, so called because it was supposed to carry 1,000 signatures. The petitioners requested that they be 'eased and relieved' of those ceremonies and practices which they considered to be remnants of the popish church. These included the use of the ring in marriage and bowing at the name of Jesus. They also asked that:

- the ministry be staffed by 'able and sufficient men';
- ministers be properly maintained;
- pluralism (the holding of more than one benefice or church living) be ended.

It was hoped that these measures would result in there being an educated preaching ministry. The proposals were extensive but moderate. There was no demand to abolish the episcopacy. The king, therefore, always keen to engage in theological debate, agreed to convene at Hampton Court in January 1604 a conference to discuss the requests put forward in the Millenary Petition.

The most famous incident of the Hampton Court Conference came after one of the Puritans mentioned the word 'presbytery'. James became agitated. He said that, if the office of bishop was abolished, he knew what would become of his supremacy: 'no bishop, no king'. Once the church hierarchy was removed, the state hierarchy would be vulnerable. In conclusion, James told

A person who is **excommunicated** is expelled from the church by the pope. It was believed that anyone who was excommunicated was thereby condemned to Hell on death.

What was a Puritan? What were the main beliefs of those known as Presbyterians?

the Puritans that 'if this is all they have to say, I will make them conform themselves or I will harry them out of this land or else do worse'.

On the final day, the Puritans were then called in and informed that the great majority of the practices to which they objected, such as the wearing of the **surplice** and the hood, were to be maintained. Nevertheless, they were promised a number of reforms, including a reduction in the number of pluralists and a new translation of the Bible. This became the Authorised Version of 1611.

A **surplice** is a white linen vestment worn over the cassock.

The conference would, James hoped, create the context in which Presbyterians could more easily be identified. In order to give reality to this hope, convocation, the church body that paralleled parliament, met in April 1604 and produced a total of 141 canons that regulated all aspects of church life. One of these canons contained an oath, which was unacceptable to the more hardline Presbyterians and thus distinguished them from the more moderate Puritans. This divided the reformers and thus diminished the opposition to James. Moreover, the reforms offered to the Puritans at Hampton Court were in exchange for conformity within the established episcopalian church. Once a minister had formally recognised James's leadership and the institution of episcopacy, James was prepared, at least after 1605, to turn a blind eye to any minister who did not comply with what the Puritans saw as the popish practices, such as wearing the surplice and hood. After all, James himself regarded these things as 'indifferent'.

For a long time historians were highly critical of James's actions at Hampton Court. It was generally believed that, because of his temper and intransigence, James had missed an opportunity of reconciling the Puritans to Anglicanism. According to this interpretation, James, by insisting that the Puritans conform to the established practices of the Church of England, created a deep-seated disaffection that was finally to erupt in the 'Puritan Revolution' of 1642.

Research that is more recent questions this interpretation of events. This school of thought argues that the king did offer concessions to the Puritans, including the idea of a preaching ministry. Admittedly, most of these reforms were not implemented. That was the bishops' fault, not James's. The main criticism that can be made of James is that he failed to overcome the bishops' obstructionism.

Certainly, it is hard to see 1604 as the point at which the Puritans become an irreconcilable element determined upon some sort of revenge. No deep fissure appeared in the church. Only some 90 ministers, around 1 per cent of the total, refused to subscribe to the 1604 canons and were subsequently deprived of their benefices. The Hampton Court Conference did not result in large numbers separating from the established church. The emigration of

Describe what took place at Hampton Court in January 1604.

radical congregations to the Netherlands is notable for its rarity. If the Puritans were disaffected with the outcome of the Conference, it is difficult to find evidence of substantial and sustained resentment. Most Catholics were prepared to continue to work for reform from within the church. In this sense, the Hampton Court Conference was a very significant event.

Catholics, the Gunpowder Plot and its consequences

It is important to have some idea of how English Catholics fared under James I if only because there were Catholic influences in James's life. He was the son of the Catholic Mary Queen of Scots and had married a Catholic queen, Anne of Denmark. James was reported to have said that he 'would be gladly reunited with the Roman Church and would take three steps in that direction if only the church would take one'. Most Catholics seemed to have hoped that James would offer them some form of toleration. In a letter to Salisbury, he had stated that he did not intend to prosecute the Catholics for their faith. Yet, James never intended to extend a general toleration to the Catholics. Indeed, anti-Catholic legislation was soon applied with renewed vigour. This was a result of several factors:

- pressures from Puritans in parliament;
- the need to use **recusancy fines** as a source of revenue;
- the election of the intransigent Pope Clement VIII.

As early as 1604, James issued a proclamation banishing priests and ordered the collection of recusancy fines. Antagonised by this persecution, a group of Catholics schemed to remove James. The Gunpowder Plot was hatched. The plot is well known but what were its consequences?

James I was terrified and MPs were angry. Further anti-Catholic measures were introduced. The most important was the Oath of Allegiance of 1606. As in his treatment of the Puritans, the king placed a priority on political allegiance to crown and to the national church. He played down the question of doctrinal and ceremonial conformity. Despite his reaction to the Gunpowder Plot, James did not insist upon vigorous application of the Oath. In his Apology of 1608, he confirmed that the Oath was designed to identify those Catholics whose loyalty could not be relied on. 'I intended no persecution of them for conscience's cause,' he wrote, 'but only desired to be secured of them for civil obedience.'

Treatment of the Catholics fluctuated over the remaining years of James's rule. Following the appointment as archbishop of Canterbury in 1611 of the anti-Catholic, **George Abbot**, persecutions increased for a time. However, from 1613 the circumstances of the Catholics steadily improved. This is because, in the second half of James I's reign, policy towards the English

Anyone who refused to attend the national church, the Church of England, was known as a recusant. A number of laws, known as recusancy laws, were passed against them and they had to pay fines known as **recusancy fines** for non-attendance at church.

George Abbot (1562–1633) was a moderate Puritan. His anti-Spanish and anti-Arminian (see pp. 57–58) views brought him into opposition at court to Robert Carr, the Howards and George Villiers. His reputation was darkened over the killing of Lord Zouch's gamekeeper in a shooting accident in 1621. In 1627 he refused to authorise the publication of Robert Sibthorpe's sermon justifying the forced loan, an action which led to his temporary suspension.

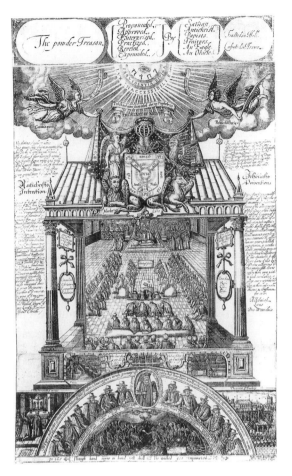

The papists' powder treason. This is an allegorical engraving, produced for 5 November 1612, 'in eternal memory of the divine bounty in England's preservation from the Hellish Powder Plot'.

How did Catholics fare during the reign of James I?

Catholics seems to have been determined by a pro-Spanish faction at court and by the king's wish that Prince Charles should marry a Spanish princess. Included in the Spanish marriage terms was the demand that English Catholics should be granted full toleration. Even after the collapse of the Spanish match (see pages 28–30) tolerance persisted. In 1625 the Venetian ambassador was able to report that 'the Catholics feel perfectly happy and many Catholic lords who had already gone away return boldly to the city.'

The middle way under pressure

Towards the end of his reign, the balance of religious forces James had carefully constructed began to break down. James seemed to develop doubts about the **Calvinist** theory of **predestination**. In 1624 he allowed the publication of Richard Montagu's *A new gag for an old goose*, a work which attacked the Calvinist belief that God alone determined whether a soul would go to Heaven or Hell. Criticised for his actions, James exclaimed that 'if this be popery I am a papist'. James began to accept anti-Calvinist arguments. In May

A **Calvinist** was a follower of the the Geneva-based reformer, John Calvin (1509–64), who was a leading figure of the Reformation. Through close study of the Bible, he came to believe that the Catholic Church was based on 'usurped instruments of tyranny and ambition'. He also developed the doctrine of **predestination** – the belief that 'by an immutable [unchangeable] counsel God hath once for all determined both whom He would admit to salvation [Heaven] and whom He would admit to destruction [Hell]'.

1618 he had issued the *Book of sports*, which permitted a large number of recreations on a Sunday. This struck a blow at one of the key beliefs of the Calvinists that Sundays should be set aside for worship. Many clergy refused to read the *Book of sports* in churches, despite being instructed to do so. Finally, foreign policy was making it increasingly difficult to maintain the religious consensus. James's attempt to play the peacemaker in the Thirty Years' War and his desire for a Spanish match for his son antagonised many Puritans, especially as Catholic powers gained the upper hand in the war. In 1622, in order to gag criticism of royal policy, he issued his *Directions to preachers*, which surrounded preachers with 'limitations and cautions', thereby further alienating Puritans.

Moderate Puritans had been able to support James so long as he appeared sound on doctrine. Once he advanced anti-Calvinists, even as a consequence of practical politics, that support began to dwindle. However, criticism of James's religious policies remained muted. If there were religious divisions in England, they rarely surfaced to take the form of argument and conflict. The same could not be said of much of Europe. Developments on the continent were to have great consequences for English politics.

Foreign policy

Introduction

England was a European state. By 1603 it was a Protestant state, which put it in a significant minority among European powers. Because it was on the periphery, England had interests beyond the continent. However, Europe had the greatest effect on England's foreign policies.

Late sixteenth-century Europe had been dominated by the struggle, part religious, part secular, between Protestants and Catholics. In 1603 England had been at war for 18 years against the leading Catholic state, the great power of the time, Spain. England had resisted attempts at invasion by the Armada. By 1603 a kind of stalemate had been achieved. Then James VI of Scotland, the old enemy of England, became the English king. What would be the aims of his foreign policy? How far would he change from the foreign policy of Elizabeth I?

The aims of James's foreign policy

The main aim of James I was peace. He also wanted to play the role of mediator, to bring peace to Europe. Not that he was a particularly active peacemaker. He adopted a passive stance towards foreign affairs and tried not to get involved in European conflicts. Several reasons why he did so have been put forward.

Some are personal reasons, for example that he simply believed in the virtues of peace rather than war. Other reasons are psychological. It has been suggested that James's aversion to all forms of violence was a reaction to the turbulent times of his childhood. Some even argue that he disliked force because he was in his mother's womb when she saw the violent murder of her secretary, Cardinal Riccio, in 1566.

Other explanations are more practical. England had no substantial armed force and only a small navy. In addition, parliament was reluctant to provide the money needed to prepare for and fight wars. Allies were hard to find. Relations with the other leading Protestant state, the Netherlands, were not always good. Trade caused deep divisions between the two powers. France was too divided and too suspicious of England to be a reliable ally. England was often alone but that did not stop James trying to mediate between warring powers.

> What are the main reasons that led James to pursue a policy of peace?

James the peacemaker

James began his reign by ending the war with Spain. The 1604 Treaty of London conceded nothing that was vital to the interests of England. Indeed, the terms agreed opened up opportunities for England to trade with Spain and the Spanish Netherlands, a development from which the English cloth industry benefited in particular. Yet, more aggressive Puritans objected to making peace with Catholic Spain, particularly when it was felt that one more attack would have provided the knockout blow.

In 1609 James helped bring about a truce to end the long-running war between Spain and the Netherlands by agreeing to guarantee the Protestant interest, should Spain end the truce.

It has been suggested that James should have tried to rebuild the anti-**Habsburg** alliance system of the 1590s, in particular by allying with France. Preferring to react to events rather than dictate them, and personally keener on peace than war, he failed to do so. In 1610, when the French king was assassinated and succeeded by Louis XIII, a monarch sympathetic to the Habsburg cause, that opportunity was lost. France agreed with Spain a double marriage treaty. Louis XIII was married to Anne of Austria, daughter of Philip III, and Louis's sister was married to the future Philip IV.

> Members of the **Habsburg** family belonged to a great Catholic European dynasty whose influence was dominant in huge tracts of territory. The Holy Roman emperor, though elected, was in practice always a Habsburg, as were the kings of Spain in the sixteenth and seventeenth centuries. The latter alone commanded an empire over which the sun never set.

James the Protestant leader

James's preference for peace had meant that he turned down the opportunity to lead an alliance of Protestant states. However, in 1611 he changed his mind. He agreed to make a defensive alliance with the Protestant Union, a group of Protestant states that had formed an alliance in 1608. James encouraged the Dutch to make a similar arrangement with the Union, which they did in 1613.

Elizabeth (1596–1662) was the eldest daughter of Anne of Denmark and James I. Her marriage to Frederick, the elector of the Palatinate of the Rhine, in 1613 was celebrated with lavish ceremonies including a sham battle on the Thames costing £9,000. Having been expelled from the Palatinate at the start of the Thirty Years' War, she became a refugee in Holland. The 'Winter Queen' eventually returned to England in 1661.

The second Cleves–Jülich crisis occurred because the position of these German territories, astride the lower Rhine and adjacent to the United Provinces, meant that they were keenly sought after by the leading European powers. A series of crises (1609–14) occurred when John William of Cleves–Jülich died in 1609 without providing an heir.

In the same year, James's daughter, **Elizabeth**, married the new elector of the Palatinate, the Protestant Frederick V. As a leader of this confessional bloc (that is, a group of countries that belonged to the same faith) James was able to mediate in disputes where all parties involved were Protestant. Thus, James played an important role in arranging peace between Sweden and Denmark in 1613. It was a function that James proved capable of performing even when he had little obvious influence upon all the participants, as in 1614 when he helped settle the **second Cleves–Jülich crisis**.

The Spanish match: negotiations begin

If James was to be an effective mediator in any future dispute involving both Catholic and Protestant elements he needed a mechanism that would permit him an influence in both camps. It was therefore necessary for him to counterbalance the effect of the marriage of his daughter to the Protestant Frederick. The most obvious way of doing so was to acquire a Catholic bride for his son. Thus, James set about marrying his younger son, Charles, to a Spanish Catholic princess. Negotiations had taken place on several occasions since 1603. 'If he [James] could now match his son with the Spanish infanta,' observes the historian Roger Lockyer, 'he would be, in his own person, the link between Catholics and Protestants, able to speak to both on equal terms and thereby bring about the reconciliation that had so far eluded human endeavour.' It was an admirable but ill-fated ambition.

James's attempts to forge a marriage alliance with Spain have received much critical comment. A number of points can be offered to support the notion that James's pursuit of a Spanish match was a 'tactical error'. Firstly, Protestant opinion in England regarded Catholic Spain as an implacable enemy. Any attempt, therefore, to co-exist peacefully with Spain and to marry the heir to the throne to one of its princesses appeared to be a betrayal of the national interest. Secondly, marriage negotiations, from 1614 onwards, highlighted anti-Catholic and pro-Catholic divisions at court. These divisions were made worse by the leisurely pace of negotiations. The comparative youth of the parties – Charles was fifteen in 1615 and the infanta six years younger – did not give the negotiations any sense of urgency. In addition, conditions imposed by the pope, for example that Charles should convert to Catholicism, nearly halted negotiations altogether.

In order to keep the negotiations alive, James was increasingly forced to appease Spain. Controversially, Sir Walter Ralegh was executed in 1618. The ostensible reason was that he had committed treason in 1603. The more likely reason was that, in 1617, against the orders of James, he had attacked Spanish possessions in the New World. It was at this point that negotiations were overtaken by events in central Europe.

What arguments have been put forward to suggest that James's pursuit of the Spanish match was 'a tactical error'?

Spanish possessions in 1640
SWEDEN
NORWAY
AND
DENMARK
Baltic Sea
SCOTLAND
IRELAND
ENGLAND
London
HOLSTEIN
MECKLENBURG
POMERANIA
UNITED
PROVINCES
BRANDENBURG
POLAND
CLEVES
JÜLICH
SAXONY
SILESIA
SPANISH
NETHERLANDS
LUX.
Prague
BOHEMIA
LOWER
PALATINATE
UPPER
PALATINATE
Paris
LORRAINE
ALSACE
BAVARIA
Vienna
AUSTRIA
WÜRTTEMBERG
FRANCHE
COMTÉ
FRANCE
STYRIA
HUNGARY
SWITZERLAND
TYROL
CARINTHIA
CARNIOLA
SAVOY
MILAN
VENICE
BOSNIA
PARMA
MODENA
Avignon
GENOA
DALMATIA
TUSCANY
PAPAL
STATES
ROUSSILLON
ARAGON
CATALONIA
PORTUGAL
Madrid
CASTILE
Lisbon
VALENCIA
Seville
CORSICA
Naples
KINGDOM
OF
NAPLES
Rome
SARDINIA
SICILY
BARBARY STATES

The Spanish European empire and the Palatinate region. These regions were at the heart of the first two Stuarts' foreign policy.

The outbreak of the Thirty Years' War

The Defenestration of Prague on 23 May 1618, when four Catholic councillors were flung out of the window of the castle that stands guard over that Bohemian town, has become, as Geoffrey Parker reminds us, in *Europe in crisis* (1979), 'the best known single event of seventeenth-century European history'. It marks the beginning of what historians have called the Thirty Years' War, eventually concluded by the Treaties of Westphalia in 1648. Protestants in Bohemia, increasingly alarmed by the anti-Protestant measures being taken by their king-elect, the Archduke Ferdinand, deposed him. They offered the Bohemian crown to Elector Frederick V, Protestant ruler of the neighbouring territory known as the Palatinate. He was a leading member of the Protestant Union and husband of James's daughter Elizabeth. On 26 August 1619 Frederick was formally elected to the Bohemian crown. Two days later, the Archduke Ferdinand was elected as Holy Roman Emperor. Ferdinand was set upon revenge. Frederick, anticipating hostilities, wrote to James I, requesting help. However, James regarded his son-in-law as a usurper, a person who overthrew kings and seized kingdoms. James, therefore, sent no aid; instead, he offered to mediate between Frederick and Ferdinand.

Before he could take any major steps to do so, Ferdinand, helped by Spanish troops, had defeated Frederick at the Battle of the White Mountain close to Prague. He was replaced as elector by the Catholic Maximilian of Bavaria. James called a parliament in 1621, the first since 1614, but James did not intend actually to fight for the Palatinate. Quite apart from the fact that he did not have the material means to do so as he had received only two subsidies from the first session of the 1621 parliament, he hoped that the prospect of England entering the fray and the imminent end of the Twelve Year Truce (1609–21) between the Dutch and Spain, would be enough to force the Habsburgs to the negotiating table.

The Spanish match: negotiations fail

In the meantime, it became even more necessary to conclude the Spanish match as it would provide an important lever that could be used on the king of Spain and, through him, his Austrian relations and, in particular, the Holy Roman Emperor, Ferdinand. James believed that the Spanish king would have sufficient influence over Ferdinand to be able to order the latter to return the Palatinate to Frederick. James made several miscalculations. He fatally overestimated the influence of the Spanish Habsburgs over their Austrian cousins. He failed to realise that Maximilian of Bavaria would not give up the Palatinate, a state he had just acquired. Finally, for James's policy to have any chance of success, it was vital that he continued to appear to be well supported at home. Yet, the pursuit of the Spanish marriage caused a domestic crisis that

Simul Complectar omnia

Gentis Hispanæ decus

Count Gondomar, the Spanish ambassador at the court of King James, portrayed as Machiavelli in T. Scott's anti-Spanish pamphlet, *Vox populi*.

created the opposite effect. Frustrated by the king's apparent inactivity, the Commons, in 1621, petitioned James to fight for the cause of the Palatinate, to enforce the recusancy laws and ensure that 'our most noble Prince may be timely and happily married to one of our own religion'. In turn, this invasion of the royal prerogative provoked the dissolution of parliament.

Historians, for example David Harris Willson in *King James VI and I* (1956), have been generally critical of James's pursuit of a Spanish match beyond 1618, and especially after 1620. They point out that Spanish terms for a marriage alliance were pitched deliberately high. For example, the demand that recusancy laws be repealed was never likely to be met because that repeal could only be legitimately effected by parliament. Consequently, so it is argued, James was strung along by the Spanish. The marriage negotiations immobilised any effective English response to the Palatinate crisis and thus acted as 'Spain's best army'.

Frustrated by the lack of progress in the marriage negotiations, Charles and Buckingham set out for Madrid in 1623 wearing false beards and calling themselves Thomas and John Smith. James now agreed to the marriage articles. Included amongst the terms was the assurance that the infanta be allowed to bring with her to England 24 priests and one bishop and that a chapel should be built for the princess, to which all Englishmen who pleased might have access. A series of private articles promised the English Catholics toleration, to be confirmed by act of parliament in due course. At no point

Why did Charles and Buckingham travel to Spain in 1623?

was the Palatinate issue mentioned. Yet, the Spanish marriage never took place. Humiliated and mistreated during their time in Madrid, both Charles and Buckingham returned to England intent upon war with Spain as a way of revenge. The ageing king was overwhelmed by the bellicose energies of his son and favourite. Preparations for war were begun.

War with Spain

In 1624 a new parliament was called. Specific appropriation clauses (see page 15) were attached to the supply it voted, attempting to ensure what seemed a popular demand, that war be declared against Spain.

England also agreed to help fund the Dutch war effort for two years and to supply 6,000 volunteers. In addition, negotiations got underway for Charles to marry the sister of King Louis XIII of France, Henrietta Maria. The price of the French marriage that finally took place in May 1625 was that James was to free English Catholics from persecution. It was an unpopular arrangement but, as Sir Simonds D'Ewes observed, 'the English generally so detested the Spanish match as they were glad of any which freed them from the fear of that'. Moreover, if it brought the French into an anti-Habsburg military alliance that would enable the Palatinate to be liberated then it was a price worth paying.

This it seemed to do. In the early months of 1625, the French agreed to supply 3,000 cavalry to an English expeditionary force of 12,000 men under the leadership of the German mercenary Mansfeld. However, Louis XIII, fearful he might antagonise Spain, refused permission for Mansfeld's ships to land at Calais. Eventually they docked in the United Provinces where a lack of provisions, disease and cold took their toll. Within six months, only 600 of the original force of 12,000 remained. It was not an encouraging background for the new king, Charles I. On 27 March 1625 his father had died and the reign of James I had come to an end.

James I's achievements

We began by outlining James I's aims: political union of England and Scotland, peace abroad and religious peace at home. The first he soon abandoned in the face of English opposition. The second he eventually had to abandon as European affairs became more complex and as he came under pressure of various sorts – family, religious and political – to intervene. The third he did achieve, despite having to face a threat as serious as the Gunpowder Plot. There were some religious divisions towards the end of his reign but they were on a limited scale, especially in comparison with the bitter religion-centred struggles on the continent.

One thing that James I certainly did not manage to achieve was 'to live of his own'. He failed to curb his extravagance and thus made the crown's financial position a great deal worse. The corruption that went with the extravagance did not improve matters. These problems caused relations with parliament to be strained, especially in 1610 and 1614. However, as long as the expense of war was not added to all other expenses the issue could be contained. The war that James I allowed himself to be dragged into at the very end of his reign did not harm his position but posed dangers for the new king, who was a different character from his father.

Summary questions

1 (a) Identify and explain any *two* domestic problems which faced James I on his accession in 1603.

   (b) Compare the success of James I's government by 1625 in dealing with at least *three* problems.

2 By what methods, and to what extent, did James fulfil his aims?

3

England, 1625–29

Focus questions

◆ What was the relationship between Charles I and parliament?

◆ What was the importance of financial issues in relations between Charles I and parliament?

◆ What part did foreign affairs play in relations between Charles I and parliament?

◆ How serious were religious divisions in the country?

Significant dates

1600　Charles, the younger son of James VI, is born in Scotland.

1612　Charles becomes heir to the throne on the death of Prince Henry.

1625　Charles I accedes to the throne and marries Henrietta Maria of France.
Charles calls his first parliament.
The Cadiz expedition is launched.

1626　Charles calls his second parliament.
War with France breaks out.
Parliament attempts to impeach Buckingham.

1627　The first expedition to La Rochelle sets sail.
A forced loan is levied.

1628　Charles calls his third parliament.
The Petition of Right is presented to Charles.
Buckingham is assassinated.

1629　The third parliament ends and Personal Rule begins.
April The Treaty of Susa is signed with France.

1630　*November* The Treaty of Madrid is made with Spain.

Overview

Charles I became king while England was at war with Spain, a war he had helped to bring about. Within two years, England was also at war with France. Wars cost money so parliaments had to be called more often. Unsuccessful

A portrait of Charles I and his family, painted by Van Dyck in 1632. Charles I is shown with Charles, prince of Wales, who was born on 29 May 1630, at his knee. Queen Henrietta Maria is seated next to the king. On her lap is the infant Princess Mary, born 4 November 1631.

wars, as these were, were unpopular. Criticism grew, especially from MPs who met more frequently. Religion became more of an issue than it had been under James I. By 1629 relations between the king and his MPs were so bad that the king decided to rule without parliament, which he managed to do for the next 11 years.

The four years between 1625 and 1629 are an important period in the history of Stuart England. How and why was it that relations between Charles I and parliament deteriorated so quickly? Who or what was responsible? Historians argue about these issues almost as much as contemporaries did then.

The new king

During his first 12 years, Charles lived very much in the shadow of his elder brother, Henry, who was generally regarded as 'the flower of the house, the glory of this country, and the admiration of all strangers'. However, this 'true lover of the English nation and a sound Protestant' succumbed to typhoid fever in 1612, at which point Charles became heir. Sir Robert Dallington chose this moment to remind Charles that 'all men's eyes are upon you'. Over the

Prince Rupert
(1619–82) was the flamboyant third son of the daughter of James I, Elizabeth, and Frederick V of the Palatinate. He acquired military experience on the continent during the Thirty Years' War. Charles I, in 1642, appointed him lieutenant-general of the horse. He was to be undefeated until the Battle of Marston Moor in 1644, though his cavalry disastrously overshot the field of battle at Edgehill in 1642 and at Naseby in 1645. He was sacked after surrendering Bristol in September 1645. Thereafter, he successfully served the royalist cause as a commander of the fleet.

Henrietta Maria
(1609–69) was the daughter of Henry IV of France and Marie de Medici. At the time of her marriage, notes J. P. Kenyon, 'she was still a gawky adolescent, with enormous eyes, bony wrists, projecting teeth and a minimal figure. At the sight of her new husband, she burst into tears.' However, after the death of Buckingham the marriage prospered. From 1640 the queen began to play a direct part in royal policy, nicknaming herself 'the She Majesty Generalissima' because of her success in rousing and directing royalist enthusiasm during the Civil Wars.

course of the next few years, Charles remained in the background. It appears that he was only brought out of himself by his friendship with George Villiers, duke of Buckingham, favourite of James. Rather unusually, the favourite of a monarch also became the favourite of the heir to the throne. This friendship was consolidated by their trip to Madrid in 1623, designed to fulfil the Spanish match.

Charles was never so popular as he was upon his return as his quest for a Spanish bride had ended in failure. Buoyed by his new popularity and filled with confidence, he took a significant role in the successful parliament of 1624, helping to prepare for war with Spain.

In March 1625 he became king. What attributes did the new king bring to the throne?

- He was a man of honour. Charles believed that some principles should be adhered to whatever the political repercussions. After the Battle of Naseby, for example, he assured his nephew, **Prince Rupert**, that 'I know my obligation to be both in conscience and honour, neither to abandon God's cause, injure my successors, nor forsake my friends.' Once Charles had invested his trust and loyalty in an individual or institution, it was complete and enduring. When he did 'forsake' Wentworth, in 1641, Charles never forgave himself. Above all, Charles demonstrated a touching loyalty and intense concern for the fate of members of his family. Charles was intensely loyal to **Henrietta Maria** and, after the assassination of Buckingham, their marriage became the greatest Stuart love match of the seventeenth century.

- He introduced a new sense of propriety and decorum to the court. In contrast to the loose practices and easy ways of the Jacobean period, 'The face of the court was much changed', remarked Lucy Hutchinson, 'for king Charles was temperate, chaste and serious, so that the fools and bawds, mimics and catamites of the former court grew out of fashion.' Charles I wanted 'to establish government and order in our court which from thence may spread with more order through all parts of our kingdoms'.

- He was a cultured king. He commissioned paintings from a number of artists, especially Van Dyck. Charles became something of an expert in art. He was also a lover of music, plays and architecture and had plans to build a new palace at Whitehall that would have been larger than the El Escorial of Philip II of Spain. Charles's artistic tastes bolstered, as well as reflected, his natural authoritarianism and love of order.

- He worked hard at fulfilling the role expected of him. For a nine-month period during 1637–38, he was present at 25 of the 80 recorded meetings of the privy council, an impressive record considering his other kingly duties. Nor was Charles a passive figure at such meetings. The privy council which met on 14 September 1626 allowed itself to be persuaded by the king to levy the forced loan. 'For a shy young man of 27, surrounded by experienced councillors, this was an impressive achievement,' writes Richard Cust in *The forced loan and English politics, 1626–1628* (1987). As Conrad Russell has remarked, Charles 'suffered from energy'.

- He chose effective royal servants. 'It is fashionable these days to consider king James superior to his son in political acumen', observes M. B. Young, 'but Charles chose far better men to serve in the highest offices of state.'

However, what were Charles's personal qualities which made it more difficult for him to be an effective king? They were several:

- He was intensely reticent and therefore a poor communicator. The king was a man of few words. He had no great liking for debate and he preferred to listen rather than talk, a consequence of his stutter. It meant that he failed to articulate his ideas, as a result of which many interpreted his actions in ways they wanted to. As he told the 1625 parliament, 'I thank God that the business of this time is of such a nature that it needs no eloquence to set it forth, for I am neither able to do it, nor doth it stand with my nature to spend much time in words.'

- He was uncompromising. There is no doubt that Charles was peculiarly inflexible in his political views, a quality that was stiffened by his belief in the divine right of kings. This is demonstrated by his unswerving attachment to Buckingham. Charles was stubbornly reluctant to bring about constructive compromise because to be seen to offer concessions was, in his eyes, an admission of weakness. From being stubborn, he could easily become vindictive. **Sir John Eliot**, one of the 'fiery spirits' who had criticised the actions of the government in the parliaments of the 1620s, was imprisoned in the Tower after the dissolution of parliament in 1629. Even when it was clear that he was dying, Charles refused to release him and, after Eliot's death, would not allow his body to be returned to his home county.

- He was obsessed with order and ritual. Those who could approach the king were carefully vetted and a hierarchy of rooms was re-established. Gone was the accessibility to the royal person that had been such a feature of the previous king's reign. Charles also reduced the number of occasions when he would touch for the 'king's evil', an act thought to cure a common disease of the lymphatic glands known as scrofula. Nor did Charles undertake leisurely 'progresses' into the countryside, as his predecessors had done. The collective result of changes such as these, according to Judith Richards in her article 'His nowe majestie', in *Past and present* (1990), was 'a monarch who, for nearly 15 years, withdrew from the vast majority of his subjects to a degree unprecedented for generations'.

Sir John Eliot
(1592–1632) emerged as the leading figure in the Commons' opposition to royal policies in the first three parliaments of Charles I. He was an outspoken critic of Buckingham and played a leading role in events which brought about the Petition of Right. Arrested after the presentation of the Three Resolutions in 1629, he was placed in the Tower where he died in 1632. Charles refused to allow his body to be taken back to Cornwall for burial by his family.

Charles I was clearly a complex character and the desire to give him certain psychological traits is often hard to resist. Many have found it easy to blame him for the outbreak of civil war during his reign, not least because his propensity to deceit inspired little trust. Even the royalist Clarendon, when writing *The history of the Rebellion and Civil Wars in England*, began his search for the origins of the Civil Wars in 1625, the year of Charles's accession to the throne. Indeed, the argument that Charles created rather than inherited many of his difficulties has retained many adherents. For L. J. Reeve, in *Charles I and the road to Personal Rule* (1989), Charles was 'woefully inadequate'. Conrad Russell concluded that 'Charles I, whatever his virtues, was unfit to be king'. 'An inept blunderer', echoes Maurice Lee Jr., in *The road to revolution: Scotland under Charles I 1625–37* (1985).

Other historians have argued, however, that it was less the man who was at fault and more the machine. Thomas Cogswell, for example, in *The blessed Revolution* (1989), has cautioned that 'it is worth considering whether the culprit [for the difficulties that Charles encountered] was the declining quality of royal leadership or a rapidly changing political universe'. For instance, he ruled Britain despite the fact that he lacked British machinery of government. Indeed, until there existed a British privy council any British monarch was likely to antagonise Scottish and Irish opinion.

John Morrill has suggested a middle way between these opinions by arguing that Charles 'is a necessary, although not sufficient cause of the Civil War'.

Before returning to such issues, we need to have a better idea of Charles's reign. We shall start with the first four years, which is a period dominated by foreign policy and its repercussions.

What were the main features of Charles I's personality?

Wars with Spain and France, 1625–29

The first four years of Charles's reign were characterised by war, first against Spain and then, from 1627, against both France and Spain. Thereafter, until 1640, discounting the Bishops' Wars (see pages 70–75), Charles pursued a policy of peace. Yet there is, nevertheless, a consistency of aim that informs Charles's foreign policy, namely that his sister, Elizabeth, and her husband, Frederick V, the elector Palatine, should be restored to the Palatinate. Moreover, if James I's reaction to the European crisis had caused difficulties in the parliament of 1621, then Charles's and Buckingham's decision to fight two wars created what one contemporary referred to as 'a crisis of parliaments'.

England always had a problem in fighting continental wars and that was in providing an effective army. As an island power, England's navy was its first line of defence and attack, which meant that the army was relatively neglected. Previously in 1625, England had paid for a mercenary force led by Mansfeld, which failed miserably (see page 30). Charles then allied with the Netherlands and with Denmark in an anti-Habsburg coalition. He agreed to pay £30,000 a month to Denmark, which would help sustain a Danish army of 36,000, already based in northern Germany.

In 1625 an Anglo-Dutch fleet set sail for Cadiz. The fleet had no specific aim other than that a blow should be struck at Spain. The attack was a catastrophe. With a thirst heightened by hot weather, the soldiers broke into farmhouses where they discovered great vats of wine. 'The whole army, except the commanders', reported one observer, 'was all drunken and in one common confusion, some of them shooting at one another amongst themselves.' Of the 12,000 troops who set out in October 1625, only 5,000 men returned.

Any effective anti-Habsburg alliance needed to include Spain's greatest enemy, France. After the failure of the Spanish match in 1623, Charles quickly negotiated a match with Henrietta Maria, the 16-year-old sister of the French king, Louis XIII. The English crown agreed to drop the laws persecuting Catholics. The French hinted that they might support its new ally against their common enemy, Spain. After a proxy marriage in March 1625, Henrietta Maria crossed the channel and met her husband. Yet, despite Charles I's marriage to Henrietta Maria, relations between England and France deteriorated rapidly. There were several reasons why this happened. These included:

- The royal marriage itself. Henrietta Maria and Charles were at first each irritated by the presence of the other. The queen brought with her a large Catholic household, which aroused concern at Whitehall.
- The treatment of the English Catholics. The marriage alliance had stipulated that the recusancy laws be relaxed. In practice, they were now being applied with a renewed vigour because of pressure from the parliament of 1625. The French were bound to be angry.
- The behaviour of Buckingham. When he had travelled to France in 1625, in order to escort Henrietta Maria to England, Buckingham had flirted with the French queen. The incident perhaps encouraged poor relations between the French king and England.
- A trade war between England and France. The English government began to seize French vessels which it thought were benefiting from the breakdown of trade relations between England and Spain. It was the arrest of a ship, the *St Peter*, in December that finally provoked the French into taking reprisals. In that month, it was learnt that the French government was contemplating a general embargo of all English property in France.
- Buckingham's desire to avenge a political defeat by the new French first minister, Cardinal **Richelieu**. Upon the collapse of the Mansfeld expedition, Buckingham told the Venetian ambassador that the French had 'deceived him by their double dealing about Mansfeld and by their equivocations over their promises'.

Richelieu (1585–1642), the principal minister of Louis XIII, did much to encourage the development of royal absolutism in seventeenth-century France.

The **Huguenots**, or French Protestants, had been granted extensive civil and religious rights in the Edict of Nantes (1598). They were dispersed throughout France but large numbers had taken up residence in the citadel port of La Rochelle.

A **Jesuit** was a member of a religious order, the Society of Jesus, which was founded in 1534 by Ignatius Loyola. The Jesuits spear-headed the Counter-Reformation – a movement for reform and missionary activity within the Roman Catholic Church, which began in the mid sixteenth century.

John Felton

(1595–1628) seems to have been inspired to assassinate Buckingham because of parliament's attacks upon the duke. Felton was hanged, castrated, drawn and quartered. The popular rejoicing that broke out at the news of Buckingham's death widened the gulf between the king and his people.

- The embarrassment caused to England by supporting the French against the **Huguenots**. In 1624 Louis XIII requested the loan of English ships to help put down an uprising by Huguenots in the port of La Rochelle. Once the Huguenots had been suppressed, Buckingham anticipated that the French would turn their attentions to the Habsburgs and assist the English in the restoration of Elizabeth and Frederick to the Palatinate. However, despite the fact that the Huguenot fleet was destroyed in September 1625 by a French squadron that included the English ships, the French gave no indication that they would help the English regain the Palatinate.

The Mansfeld and Cadiz expeditions were evidence of England's inability to fight a foreign war. By the end of 1626 England was not only continuing the war with Spain but was about to go to war with France as well. Henrietta Maria, whose resolute Catholicism was sustained by the influence of her **Jesuit** advisers, continued to regard her husband as a heretic. In 1626, his patience worn thin, Charles breached the terms of the marriage agreement by expelling his wife's French attendants. 'The Devil go with them', he wrote to Buckingham in a tone of both exasperation and triumph.

Richelieu appeared to be growing ever more devious, and at the expense of England. In 1626 France and Spain concluded the war they had been fighting in northern Italy. Then Richelieu decided to build a substantial fleet and to acquire trading posts in the New World. Both of these developments were harmful to the interests of England. To cap it all, the French then seized the entire English wine fleet of some 200 ships.

To Buckingham and Charles it thus seemed apparent that there would never be any prospect of the French joining an anti-Habsburg alliance while Richelieu continued in office. They, therefore, revived a scheme to depose him by lending support to his internal enemies, especially the Huguenots. In June 1627, with Buckingham in personal command, a fleet of nearly 100 ships left Portsmouth to support the Protestants of La Rochelle, besieged by Richelieu's forces.

The expedition met with a military disaster even greater than the Cadiz and Mansfeld expeditions. When the English finally attempted to take La Rochelle by storm, the scaling ladders were found to be five feet short and the attackers could only cast 'their threatening eyes about [as] they remained unmoveable till they were shot and tumbled down'. Yet, military disaster served only to solidify English strategy. Another English fleet set out for La Rochelle in the spring of 1628. It was as unsuccessful as its predecessor. Buckingham resolved to lead yet another attempt. In August 1628, as he prepared the fleet in Portsmouth, **John Felton**, a demobbed soldier with a grudge against Buckingham, stabbed him to death. The expedition still sailed but it was no more

John Felton assassinates Buckingham at Portsmouth, on 23 August 1628. Felton claimed that he had been encouraged in his action by parliament's criticisms of the duke. Parliament's dislike of the duke was probably an important factor in the poor relations between Charles and parliament. It seems that Felton nearly got away with the deed. When cries went up for 'A Frenchman! A Frenchman!', Felton, mishearing the shouts, thought that his name was being called. He thus presented himself to Buckingham's men, saying, 'I am the man.'

successful than the previous two. La Rochelle surrendered to Louis XIII in October 1628.

Not for two centuries had England faced a war with France and Spain simultaneously. The rare attempt to fight the two great powers of western Europe at the same time and the disastrous military campaigns that followed had major consequences. It caused a financial and political crisis in England, culminating in Charles's acceptance of the Petition of Right in 1628 (see page 42). The temptation has been to blame Charles and Buckingham for the policy of wars on two fronts. However, Roger Lockyer has cautioned against doing so. He points the finger of blame at the Commons for refusing to pay for a war which it had demanded, first in 1621 and then again in 1624. He concluded that MPs 'blamed Buckingham for failures for which they themselves were in large part responsible, and after his death they blamed Charles for refusing to support the Protestant cause, despite the fact that when he had done so, with their avowed approval, at the beginning of the reign, they had washed their hands of the whole business'.

Military exhaustion, lack of success, debt and the death of his principal adviser left Charles with no alternative but to conclude peace with both France and Spain. The king was fortunate that Richelieu was equally keen to make peace with England. When France and England signed the Treaty of Susa in April 1629 they agreed that neither country would interfere in the affairs of the other. Charles's sense of wounded pride probably explains why it took rather longer to make peace with Spain. The Treaty of Madrid was signed in November 1630. According to its terms, the English agreed to work for peace between Spain and the Dutch while Spain said it would work towards the restoration of Frederick.

The dramatic events in Cadiz, La Rochelle and Portsmouth had a great impact on English politics and it is to these that we now turn.

Describe each of the following:
• the Mansfeld expedition;
• the Cadiz expedition;
• the expeditions against La Rochelle.

King and parliament, 1625–29

The 1625 parliament

Charles's first parliament met on 18 June 1625 against a background of failure of foreign policy, economic problems and an outbreak of plague. The Commons voted Charles two subsidies (about £120,000), a reasonable sum in the circumstances though well short of the £1 million which Charles needed to wage the war against Spain.

Tradition had it that the monarch's right to collect customs duties known as tonnage and poundage, equivalent to about 50 per cent of the crown's ordinary income, was confirmed by the first parliament of the new reign. However, the Commons in 1625 voted Charles the right to collect these duties for only one year. Charles, therefore, unable to relinquish such a substantial part of his income, resorted to the collection of tonnage and poundage without the authority of parliament. Some historians argue that the Commons, faced with a monarch who might be on the throne for the next 40 years, had regarded this as an opportunity to re-examine the question of customs and impositions, which many still regarded as illegal. By granting tonnage and poundage for one year only, they hoped to be able to reconsider the matter at a later session. Such a breach with precedent was distasteful to the king. Roger Lockyer considers that the affair 'did as much as any single issue to poison the atmosphere at the outset of Charles's reign'.

Plague in London forced Charles to move the parliament of 1625 to Oxford. Having already made their grant of subsidy and, since it was against precedent for the same session to offer more supply, many MPs questioned the purpose of this Oxford meeting. Some believed that Buckingham would use a refusal to grant any more supply as an excuse for his disastrous performance as lord admiral, a role for which he was coming under increasing attack. The atmosphere in parliament was also affected by a revival of concern about religion, compounded by the presence of a Catholic queen. Many MPs were fearful of what they perceived to be a relaxation in the recusancy laws. Richard

Montagu, who had already come to attention in 1624, had now produced a more forceful exposition of his views in *Appello Caesarem*. His stress on the Catholic elements in the Anglican Church agitated the already alarmed Commons. Some MPs tried to have him arrested. However, he escaped their grasp when Charles appointed him a royal chaplain. A few weeks later, Charles dissolved his first parliament. He soon decided to call another.

The 1626 parliament

Charles's second parliament met in February 1626. It was called because Charles needed more subsidies to fight the war against Spain. MPs were reluctant to grant supply until their grievances had been met, the greatest of which was Buckingham. Before parliament met, Buckingham had hosted meetings at York House of anti-Calvinist and Calvinist representatives. The latter wanted the writings of Montagu declared erroneous. However, Buckingham made it clear there was to be no firm stand taken against the anti-Calvinists.

In an attempt to exclude troublemakers from parliament, Charles appointed as sheriffs a number of MPs, thus preventing them from sitting in parliament. The main effect of this action, however, was to bring forward men, such as Eliot, who were even more antagonistic to Buckingham than those excluded. Charles chose to reinterpret his prerogative and, even as parliament was sitting, redefined parliamentary privilege of MPs by arresting Sir John Eliot and **Sir Dudley Digges**. However, he was forced to release them when the House refused to do any more business until they were set free. When the Commons proceeded with moves to impeach Buckingham, in order to save his first minister, Charles dissolved parliament in June 1626. It had achieved nothing except to widen the rift between king and parliament.

> **Sir Dudley Digges** (1583–1639) was a leading opponent of Buckingham and played an important part in preparing the Petition of Right.

Prerogative rule, 1627

Charles was still at war with Spain, about to go to war with France, in addition to which he had promised to pay Denmark £30,000 a month as part of an anti-Habsburg alliance. He had to find extra-parliamentary means of raising money. The most successful was the forced loan. By July 1627 more than £240,000 had been received, a greater yield than had been expected from anticipated subsidies in the 1626 parliament. He also made many families accommodate soldiers as they prepared for the La Rochelle expedition. This compulsory billeting of troops raised great animosity, as did the imposition of martial law in some areas. To some, these moves were an abuse of the royal prerogative.

The very success of the loan raised the fear that the king might dispense with parliaments altogether. A total of 76 men were arrested for refusing to pay the loan, of whom five took their cases to court by issuing writs of **habeas corpus**, which demanded a reason for their detention. The Five

> **Habeas corpus** is a writ in common law ordering the person to whom it is addressed to deliver a certain man or woman in his custody to a court.

What were the main
events in the
parliaments of 1625
and 1626?

Knights' Case confirmed that the five had been imprisoned 'by special command of our Lord the King'. Notwithstanding this judicial support for his action, Charles insisted on the publication of the sermons in favour of the forced loan (see marginal note on page 22).

The parliament of 1628–29

Despite the success of the forced loan, the sums raised fell far short of what was required to pay for two foreign wars. In March 1628 Charles met his third parliament, which he asked to grant supplies, though how much he did not say.

Within a month, MPs had decided to give the king five subsidies and did not continue with their attack upon Buckingham, recognising that to do so might bring a swift end to parliament. However, they made the grant of subsidies dependent upon the king's acceptance of a Petition of Right. The petition stated that:

What were the
demands included in
the Petition of Right?

- no one should be forced to make a loan or pay a tax that did not have the consent of parliament;
- no one could lose their liberties or property except according to the law of the land;
- martial law and the billeting of soldiers should not occur.

The king's response fluctuated. First he was evasive, then he approved the petition and then he changed his mind. MPs blamed Buckingham in particular, who became the 'grievance of grievances'. Within weeks, Buckingham was dead, assassinated by John Felton.

The demise of Buckingham did little to improve relations in parliament. MPs now concentrated their attention upon the king's continued collection of tonnage and poundage despite their collection now being illegal. They also criticised the continued advancement of anti-Calvinists in the church. Even though Charles had ordered the suppression of Richard Montagu's *Appello Caesarem*, he still nominated Montagu as bishop of Chichester and William Laud as bishop of London.

It is hard to see why Charles recalled parliament for a second session in January 1629 as he already had five subsidies. Perhaps he hoped for a formal grant of tonnage and poundage. On 2 March 1629 when the Commons expressed a desire to proceed against customs officers who had seized the property of one of their members for not paying tonnage and poundage, the dispute blew up once more. Expecting an early dissolution, some MPs held down the speaker while the Commons presented the Three Resolutions. These declared:

- 'whosoever shall bring in innovation of religion, or by favour or

Parliament is shown in session in 1629, shortly before it was dismissed by the king.

countenance seek to extend or introduce Popery or **Arminianism** . . . shall be reputed a capital enemy to this Kingdom and Commonwealth;

- whosoever shall counsel or advise the taking and levying of the subsidies of tonnage and poundage not being granted by parliament . . . shall be likewise reputed an innovator in the Government and a capital enemy to the Kingdom and the Commonwealth;
- if any merchant or person whatsoever shall voluntarily yield, or pay the said subsidies of tonnage and poundage not being granted by parliament, he shall likewise be reputed a betrayer of the liberties of England.

The king ordered the arrest of nine MPs including John Eliot, **Denzil Holles** and Benjamin Valentine. Parliament was dissolved. It was not to meet for another 11 years.

Arminianism was another name for anti-Calvinist beliefs. This is because anti-Calvinists were thought to follow the teaching of a Dutch heretic called Arminius (see pp. 57–58).

Denzil Holles (1599–1680) was one of the Five Members whom Charles sought to impeach in January 1642. He emerged as the leading spokesmen of the Political Presbyterians (see p. 97). He was to spend the 1650s in exile, though returned to England at the Restoration.

4 Politics and religion, 1603–29: a summary

These 26 years have been considered as two separate and unequal periods: the whole of the reign of James I and the first four years of the reign of Charles I. It is important in understanding the whole period to bring those unequal halves together. There are some common themes that enable us to do so.

One is war. At both the beginning and the end of the period England was at war with the same country, Spain, and was aiming to bring those separate wars to an end. There were differences between the two wars. In 1603 the conflict was 18 years old and had involved the defence of the country against the world's greatest power of the time, as symbolised by the defeat of the Spanish Armada. In 1629 the war was just four years old, and had begun at the very end of the reign of James I, when Charles and Buckingham had persuaded the ailing king of the need for war. It involved attempts to restore James I's daughter to her rightful position in the Palatinate and two unsuccessful expeditions, one to the continent, led by Mansfeld, the other to Cadiz. In 1629, unlike 1603, England was at war with France as well as Spain. Its causes were varied; several concerned Buckingham. None involved the defence of the realm. This war went badly, as shown by the raids on La Rochelle. In April 1629 England made peace with France.

Thus England was at war for only some five years of the twenty-six being considered, at the start and the finish of the period. In between, James I aimed to avoid war. He still wished to play a role as a peacemaker in Europe. This did not mean too much in the early part of his reign. Long-running conflicts between Spain and France and Spain and the Netherlands were coming to an end but, from 1618, tensions flared up once more between Catholic and Protestant, between the Habsburgs and their many enemies. England was directly involved because of the marriage of James I's daughter to the elector Palatine. James tried to keep the peace but failed. The trip to Madrid in 1623 symbolised the failure of James I's even-handed approach to continental struggles. The parliaments of 1621 and 1624 were critical of James's failure to act on behalf of his daughter and Protestantism. Buckingham and Charles wanted action as well. In 1624 England slid into war with Spain. It was a popular, but ill-conceived, war. No one had a clear idea of aims and strategy. Furthermore it broke out just as James I's reign was coming to an end and a new reign beginning. It was a difficult time to fight any war, let alone one as badly planned as this one.

Foreign affairs played an important part in relations between crown and parliament especially when England went to war. If those wars were waged successfully, as most of Elizabeth I's had been, then those relations remained on a level footing. If the wars were a failure, relations became very strained. The wars of the 1620s went very badly for England. These failures increased parliamentary criticism of the crown – or, to be more precise, the crown's ministers. It was still not possible to hold the crown responsible. If the government failed it was because the king was wrongly advised. Charles I's main adviser was Buckingham, his favourite of many years. By 1626 MPs were sufficiently angry and sufficiently bold to try and impeach Buckingham. Such a controversial move meant the early dissolution of parliament. Failure overseas was starting to affect government at home.

Why was the English war effort of the 1620s so strikingly unsuccessful? One reason was poor strategy, badly planned. Another was a lack of sufficient funds, for war was an expensive business. This leads on to a consideration of public finance. That the monarch was expected to 'live of his own' ordinary revenues in peacetime was one of the unwritten rules which everyone accepted. Doing so was becoming more difficult, as the value of the income from ordinary revenues, such as rents from royal lands, was reduced by inflation. Elizabeth I had tried to keep to this unwritten rule. Wartime was, however, different and the crown could ask parliament for extraordinary revenue in the form of subsidies. Those subsidies were a property tax upon the landed class from whom MPs were chosen. MPs were reluctant to impose upon their own kind too great a tax burden. Furthermore, the value of subsidies was also being eroded by inflation. The crown was never given enough money to fight the campaigns of the 1620s with any real chance of success. It was not that MPs did not provide subsidies. In all but one of the five parliaments of the 1620s they did so. The exception was the 1626 parliament. The problem was that MPs did not provide enough money to fight a successful war. They willed the end but not the means and their reluctance to provide sufficient funds caused the crown to turn to other, less acceptable, ways of finding the money. The best example comes after the 1626 parliament, when the king used a forced loan to raise further funds. In doing so, he further antagonised the landed class. When he next called parliament, in 1628, MPs wanted to impose on the crown tighter rules concerning the raising of money and so drew up the Petition of Right. Charles had to agree but he did not accept the new restrictions. MPs came to realise this and passed three more resolutions.

One of those resolutions involved the third theme of the period, religion. James I had raised hopes of Puritan reform only to dash them but his refusal to require too strict a uniformity ensured that he aroused no alarms or fears, unlike Charles's support of anti-Calvinism. Charles was not keeping to his father's middle way. By veering towards what many people saw as the papist side he confirmed all the worst suspicions and doubts of the Puritans – and this was despite going to war with the two leading Catholic powers.

James I had avoided war and had been cautious over religious issues, which meant that his financial problems did not become too great an issue. Charles had plunged into wars and had been less cautious over religion. Thus, by 1629, he was facing three major problems, not one. Relations with parliament became very strained as a result. Charles I believed parliament was being unreasonable, if anything making problems worse, and so he decided to govern without parliament. He believed that a period of stable, effective government would soon change things for the better.

Summary questions

1 What were the *three* major problems that Charles faced in 1629?

2 Identify and explain any *two* particular issues which caused problems between Charles and his parliaments, 1625–29.

3 Compare the importance of the following *three* factors as explanations for Charles dispensing with parliament in 1629:
   (a) MPs were increasingly invading the royal prerogative;
   (b) parliaments were providing insufficient finance;
   (c) the personality of Charles I.

Personal Rule and civil war, 1629–49

5 Personal Rule, 1629–40

Focus questions

◆ How was Charles I able to govern without parliament?

◆ What was Thorough?

◆ What financial policies were followed in the 1630s?

◆ What religious policies were followed in the 1630s?

◆ How and why did Personal Rule end?

Significant dates

1629	Wentworth becomes president of the Council of the North. Charles decides to rule without parliament.
1630	Peace is made with Spain.
1631	Books of Orders.
1632	Wentworth is appointed lord deputy of Ireland.
1633	Laud is appointed archbishop of Canterbury.
1635	Ship money is extended to inland counties.
1637	John Hampden refuses to pay ship money. Prynne, Burton and Bastwicke are mutilated.
1639	The First Bishops' War breaks out.
1640	Charles I calls his first parliament since 1629.

Richard Weston, earl of Portland (1577–1635), was a Catholic who had been appointed chancellor of the exchequer in 1621 and lord high treasurer in 1628. He was the main figure behind the fiscal devices adopted after 1629 and therefore hugely unpopular.

Henry Rich, **Lord Holland** (1590–1649), was employed to negotiate the marriage of Charles and Henrietta Maria. He was beheaded by parliament in 1649.

Overview

After the extraordinary events in England of 2 March 1629 (see pages 42–43) a period of rule without parliaments was neither unexpected nor unprecedented. After all, the frequency of English parliaments in the 1620s had been exceptional. During the course of the previous decade, from 1611 to 1621, a parliament had been called in England on only one occasion (1614).

By making peace with both France and Spain and by increasing the efficiency as well as extending the impact of feudal fiscal devices, like wardship and purveyance, Charles created conditions in which he could rule without calling a parliament in England throughout the 1630s. Thus, until 1640, when the prospect of a Scottish invasion of England necessitated the meeting of a parliament, Charles enjoyed an 11-year period of Personal Rule.

The king's decision to govern without parliament in 1629 did not mean that he had resolved never to recall that body. It is true, however, that Charles was wary and suspicious of parliaments. Charles fervently believed that parliaments, by failing to support the war efforts against France and Spain, had damaged his royal authority, honour and dignity – the very qualities that he believed any monarch should strive to protect. In this sense he probably regarded it as his duty to do without parliaments, at least until the 'ill affected men' in the Commons such as Eliot, Valentine, Strode and Denzil Holles had learned their lesson by looking at the four dark walls of a prison cell. 'We shall be more inclinable to meet in parliament again', declared a royal proclamation of 27 March 1629, 'when our people shall see more clearly into our intentions and actions [and] when such as have bred this interruption shall have received their condign [well-merited and severe] punishment.'

Until that happened Charles set about achieving his two main aims:

- providing well-ordered and efficient government, what Laud and Wentworth came to refer to as 'Thorough';
- raising sufficient money in order to avoid the recall of parliament.

How did he intend to achieve these aims? How far did he do so?

The nature of Personal Rule

'Personal Rule' did not mean that Charles governed entirely by himself. Faction and patronage were as much part of his Personal Rule as they had been with parliaments in the 1620s, perhaps more so now that Buckingham was dead. After his assassination in 1628, Charles did not take another favourite. Factional politics were fully restored.

Until the mid 1630s, the leading group sympathised with Spain and Catholicism and are, therefore, referred to by historians as the Spanish faction. This group was headed by Sir **Richard Weston** (later earl of Portland) as lord treasurer, until his death in 1635. Thereafter other factions emerged. One of the most important of these was the French group, or queen's party. Centring on Henrietta Maria, and including men like the **Lords Holland** and **Coventry**, this element aimed at replacing sympathy for Spain with attachment to France.

Two other important members of the king's government during this period were **Sir Thomas Wentworth** and **William Laud**. Wentworth had been a critic

Sir Thomas Coventry, **Lord Coventry** (1587–1640), attempted to mediate between Charles and the parliamentary leaders in 1629 and assented to the levying of ship money in 1634. He was lord keeper of the great seal from 1625 to 1640.

Sir Thomas Wentworth, earl of Strafford (1593–1641), sat in four of the five parliaments of the 1620s. In 1627 he was briefly imprisoned for refusing to pay the forced loan. After 1629 he became a servant of the government and implemented Thorough, first in northern England as president of the Council of the North (1629–32) and then as lord deputy of Ireland. He was instrumental in advising Charles to call the Short Parliament in 1640 and to prosecute the war against the Scots. He was beheaded on 12 May 1641.

William Laud (1573–1645) was the son of a clothier – his enemies claimed that he was 'dragged forth from the dunghill' – and rose to be archbishop of Canterbury from 1633 until his execution in 1645. James had refused to advance Laud beyond the bishopric of St David's because he considered him to have 'a restless spirit, and cannot see when matters are well, but loves to toss and change and bring things to a pitch of reformation floating in his own brain'.

The **Council of the North** acted as an extension of the privy council and was based in York. It exercised legal and administrative power in a region remote from Westminster.

Identify the main factions and personnel associated with Charles I's period of Personal Rule.

of the king's government in the parliaments of 1626 and 1628 before becoming lord president of the **Council of the North** in early 1629. In 1632 he became lord deputy of Ireland. Both posts meant that Wentworth was physically removed from the affairs of court. William Laud, a cleric, became bishop of London in 1628 and archbishop of Canterbury in 1633. He was emotionally distant from the royal court. For these reasons, despite their differences, the two men became close allies and corresponded frequently throughout the 1630s. They became associated with the policy of Thorough, more efficient and more effective government pushed through from the centre. Their forthright approach to resistance only angered the opposition, who came to see them as a dangerous partnership at the heart of government.

The policy of Thorough

Thorough in England

The Books of Orders, 1631

In the form of the Books of Orders of 1631, there occurred what J. P. Kenyon has called 'the most ambitious scheme for the supervision of local government in the century'. In January 1631 a total of 314 books of instructions were sent to key figures in local government, especially justices of the peace, whom the royal court believed had neglected their duties. The Orders commanded justices of the peace to report monthly to the privy council. If the justices of the peace proved unworthy, they were to expect 'punishment in our court of **Star Chamber**'.

Amongst other things, the Orders contained instructions regarding:
- the collection and use of poor rates;
- the upkeep of roads and bridges;
- the movement of goods and the control of local markets;
- the treatment of beggars.

Star Chamber was a court composed of members of the privy council and judges sitting as a court of law that dealt with criminal offences, particularly those involving breaches of public order. During the 1630s it became generally unpopular because of the savage penalties it imposed on Puritan critics of royal policies. It was abolished in 1641.

They were issued in 1631, following economic recession and poor harvests, and provoked fears of the breakdown of society as unemployed and hungry labourers wandered from parish to parish. Eight of the twenty-four incidents of food rioting in Kent between 1558 and 1640 occurred in 1630–31. It was probably a fear of the mob and a desire to preserve established order that persuaded Charles to issue the Books of Orders.

Assessing the impact of the Orders has proved difficult, though most historians agree that they alleviated the worst of the social consequences of the economic crisis of 1629–30. Kevin Sharpe believes that effective imposition of the Books of Orders helped to secure social stability to a degree that was the 'envy of other European monarchies' and that 'it is a testament to the general stability and health of the regime that for most of the decade co-operation was secured'. Angela Anderson suggests that 'by 1635 . . . a pattern had been successfully established by which energetic central government could affect and improve the administration throughout the country'. However, a detailed record of the workings of the Orders across the country does not exist since few private papers of justices of the peace active in the 1630s survive. Nevertheless, one estimate has suggested that as few as one tenth of the reports that should have been submitted by the justices of the peace to the council were actually submitted. This leads W. K. Jordan, in *Philanthropy in England 1480–1660* (1959), to a conclusion that is the very opposite of the views of the historians presented above. It certainly seems that the council was unable to monitor justices of the peace, particularly when the crown was also burdened with levying ship money (see page 55). Moreover, as the 1630s advanced and the economic depression lifted, it became less necessary to impose the Books of Orders anyway.

Reform of the militia

The militia was made up of the county-based soldiers who were mobilised only during times of national emergency. The inadequacy of the militia had become particularly apparent during the wars against France and Spain. In 1629 the council therefore issued orders for the regular training and equipping of the county bands, a process that was to be overseen by the **lords lieutenant and deputy lieutenants**. However, the peaceful 1630s did not inject any sense of urgency into the reform process. Moreover, there was now a real doubt as to the legality of the council's actions; the parliamentary statute allowing the setting-up of local militias had been repealed in 1604. John Bishe of Brighton, for example, refused to attend militia musters on the grounds that 'there was no law to enforce them'. Despite the fact that Kevin Sharpe has argued that the changed foreign circumstances in the middle of the 1630s rejuvenated the reform process, the inadequacy of the militia in the Bishops' Wars seems testimony of the council's failure.

Lords lieutenant and deputy lieutenants were royal appointees, responsible for maintaining security and organising the local militia within each county.

What was the purpose of a) the Books of Orders and b) the local militia?
How effective were they?

Thorough in Ireland

Wentworth's time in Ireland was an important period in the history of Anglo-Irish relations. They marked a major attempt by the English state to impose a particular kind of ordered government on a territory that had its own traditions of government.

One reason for attempting to do this was that Charles I could not afford to have Ireland as a drain upon the English exchequer. Wentworth employed three particular strategies in his quest to make Ireland financially independent of England:

A picture of Thomas Wentworth, earl of Strafford, that shows his arrogance and determination. This portrait is in the style of Van Dyck.

The **Book of Rates** contained the official valuations of items that were liable to customs duties.

- He called the Irish parliament in 1634–35. It agreed to a vote of six subsidies. A similarly careful supervision of its next meeting in 1640 resulted in a grant of four subsidies.
- He doubled the amount of income received from customs. A new **Book of Rates** helped to increase income from this source from £40,000 in 1633 to £80,000 in 1640.
- He converted all doubtful claims to land into tenures from the crown, thus increasing revenues from crown lands. This was done by setting up a Commission for Defective Titles in 1634, a body that would systematically revise the terms on which land was held from the crown. The monarch could then demand his feudal dues.

According to Hugh Kearney, the collective effect of these measures was that 'for the first time since the later middle ages the English government was not called upon to make a substantial contribution to the Irish exchequer or to give way on important issues in return for a subsidy from the Irish parliament'. However, this was achieved only at the cost of alienating each of the two main groups in Ireland: the Old English and the New English.

The Old English were the descendants of the English who had settled in Ireland in the middle ages. They were distressed by Wentworth's manipulation of the Irish parliament. He offered only a selective granting of **The Graces:** he refused to pass those that diminished the king's title to land. They opposed Wentworth's policy of plantation, which meant importing a Protestant population at the expense of the existing population. In Galway, the Old English were fined for refusing to support the policy. By challenging existing land ownership, Wentworth created a great deal of resentment and fear. Indeed, Kearney has concluded that 'part of the explanation for the rising of the Old English in rebellion in 1641 must be attributed to Wentworth's decision to proceed with the plantation of Galway at all costs and to the ruthless manner in which he crushed all opposition'.

The New English were those English and Scottish settlers who had arrived in the past 50 years and who were Protestant. They resented his attempts to impose High Church Laudianism on Ireland. Since Wentworth sympathised with Laud's ambition to improve the fabric of the church, the lord deputy considered it important to resume those church lands and properties that had been impropriated (acquired) by laymen. Wentworth clashed with **Richard Boyle, earl of Cork,** the leading New English landowner. In 1634 Cork was summoned before the Court of Star Chamber. He was eventually fined £15,000. **Sir Francis Annesley, Lord Mountnorris,** who received about £20,000 from the customs farm in 1635, was court-martialled on a trumped-up charge of treason. In such ways did Wentworth antagonise the group which should have been his natural ally, the Protestant New English.

Wentworth also alienated the City of London. The corporation of London, which had received a large grant of land in Londonderry for a very low rent, failed to fulfil its obligations towards the area. In 1635 it was fined £70,000. This created a dangerous resentment. When, in 1639, the king needed the support of the City it offered him only £5,000.

Governing Ireland was always difficult. Events in Scotland after 1637 made it more so. The success of the Covenanting Scots (see pages 74–75) bred a common interest between the regime in Scotland and the Scots in Ulster. As David Stevenson has pointed out, in *The Scottish Revolution 1637–1644* (1973), 'successful Scots' defiance of royal power had roused intense excitement among those of the **native Irish** who were not reconciled to conquest. The Scots had revealed the fragility of royal and English power, and many of the Irish resolved to follow their example.'

The Scottish crisis led to Wentworth's recall from Ireland in 1639. Wentworth had now achieved what he most wanted, to be the prime servant of his king. He became the earl of Strafford. Wentworth's recall to England in 1639 created a political vacuum in Ireland which helped cause the Irish Rebellion of

In 1628 Charles I and the Irish landlords struck a bargain whereby the landowners would pay £120,000 over three years, in return for which the crown would not lay claim to certain lands. This was known as **The Graces.** It was meant to be approved by the Irish parliament but never was.

Richard Boyle, earl of Cork (1566–1643), by coercing landholders and defrauding the state, had become one of the richest men in Ireland by the 1620s. However, Wentworth was determined to make an example of Cork as the New Englishman who had most defrauded the crown. As part of this process the earl was fined £15,000 and forced to move an enormous family tomb he had built in a prominent position in St Patrick's Cathedral, Dublin.

Sir Francis Annesley, Lord Mountnorris (1585–1660), was one of the New English. He was court-martialled and condemned to death for insulting his commanding officer. The Long Parliament made Mountnorris's case a prime instance of Wentworth's arbitrary government.

The **native Irish** (or Gaelic Irish) were Catholic Irish who could trace their descent from before the time of the Conquest in 1066.

Identify the groups who were alienated by Wentworth's policy of Thorough.

Francis Cottington
(1578–1652) was master of the Court of Wards from 1635 to 1641 and a treasury commissioner from 1635 to1636.

William Juxon
(1582–1663) was bishop of London from 1633 to 1649 and lord treasurer from 1636 to 1641 – the first clerical lord treasurer since the reign of Edward IV. He attended the king at his trial and received his last words on the scaffold. He was archbishop of Canterbury from 1660 to 1663.

October 1641. While he ruled Ireland, he maintained order and peace but the methods he used stored up problems which came to the surface once he was gone.

Balancing the books

Richard Weston, **Francis Cottington** and then **William Juxon** employed various devices in the 1630s in an attempt to put English royal finances on a sounder basis by reducing expenditure. The most important factor which explains why the financial position of the crown improved in the first part of the 1630s was the consequence of avoiding war. Whereas the 1620s had seen about £500,000 spent on military and naval preparations, by 1635 that figure was only £66,000. They cut back on royal expenditure at court – for example, pensions and annuities were reduced by 35 per cent. They raised ordinary revenue by 25 per cent to more than £600,000 per annum by 1635. This cut the annual crown deficit to just £18,000. The total debt, the result of accumulated deficits, remained more than £1 million.

More importantly, Weston and Cottington increased income and by a variety of means. These included the following:

- Applying recusancy laws more rigorously. By 1635 they were bringing in £27,000 per annum as opposed to only £5,000 in 1630.
- The sale of crown lands. This brought in a total of £650,000 between 1625 and 1635.
- Applying half-forgotten feudal dues. For instance, distraint of knighthood was a medieval device whereby all those with land worth £40 per annum or more (by the 1630s, a substantial number because of the effect of inflation) were obliged to be knighted in service to the monarch. It was decided to fine anyone who, despite their qualifying circumstances, had failed to do this at the time of the king's coronation. By the end of the 1630s, fines from this source had raised a total of £174,000 from 9,000 individuals. Meanwhile, greater use of purveyance, the crown's right to purchase commodities at reduced prices, brought in £30,000 per annum between 1630 and 1635. Fines were also imposed on those subjects who could not prove that they owned land once held by the crown by the Commission for Defective Titles.
- Weston's successor, William Juxon, exploited more feudal devices. Fines were imposed for living within the (expanded) boundaries of royal forests, producing a total of about £40,000. Wardship revenue was also collected more carefully in the mid 1630s, bringing in about £55,000 per annum – three times as much as it had in 1613.
- Exploiting a loophole in the 1624 act which had banned the grant of

monopolies to individuals. Companies were not included in the act. Thus, in 1632 Charles licensed the manufacture of soap to a company in return for £4 per tonne of soap sold.

- Levying ship money. The crown had the right to demand money from coastal towns and counties during national emergencies in order to build a fleet. Between 1634, when ship money was first levied in the 1630s, and 1640, nearly £800,000 was paid in ship money. This was considerably more than the total value of subsidies received during the whole of Charles's reign. This extraordinary sum is explained by two factors in particular. In 1635 it was extended to inland counties of England and Wales on the basis that it was 'just and reasonable' that all who might benefit from a fleet that kept the shores safe from foreign invasion and pirates should contribute. However, this was against precedent and some argued, therefore, that ship money was unconstitutional (see below). The second reason why ship money raised so much money was that it was based upon new methods of assessment which affected more people than a parliamentary subsidy – in Essex, for example, four times as many.

[handwritten margin note: –unprecedented levying of fees –raise LOTS of revenue]

The growth in tonnage and poundage and impositions, moreover, should not be forgotten. Peace had a very beneficial effect on trade and, therefore, upon the king's income from customs duties. In 1635 these totalled £358,000.

By 1637 the collective effect of these financial expedients was that the annual revenue was more than £1 million, 50 per cent higher than it had been in real terms in 1625. Even the crown jewels, pawned in the 1620s, had been redeemed by the end of the 1630s.

What response was there to these various financial devices, some of questionable legality? In 1634 Sir David Foulis had attempted to gain support in Yorkshire against the levying of distraint of knighthood. However, his campaign met with little sympathy, possibly because his actions were more part of his rivalry with Wentworth than any principled resistance to the government levy. On the other hand, the significantly large number of people affected by this tax, and the fact that the Long Parliament which met from November 1640 abolished it, suggests that distraint of knighthood had created disaffection.

The greatest number of complaints were provoked by the levying of ship money. Most complaints concerned the level of the duty rather than the principle of the tax itself. The greatest challenge to the levying of ship money was posed by John Hampden. In 1636–37 he refused to pay ship money. He challenged in the courts the ruling already made in favour of Charles – that the king in times of national danger was able to command his subjects to pay a levy without recourse to a parliament. Though five out of the twelve judges gave judgement in Hampden's favour, the court ruled in favour of the crown. Yet even this close outcome did not affect the receipts from ship money; the case only encouraged the delay of payment while people awaited a judgement. Thus, until the end of 1638, more than 90 per cent of ship money was paid – about £200,000 per annum. It was only the attempt to fight the Scots in the First Bishops' War (see pages 71–72) without calling a parliament – the first occasion that a war had been fought without a parliament since 1323 – that induced a taxpayers' strike and resulted in the amount falling to 20 per cent. 'We are assured by Whig historians', observes J. P. Kenyon, 'that [ship money] aroused the most furious opposition in the provinces, and this "fact" is generally accepted. In fact, there is scarcely any evidence for it, and what there is is associated with predictable individuals like the earl of Warwick and Lord Saye and Sele.' For the greater part of the 1630s, Englishmen paid their taxes, probably grumbling in the process, but they did pay.

By what means did Charles raise revenue during the 1630s? What evidence is there of resistance to these devices?

Laud and religious policies

From 1618 onwards, but more especially from 1625, it is possible to perceive an increase in activity at both ends of the religious spectrum in England, the patronage given to the anti-Calvinists ultimately provoking a Calvinist reaction. The fact that the anti-Calvinists labelled their Calvinist opponents as Puritans meant that those who had previously regarded themselves as being in the centre of the religious spectrum now found that they had been made extremists. 'It is difficult for us to grasp', argues Nicholas Tyacke, in *Anti-Calvinists; the rise of English Arminianism c.1590–1640* (1987), 'how great a revolution this involved for a society as steeped in Calvinist theology as was England before the Civil War.' Calvinists now had to decide whether or not they could continue to worship within the Church of England. A number – perhaps as many as 15,000 during the whole of the 1630s – concluded that they could no longer do so and emigrated to the New World. Those who remained had to try and resist the advance of their enemies. After 1629, when Charles decided to rule without calling a parliament, this became increasingly difficult. Not only did the absence of parliament deprive them of a platform for their views but the two archbishoprics were occupied by anti-Calvinists. In 1632 Richard Neile gained York and, in the following year, William Laud became archbishop of Canterbury. They determined on the following:

- To diminish the importance given to the notion of predestination. Instead they placed greater stress upon the belief that the grace of God was freely available to all. In other words, they sought to play down the established theological belief of the Calvinists that God had preordained the fate of every human soul – that at its conception it was already ultimately destined

A portrait from Van Dyck's studio of Archbishop William Laud. His avuncular expression belies a ruthless determination to get his own way.

for either Heaven or Hell. This was half way to the Catholic belief that God's grace could be won by an individual through the doing of good works.

- To give a greater significance to the sacrament of holy communion. This in turn meant that religious ceremony assumed greater importance than religious preaching, that the communion table was more important than the pulpit.
- To restore the sense of a 'beauty of holiness' in the church by refurbishing stained glass windows and generally beautifying church fabric.
- To enhance the authority of the clergy and the ecclesiastical hierarchy, thus enabling the church to play a central role in the life of the state.

– cloth religion in beautiful robes

What were the main features of the anti-Calvinist programme?

The problem of terms

Discussion of religious issues during the reign of Charles I is bedevilled by problems relating to a definition of terms. Historians have proposed a variety of terms in which the church policy of Charles and Laud might best be discussed and understood. The one that receives most frequent use, and one that was familiar to contemporaries, is 'Arminianism'. Arminius (1560–1609) was a Dutch theologian who believed that salvation, or passage to Heaven, could be attained by securing God's favour, or grace, and that this could be achieved by doing good works. By playing down the widely established Calvinist notion of predestination, men such as Lancelot Andrewes, Richard Neile and William Laud can be classed as Arminians. But this group tended to put an emphasis upon the importance of ceremony, the episcopal government of the church and the sacraments, none of which featured in the writings of Arminius. Furthermore, there had been a party of this kind in England from the late sixteenth century, before Arminius was heard of. It is, therefore, suggested that the group that achieved dominance in the English church in the late 1620s and 1630s might best be referred to as English Arminians, and that the policy they pursued in the 1630s is best described as Laudianism. However, this perhaps lends too much importance to Laud alone. Julian Davies, in *The Caroline captivity of the church: Charles I and the remoulding of Anglicanism* (1992), arguing that the king was the driving force behind the religious changes of the 1630s, has suggested the term 'Carolinism'. Yet historians have generally found it impossible to prove who had the greater responsibility for the religious reforms of the 1630s, the king or the archbishop. It was probably a symbiotic relationship. Ultimately, the most appropriate term to use when talking about the religious policies of Charles and Laud is 'anti-Calvinism'.

Why Charles supported the anti-Calvinists

There are two main reasons, religious and political, why Charles supported the anti-Calvinists. Firstly, the importance that they placed upon order and ceremony appealed to a king who, as shown by the nature of the royal court, was obsessed with rank and decorum. The 'beauty of holiness' was as important to Charles as it was to Archbishop Laud. Secondly, as Roger Lockyer has observed, 'because they [the anti-Calvinists] realised that their opponents dominated parliament they tended to exalt royal authority.'

The balancing of different opinions in the church, the *via media* that James had effected with great success until the outbreak of the Thirty Years' War, collapsed after 1625 as Charles attached himself to the anti-Calvinist cause. In February 1626 the royal favourite, Buckingham, perceiving which way the religious wind was blowing, also attached himself to the anti-Calvinist element at a religious conference held at his London home, York House. After he was appointed chancellor of Cambridge University later that year, he forbade all predestinarian teaching at the university. There was a flurry of anti-Calvinist appointments in 1628 including Richard Neile to Winchester and William Laud, who had preached at the opening of parliament in 1625 and 1626, to London on 4 July. Following the temporary suspension of archbishop Abbot in 1627 for refusing to license a sermon by an anti-Calvinist, the anti-Calvinists were left in virtual control of the church.

Laud's character and beliefs

Laud proved himself indefatigable in implementing anti-Calvinist reforms (see pages 59–61), even at the expense of his health. He ordered bishops to

Why did Charles promote the anti-Calvinists?

reside in their **see** and produce regular inspection reports. However, an obsession with the detail of these visitation reports and the day-to-day operation of the church tended to obscure Laud's larger purpose. This weakness was compounded by his general inability to get along with others. He seems to have suffered from a dangerous impatience, something that was perhaps exacerbated by his advancing years for, at sixty when appointed as archbishop, he perhaps realised that his time was limited. Nor was Laud ever personally close to the king. Despite the fact that Laud owed his promotion to Charles, the archbishop always felt insecure, especially when the queen's party gained influence at his expense in the late 1630s. Laud reacted badly to criticism and was particularly sensitive to remarks about his low birth (he was the son of a Reading clothier). Criticism from members of the political nation seems to have developed in him a sense of insecurity so strong that it probably accounts for his astonishingly selfless commitment to public service. Yet his quest for efficiency, attention to detail and zeal to get things done – the policy of Thorough – also meant that 'he was appallingly active, appallingly visible and an appalling nuisance'.

What were Laud's religious beliefs? He was not Catholic. For example, he supported recusancy fines. In a scholarly confrontation with a Jesuit, published in *A relation of the conference between W. Laud and Mr Fisher*, the archbishop firmly refuted the doctrines of Roman Catholicism. 'It is ironic', remarks Kevin Sharpe, 'that one of the best defences of the Church of England against Rome was penned by a prelate charged with popery.' Yet rumour abounded that Laud was in the pay of the pope. Being offered a cardinal's hat cannot have helped (even though the offer was unlikely to have had papal sanction). The innovations in church fabric and services must have appeared to many as a move away from accustomed Protestant practice. He was not an Arminian, at least in the sense that he did not follow all the teachings of the Dutch theologian Arminius. At his trial, he argued that he had 'nothing to do to defend Arminianism'. Laud, however, did agree with Arminius' rejection of Calvin's dogma of predestination, the notion that one was damned or saved even before birth according to God's will. Laud's theology is therefore best seen as anti-Calvinist. He regarded himself as being a staunch supporter of the Protestant Church of England. Laud wanted to return the church to the pure state it had been in before it had acquired elements of Roman superstition.

The Laudian programme and its impact

The Laudian programme was directed at providing two things in particular:
- the provision of order and decency in church services;
- the imposition of religious uniformity.

See is another word for diocese, the area over which a bishop has jurisdiction.

Edward Hyde, earl of Clarendon (1609–74), having emerged as a leading royalist from 1642, went into exile with Charles II during the 1650s. He was instrumental in facilitating the Restoration in 1660 and governed as lord chancellor until 1667 when he was driven into exile. He wrote *The history of the Rebellion and Civil Wars in England*.

As **Edward Hyde, earl of Clarendon**, observed, many churches were 'kept so indecently and slovenly'. The condition of St Paul's Cathedral was considered to be 'a scandal to the nation'. When a yeoman from Warwickshire was charged with defecating in St Paul's Cathedral his defence was that he had not realised that he was in a house of God. Meanwhile, the 1633 visitation report of the archbishop of York had stated that in most places churches 'are very miserable and ruinous in the fabric'. On the basis that the physical state of a church was an indication of its spiritual well-being, Laud instigated a reform programme designed to enhance the interior beauty of churches, to emphasise what he called 'the beauty of holiness'. The archbishop, therefore, ordered a number of changes to the fabric of churches including the decoration of fonts, the renewal of stained glass and the rehabilitation of organs. Perhaps the most significant change came from the ruling that the communion table should be removed from the centre of the church and be set 'altarwise', that is, in a north–south orientation, in the east end of the chancel and railed.

Laud also insisted that changes be made to the act of worship, or liturgy. For the large part, this was in order further to instil notions of order, decency and deference. 'Without ceremony', Laud remarked, 'it is not possible to keep any order or quiet discipline.' The importance of the Book of Common Prayer was stressed, which in turn led to an emphasis upon prayer at the expense of preaching. The pulpit was removed from its hitherto pre-eminent position and the sacraments, the bread and the wine, were given new importance and reverence. There was thus a renewed concern with bowing towards the altar and kneeling during communion. Keen that other holy days of the church should not take second place to Sundays, which many Protestants felt should be set aside for worship and spiritual meditation, the king reissued the *Book of sports* in 1633. This permitted people to engage in a wide variety of 'lawful recreations' on a Sunday, 'having first done their duty to God' – that is, having attended church.

Laud wanted a strong element of uniformity and central control over the clergy. This uniformity could best be achieved by enhancing the prestige and the power of the church hierarchy, especially the authority of the bishops. He did this in several ways. Firstly, he ordered bishops to reside in their diocese and stipulated that they visit each of their parishes at least once every three years, sending a detailed report of their activities to their archbishop. In turn, the archbishops were to report directly to the king. Regular inspections, or visitations, were also instituted. Secondly, a campaign against unlicensed preachers was launched. Only those who wore the surplice and hood gained a licence to preach, in contrast to the lenient policy of James I. The most prominent victim of this campaign was the Feoffees of Impropriations, an institution organised by a group of laymen who had purchased tithes which were then used to support godly and learned preachers. In that the Feoffees' purpose was to enhance the quality of ministers, they possessed a similar aim to Laud. However, since the preachers 'were chosen often to reflect the preference of their patrons', writes Kevin Sharpe, 'rather than to uphold the articles and canons of the church' they served as an impediment to the quest for uniformity. Laud regarded the Feoffees as 'the main instruments of the Puritan faction' and they were therefore dissolved in February 1633.

What were the main features of the Laudian reform programme?

Laud's reforms provoked resentment for several reasons: their economic cost; their social implications; the challenge to religious orthodoxy and the threat they posed to political stability.

Laud's desire to 'see the bishops decently supplied ... according to their place and dignity' meant that parishioners were met with demands to contribute sums of money to fund a religious policy of which many were suspicious. The refurbishment of churches was as expensive as it was extensive. Since 36 per cent of the livings in England had been impropriated, the financial demands that fell upon the laity were increasingly burdensome. In addition, those with a vested property interest now found themselves threatened by a church which had realised that uniformity could only be achieved by economic independence. The leases of episcopal lands were re-examined and, from 1634, no lease of more than 21 years was to be made.

Many gentry were appalled by the new emphasis given to the altar, because this often resulted in the removal of the established gentry's pews, significant as a symbol of importance and power in the local community.

The Laudian programme inspired resentment on religious grounds. For example, the *Book of sports* ordered the very opposite of established Puritan belief in the importance of Sabbatarianism, the notion that Sundays should be set aside for worship and spiritual meditation. The removal of the communion table to the east end of churches and its railing-off in that position carried disturbingly popish connotations. This caused alarm at a time when the Catholic Habsburgs seemed to be sweeping all before them in the Thirty Years' War. The new emphasis placed upon the sacraments, the diminished role of preaching and the practices of kneeling and bowing towards the altar all appeared to be evidence of a design to take the Church of England back to Rome.

Political resentment against the religious programme was mainly a result of the advancement of churchmen in what had for long been secular institutions. For example, when Bishop Juxon was appointed lord treasurer in 1636, he became the first cleric to hold that post since the fifteenth century. Not only were bishops encroaching upon responsibilities that had been traditionally fulfilled by the nobility and gentry, but there was indignation that many

An engraving of a supposed dream of Archbishop Laud. Pornographic detail and the showing of various atrocities lend spice to this piece of propaganda against the archbishop.

For what reasons did the Laudian programme provoke resentment?

John Lilburne
(1615–57) fought for parliament during the period 1642 to 1645 but, thereafter, expressed his distrust of the army leaders in a number of pamphlets. He emerged as a leading voice in the Leveller movement and was forced into exile in 1652. Upon his return in 1653, he was confined in the fortress of Mont Orgueil, in Jersey, and then moved to Dover Castle until 1655. He became a Quaker (see p. 188).

of them were low born, 'dragged forth from the dunghill', as was said of Laud. Nowhere was this new clerical influence more obvious than in the use of the secular courts for religious ends, notably Star Chamber. Already, in 1627, Laud and Richard Neile, archbishop of York, had been made privy councillors and therefore sat in Star Chamber. There they dealt out harsh punishments to those who criticised the religious changes, notably Prynne, Burton and Bastwick in 1637 (see pages 65–66) and **John Lilburne** in the winter of 1637–38.

The Laudian church reached its apogee in the spring of 1640. Acting against precedent, but according to the king's wishes, convocation, an assembly of the clergy that traditionally met when parliament met, continued to sit beyond the dissolution of the Short Parliament. The canons produced by convocation in 1640 amount to a definition of the ecclesiastical policies of Charles and Archbishop Laud. Of these canons, the one which caused most alarm was the sixth. It demanded that the clergy take an oath that they would never consent 'to alter the government of this church by archbishops, bishops, deans, and archdeacons etc'. The ambiguity of the so-called Etcetera Oath advanced the fear of many contemporaries that there was a popishly inclined faction at the heart of government determined to reunite England with the Catholic

Church. The increasingly pervasive belief that there was a popish plot afoot was in large part a consequence of the programme of religious changes implemented by Charles and Archbishop Laud.

Though the government argued that the canons represented renovations of practices, such as the insistence upon kneeling, bowing and wearing of the surplice which had appeared in the canons of 1604 (but not imposed), many in the Commons believed that they amounted to innovations which smacked of popery. However, revisionist historians such as Kevin Sharpe and Peter White have claimed that the actions of Charles and Laud in the 1630s were not innovatory. They argue that the 'innovations' in the church in the 1630s were an inevitable consequence of the strict enforcement of the injunctions of 1559 and the canons of 1604. What was innovatory, they suggest, was the vigour with which the royal policy was enforced (see Peter Lake, 'The Laudian style: order uniformity and the pursuit of holiness in the 1630s', in Kenneth Fincham (ed.) *The early Stuart church 1603–1642* (1993)).

There is no doubt that the changes of the 1630s did provoke consternation and resentment. 'There is a growing body of evidence', observes David L. Smith, 'to suggest that many people felt profound reservations about the religious policies of the Personal Rule, but thought it best not to air them in public.' Many recorded their concerns in their private diaries, others chose to emigrate. John Morrill believes that the religious policies of the 1630s resulted in a 'coiled spring' of resentment by 1640. Laud's implementation of the anti-Calvinist programme, therefore, polarised opinion, provoked fierce debate and agitated those who populated other than the centre of the religious spectrum. Indeed, Nicholas Tyacke has argued that the Civil Wars of the 1640s were instigated not by the 'Puritan Revolution' found in the pages of the older historiography of the period but, at least in part, by a Puritan counter-revolution set in motion by the 'rise of Arminianism'.

However, some historians have warned against the view that the Laudian policies of the 1630s provoked dangerous religious resentment and political disaffection. They argue that resistance, by its very nature, tends to be reported while acquiescence goes unnoticed. It is true that, before the advent of the Scottish troubles in 1637, there were few religious protests. In the light of this, it has been argued that anti-Calvinism was either popular or poorly implemented. Ronald Hutton, in 'Archbishop Laud in perspective', *History sixth* (1990), has pointed out that in the dioceses of Lincoln, Durham, Gloucester and Worcester 'almost all of [the Laudian reform programme] was either very slowly implemented or ignored because the bishops who held these sees did not want it'. Hutton also notes that the 'numbers of those prosecuted and punished were small and tended to be from the south east'.

From this perspective, Laud is seen, not as the cause of an increasingly powerful religious dissent that developed as the 1630s went on, but as a kindly old man whom we have all misunderstood.

The Laudian reforms acquired political connotations because they were taken to be evidence that a popish plot was afoot, that a fifth column committed to the overthrow of religion and established liberties had infiltrated the court. In his speech to the Short Parliament, on 17 April 1640, **John Pym**, amongst other things, spoke about religious grievances. He told MPs of 'the great encouragement which is given to them of the popish religion by a universal suspension of all laws that are made against them, and some of them admitted into public places of trust and power'. However, as Kevin Sharpe has noted, 'suspicions of leniency bore little relation to the Catholics' experience'. For example, a proclamation of August 1628 commanded the detention of all Jesuits and punishment of those who received them. Those who were noticed to be absent from church services over a period of six months were to be brought before JPs. Moreover, the research of F. C. Dietz has revealed that income from recusancy fines rose from £6,000 in 1631 to £32,000 in 1640. Nevertheless, Pym's concern that Catholics were being 'admitted into public places of trust and power' was seemingly apparent amongst Charles's chief ministers. Sir Richard Weston (earl of Portland, 1633), Sir Francis Cottington and Sir Francis Windebanke, in the words of one historian, were 'Catholics under the skin'. Yet they tended to be tarnished with the brush of association. For example, the wives of Windebanke and Weston were acknowledged Catholics – as was of course the wife of the king. Most important of all, and despite his attraction to Catholicism's sense of hierarchy and decorum, there is no evidence that the king was contemplating extending open toleration to English Catholics. 'No man was more averse from the Romish church than he was', wrote Clarendon of Charles, 'nor better understood the motive of their separation from us.'

Why was there a general belief in the existence of a popish plot? The answer lies, at least partly, in an appreciation of the importance of Henrietta Maria. The presence at court of a Catholic queen meant that her household became a focal point for Catholics. The opening of her new chapel at Somerset House, decorated according to the Catholic liturgy, was celebrated by an audience of 2,000 people. Moreover, for the first time since 1558, papal agents were welcomed at court, Gregorio Panzani from December 1634 and then, from 1636, his replacement, George Con. In 1638 Con was joined by the Catholic queen mother, Marie de Medici. The arrival of these personages prompted a number of high profile conversions at court, particularly women, such as the countess Newport and Olive Porter, wife of Endymion Porter, courtier to Charles. 'Our Grate women fall away every day,' lamented one newsletter. Nor was it only women. Walter Montagu, son of the earl of Manchester, caused a breach with his father by converting to Rome. These events not only took place against the background of the Thirty Years' War, perceived by many to be a straightforward fight to the finish between Catholicism and Protestantism, but a war in which England for much of the time seemed to be pursuing the friendship or neutrality of Catholic Spain.

In all, the atmosphere at the court and foreign circumstances meant that, for many people, the religious policies of Charles and Laud appeared to be an attempt to reintroduce 'popish rites' – a fear which seemed to be confirmed by the Etcetera Oath. A large proportion of the political nation was therefore encouraged to believe that there was a popish plot afoot. Since anti-Calvinism appeared to have the support of the king, these views had some credence. And since it was generally believed that the crown could do no wrong, 'the only way to question its supremacy', notes Hugh Trevor-Roper, in *Catholics, Anglicans and Puritans*, chapter 2 (1989), 'was to raise the cry of "No Popery!"'.

> For what reasons did a large proportion of the political nation believe that there was a popish plot afoot in the 1630s?

Eleven Years' Tyranny or Personal Rule?

The case for the 'Eleven Years' Tyranny'

Charles's Personal Rule has often been called the 'Eleven Years' Tyranny'. The phrase is clearly critical of Charles's government of England and, by implication, sympathetic to the parliamentarian cause. How justified is the label? As so often, there is evidence for and against the term.

The case for is based on several policies of Charles. The first was his attempts to censor books and newspapers. In 1632 the privy council had issued a decree in Star Chamber against the production of news sheets (or *carantos*) and banned them from sale. Laud, after his appointment as archbishop of Canterbury, played an important role in prosecuting those who produced religious tracts. William Prynne, who wrote his **Histriomastix** in 1632, was sentenced by Star Chamber the following year both to the pillory and the loss of parts of his ears. In 1636 a Puritan wrote that 'our presses formerly open to truth and piety are closed against them both of late'.

> *Histriomastix* was a Puritan diatribe against the theatre that included a specific attack upon Queen Henrietta Maria – who regularly performed in plays – under an index reference of 'women actors, notorious whores'.

The second policy was the severe punishments ordered by Star Chamber. For instance, in 1637 William Prynne, Henry Burton and John Bastwick, the first of whom had already suffered harshly in 1633, were sentenced to the loss of both ears in the pillory, a fine of £5,000 and life imprisonment. In addition, Prynne was branded 'S. L.', seditious libeller, 'for writing and publishing seditious, schismatical and libellous books against the Hierarchy'. Harsh treatment of individuals who were regarded as gentlemen (Prynne, Burton and Bastwick were respectively a lawyer, clergyman and physician) probably bred disrespect for the regime rather than outright discontent.

Prynne, Burton and Bastwick were convicted in 1637 by Star Chamber for publishing Puritan attacks upon the Laudian church. They were fined £5,000 each and placed in a pillory where they had their ears cut off. Prynne was also sentenced to be branded on each cheek with the letters 'S. L.', meaning 'seditious libeller'. He claimed, however, that they stood for *stigmata Laudis*, 'the scars of Laud'. The punishment of Prynne, Burton and Bastwick seems powerful evidence that the 1630s were a period of 'tyranny'. More recently, however, Kevin Sharpe has pointed out that a contemporary observer noted that these men 'covet a kind of puritanical martyrdom or at least a fame of punishment for religion'.

The third policy was to threaten the judges. Charles had few qualms about putting pressure upon them to gain the outcome he desired. John Morrill, having examined the period 1626 to 1629, concluded that the king's behaviour during that period 'surely constituted a formidable prima facie case of legal tyranny' and that 'the 1630s sustained if they did not intensify levels of anxiety'.

The case for 'Personal Rule'

With regard to censorship, Kevin Sharpe argues that the Star Chamber decree of 11 July 1637, which some see as the apogee of Caroline censorship, 'subsumed and systematised [rather] than innovated'. Moreover, it is argued that censorship was not in fact particularly severe because it was hard to enforce. It was impossible, for example, for the government to control the import of books into England. Many of the plays of the 1630s, even those at court, were critical of Caroline politics.

The view that the Star Chamber was the key component of a harsh and insensitive government has been challenged. J. P. Kenyon has shown that it was not an instrument of the state. Indeed, the majority of cases were brought by private individuals and not the government. The apparent brutality of its sentences has also been questioned. Of the 236 judgements during the period 1630–41 only 19 involved sentences of corporal punishment. Many fines were later reduced or remitted. In the case of Prynne, Burton and Bastwick contemporaries observed that they were bent upon 'puritanical martyrdom'. This has led Sharpe to conclude that 'traditional accounts that make the trial sound like a travesty of justice are themselves a travesty of the truth'. Kenyon has remarked that 'in the absence of a prison system all seventeenth-century courts had to impose fines, corporal punishments or public penance: this was especially so of Star Chamber which could not impose the death penalty'.

Even the charge that Charles interfered with the judiciary has been reduced by Sharpe to only 'a small number of incidents compared with, say, the 1550s or the later Stuart decades'.

The alternative to firm government was anarchy. Since the political nation feared the latter, most were prepared to tolerate the former. Compared to what had happened in the 1620s, what was happening on the continent and what was to occur in the 1640s, the 1630s were a time of peace and prosperity. Writing in the 1660s, Clarendon described it as a time of 'greatest calm and the fullest measure of felicity that any people in any age . . . have been blessed with, to the wonder and envy of all parts of Christendom'.

Summary questions

1 (a) Identify and explain any *two* problems which Wentworth encountered in his attempt to impose a policy of Thorough upon Ireland.

   (b) Compare the success of Charles I's government in dealing with at least *three* problems during the 1630s.

2 To what extent is it appropriate to describe Charles I's rule without parliament, 1629–40, as 'The Eleven Years' Tyranny'?

6 The outbreak of civil war, 1637–42

Focus questions

◆ Why was Charles defeated in the Bishops' Wars?

◆ Why was there no settlement between the king and parliament in 1641?

◆ Why did civil war break out in 1642?

Significant dates

1637 An attempt to read the new Scottish Prayer Book in Edinburgh provokes riots.

1638 *February* The National Covenant is drawn up in Scotland.
August The Scottish parliament assembles.
November The Scottish General Assembly abolishes episcopacy.

1639 *March to June* The First Bishops' War breaks out and concludes with the Pacification of Berwick.

1640 *April to May* The Short Parliament meets.
June The Laudian canons are issued.
August to October The Second Bishops' War breaks out and is concluded by the Truce of Ripon.
November The Long Parliament meets.
Thomas Wentworth, earl of Strafford, is imprisoned.

1641 *February* The Triennial Act is passed.
May The First Army Plot is revealed.
The Act Against Forcible Dissolution is passed.
Strafford is executed.
October The Irish Rebellion breaks out.
The Second Army Plot is revealed.
November Parliament debates the Grand Remonstrance.

1642 *January* Charles I attempts to arrest the Five Members.
Charles I leaves London.
March The Militia Ordinance is issued.
June Charles I issues the Commission of Array.
Parliament issues the Nineteen Propositions.
August Charles I raises his standard at Nottingham and the Civil Wars begin.

Overview

Personal Rule in England lasted until 1640, when Charles called the first parliament since 1629. Three years earlier, in 1637, trouble between the king's government and his subjects broke out in Scotland. This set in motion the sequence of events which led inexorably to the recall of English parliament and then to the outbreak of civil war in England. We need to retrace our steps, to explain why trouble broke out in Scotland in 1637 and how it came to affect English affairs. Then we must consider why the political conflict in England was not resolved peacefully. Finally, we need to examine the different ideas that have been developed to explain why England went to war with itself in 1642. The subject has fascinated historians ever since the seventeenth century. New ideas are still being developed on this subject which reveal much about the historical process.

The **English Prayer Book** was resented by the Presbyterians who objected to the sections that stipulated additional saints' days, festivals and certain ambiguous comments about the use of 'ornaments'. Its illustrations of angels were also offensive to Scottish consciences.

From the Prayer Book crisis to the First Bishops' War, 1637–39

In 1637 Charles I ordered a revised version of the **English Prayer Book** to be used in church services in Scotland. In the Cathedral of St Giles, in Edinburgh, a crowd of several hundred, most of them women, rioted against the prayer

Riots in the Cathedral of St Giles, Edinburgh. Jenny Geddes is supposed to have initiated the fracas by throwing her stool in protest at the attempted reading of the new Prayer Book. After a second riot, the king announced his determination to have the book enforced: 'I mean to be obeyed.'

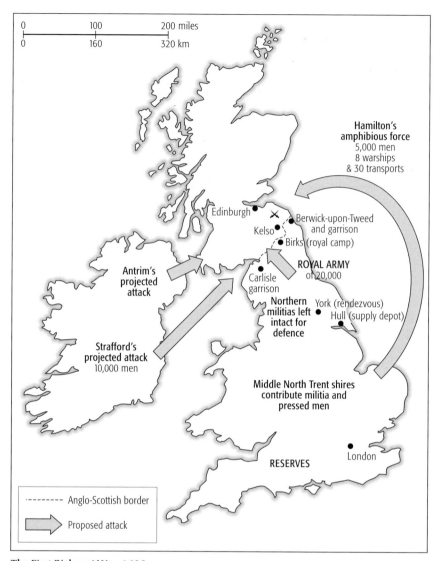

The First Bishops' War, 1639

book. (Some believed the women were in fact male apprentices in disguise.) They hurled stools at the clergy, who beat a hasty retreat. Charles I stood his ground. The Scots objected to the changes in the church liturgy contained in the book and to its introduction without proper consultation. They suspected an English plot to turn the Scots away from the path of Protestantism towards that of Catholicism. They thought Laud was behind this plan. By February 1638 the most suspicious had drawn up the National Covenant, a pledge to 'maintain the true religion of Christ Jesus . . . and [to] abolish all false religion'. People flocked to sign. Charles now began to offer concessions, such as calling the Scottish parliament, and even withdrawing the prayer book. Yet it was clear that these concessions were only begrudgingly granted and, therefore, when Scottish church leaders met in the Glasgow Assembly at the end of 1638, they resolved to abolish episcopacy in Scotland. Faced with a revolt against his authority, Charles decided to use force to stamp it out. Before we consider how he did so, we need to explain why the crisis had blown up so quickly.

He had started off on the wrong foot. As soon as he became king in 1625, Charles insisted upon obtaining an Act of Revocation, a cancellation of all grants of property made by the crown during a **minority**. However, Charles had not had a period of minority rule. He, moreover, chose 1540 as the date from which lands should be redeemed. The Revocation would apply to land that had been acquired from the church as well as from the crown. Landowners who had benefited from the secularisation of church lands would be affected. Charles had good reasons for introducing the scheme. He wanted to restore property and income to the church and to increase the income of the crown. However, these were never explained and neither was the prospect of compensation. Instead, it appeared to be a devastating blow to the interests of landholders. Although the Revocation quickly proved to be something of a dead letter, a contemporary nevertheless considered it to have been 'the ground stone of all the mischief that followed after, both to the king's government and family'.

A **minority**, or a period of minority rule, occurs when the monarch dies leaving an heir to the throne who is a minor – that is, aged 14 or below.

Charles, moreover, generally neglected Scotland. For the first eight years of his reign he had never visited Scotland and had ruled by laws enacted by proclamation. When he did finally visit Scotland in 1633, to be crowned king (seven years after being crowned king of England), he aroused more fears about his intentions. The coronation ceremony contained many Laudian features, such as a separate altar to which the clergy bowed, which many saw as a form of popery. Charles's stay in Scotland was as brief as possible. He made few public appearances and was soon back in England.

Identify three mistakes made by Charles in his government of Scotland during the period 1625–33.

Thus, it is little surprising that, in 1637, he misjudged the reaction of the Scots to his plans for religious uniformity. He was an absentee monarch who had chosen to reform perhaps the most sensitive aspects of public life and in a direction that ran counter to Scottish opinion. In 1637–38 he combined belated concessions with a hard line approach to what had become a Scottish rebellion. He soon issued orders to the counties of England to raise forces from the **trained bands** to fight the Scots. Note that he did so without calling an English parliament, the first time a monarch had tried to go to war without doing so since 1323. The treasury released £200,000 to finance the campaign. By the spring of 1639, Charles had a force of some 20,000 camped on the Scottish border. Whether he expected or hoped that the threat of war, including a trade blockade by the navy, would cause the Scots to cave in without fighting is impossible to answer. The two armies squared up to each other without

Trained bands were selected members of local militias who, from Elizabethan times, received special training to prepare them to defend their counties. They were controlled by the lords lieutenant.

coming to blows. In June 1639 the two sides agreed to settle. By the terms of the Pacification of Berwick, the armies were disbanded and Charles agreed to the calling of another Scottish parliament and General Assembly. The so-called First Bishops' War was concluded before it had begun. The crisis in Scotland, however, was far from over and the one in England was just starting.

The Short Parliament and the Second Bishops' War, 1640

The Scots continued to challenge royal rule as the assembly and parliament confirmed the decision to scrap the episcopacy. They did not disband their army. Charles had to do something. He wanted someone effective by his side. He recalled Wentworth from Ireland in 1639, made him earl of Strafford and gave him a leading role in his government. Strafford was not dominant, however. Henrietta Maria, who was emerging as a political force of some importance, opposed his return. Strafford, however, who had opposed war with Scotland in the first place, was among those who persuaded Charles to call a parliament in England for the first time since 1629. If Charles was to crush the Scottish rebellion, there was no alternative; equipping an army was estimated to cost almost £1 million a year.

Parliament assembled in April 1640. It was opened by Charles, who made a brief speech that, in the circumstances, was too brief. After 11 years and in the middle of a crisis in Scotland, MPs expected something more. Charles offered to give up ship money in exchange for the immediate grant of 12 subsidies. However, instead of discussing the royal request, MPs fell to debating the grievances that had accumulated since 1629: royal actions against parliament, against Protestantism and against property. Attempts to reach a compromise came to nought, in large part a consequence of the efficiency with which John Pym articulated the grievances of MPs. On 5 May Charles dissolved the Short Parliament. He wanted to deprive his opponents of a platform from which they could articulate their concerns.

In his account of these years, Clarendon, observing that there were many in this parliament who were prepared to lend the king support, considered Charles's abrupt dissolution of this parliament on 5 May to be his gravest error. 'Not least', observes Derek Hirst, 'it helped the English catch up with the ideological sophistication of their neighbours.'

There was one significant outcome of the end of the Short Parliament. The convocation, the assembly of the Church of England, traditionally met when parliament met and ended when parliament ended. In 1640 tradition was broken. The convocation was kept in session. There were two reasons for doing so. One was financial. The convocation voted an annual subsidy of £20,000 for six years. The other was religious. The convocation passed a new

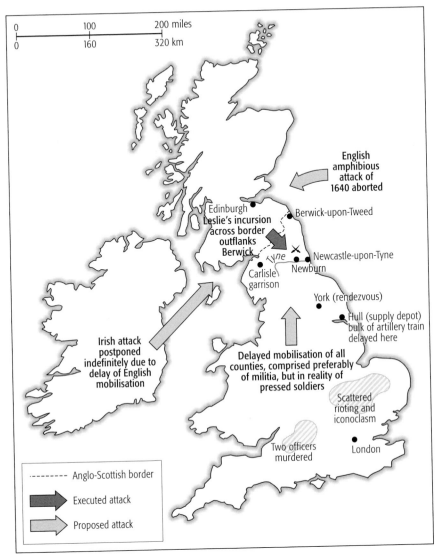

The following labels appear on the map:

- English amphibious attack of 1640 aborted
- Edinburgh
- Berwick-upon-Tweed
- Leslie's incursion across border outflanks Berwick
- Newcastle-upon-Tyne
- Tyne
- Newburn
- Carlisle garrison
- York (rendezvous)
- Hull (supply depot) bulk of artillery train delayed here
- Irish attack postponed indefinitely due to delay of English mobilisation
- Delayed mobilisation of all counties, comprised preferably of militia, but in reality of pressed soldiers
- Scattered rioting and iconoclasm
- Two officers murdered
- London

Scale: 0 – 100 – 200 miles / 0 – 160 – 320 km

Legend:
- - - - - - - - Anglo-Scottish border
▶ Executed attack
▷ Proposed attack

The Second Bishops' War, 1640

set of canons that defined the ecclesiastical policies of Charles and Archbishop Laud, including the so-called Etcetera Oath which many MPs found deeply alarming (see page 62).

In the aftermath of the Short Parliament, English MPs and Scottish Covenanters came to realise that their separate interests could best be served if they worked together to coerce Charles. Thus, there is some evidence that the English opposition encouraged the Scots to go to war against Charles.

The Second Bishops' War began in August 1640. There appeared to be much that favoured the king's cause:

- Charles had established military bases in England and Ireland; the latter could provide an army of 10,000.

What did Charles hope for from the Short Parliament?
What concession did he offer MPs?
What was convocation and in what way was it particularly significant in 1640?

This satirical picture, directed against Laud, suggests that the canons produced by convocation in 1640 were intended to blow up the Protestant religion.

- Thanks to ship money, Charles had a fleet that he could use to blockade Scotland.
- Charles could expect support from Scotland, especially from the Catholic Highlands and from the territory around Aberdeen.
- The Covenanting regime was inexperienced in fighting a war.

Nevertheless, it was the Scots who quickly gained the upper hand. The Scottish forces invaded north-east England and occupied Newcastle. This time, there was some military action, at Newburn, though hardly a set-piece battle. Charles summoned a Council of Peers rather than a full parliament and to York rather than London but the council requested the recall of parliament. Charles's agreement to the Truce of Ripon, in October 1640, made the recall of parliament essential. The truce stipulated that Charles would pay £850 a day towards the expenses of the Scottish army, which was to remain in north-east England until a settlement was agreed and confirmed by an English parliament. Bankrupt, Charles had to call another parliament within a few weeks of prematurely dissolving its predecessor. It assembled in November 1640 and was not finally dissolved until 1660. Hence, it became known as the Long Parliament.

Why had English expectations of military success proved mistaken? There were several reasons:

- The poor quality of the English troops. They were raw, ill-disciplined 'beggarly fellows'. 'Our soldiers are so disorderly that they shoot bullets through our tents,' recorded one officer.
- Not enough weaponry. As Conrad Russell has observed, 'the lack of arms clearly contributed to the lack of fighting spirit amongst the English troops'.
- Poor leadership. The earl of Arundel was appointed lord general in 1639,

though Clarendon considered that he 'had nothing martial about him but his presence and his looks'. His replacement, the earl of Northumberland, was more promising but was ill for much of the campaign. Moreover, most of Charles's commanders were lords, knights and gentlemen who had never experienced battle.

- Not enough money. The Short Parliament of 1640 offered no subsidies and the financial devices of the 1630s provided insufficient revenue to allow Charles to wage effective war.
- Opposition from English Puritans. Charles had assumed that traditional English hatred of the Scots remained greater than English hatred of royal government without parliaments. However, to many of the English, the Covenanters were seen as liberators, not enemies. By pursuing an anti-Calvinist programme both in England and Scotland, Charles had created a sizeable minority in each country that were opposed to him and for the same reason. Indeed, recent research has suggested that some of the English political nation was actively colluding with the Scots.

Why was Charles defeated in the Bishops' Wars?

The Bishops' Wars had important consequences for the course of events in England. Firstly, the Covenanters' successful challenge to royal authority in Scotland provided England with an example to follow. The Scottish Triennial Act (June 1640), which ensured that a 'full and free' parliament was to be held at least once every three years, provided a precedent for opposition MPs in the Long Parliament. Secondly, the Covenanters recognised that their security and long-term goals depended upon constraining or dismantling Charles's power in England. In particular, since they were effective agents of the crown and therefore able to mobilise royal resources, it was central to the Covenanting programme that bishops should be abolished.

The Long Parliament, November 1640 to September 1641

Having ruled without parliaments for 11 years, Charles now had to call a second parliament in the same year. Lacking any resources, yet obliged to pay a large indemnity to the victorious Scots, Charles was unable to dissolve this parliament abruptly. Consequently, the critics of Caroline government, led in the Commons by John Pym, were provided with a platform from which they attacked, and ultimately dismantled, hated aspects of the Personal Rule.

At the first meeting of the Long Parliament on 3 November 1640, MPs were united in their determination to move against the personnel and policies of the Personal Rule. This determination was articulated in a great set-piece speech by Pym in which he talked of there having been a design to 'alter the kingdoms both in religion and government'. It was generally believed that, once this reform had been accomplished and evil councillors removed, harmony would be restored between king and parliament. At this stage, the vast majority of MPs had no desire to criticise the crown or to limit the king's authority. Their intention was to restore the old order, which the evil councillors had overturned.

Two of those councillors, secretary of state Windebanke and lord keeper Finch, recognising the way the wind was blowing, fled to the continent in December 1640. Impeachment proceedings were begun against all but one of the surviving judges of the 1630s. Archbishop Laud was also impeached and, from November 1640, was languishing in the Tower. There he stayed until his execution in January 1645. The other chief exponent of Thorough, Strafford, was also arrested. He was charged with high treason. The specific charge was that, following the failure of the Short Parliament, he had advised Charles that he was 'loosed and absolved from all rules of government'.

The impeachment of Strafford took place in Westminster Hall, where for three weeks Pym led a large number of MPs in trying to convince the Lords of Strafford's guilt. The Lords were unconvinced. Impeachment was faltering so radical MPs introduced a bill of attainder to ensure Strafford was found guilty. The bill was a substitute for a court hearing, simply declaring an individual guilty of treason. If passed by Commons, Lords and crown, it would become law and Strafford could be put to death. As the London mob began to demonstrate outside the Houses of Parliament, Pym revealed details of the so-called First Army Plot – a scheme whereby a group of army officers was to capture the Tower, release Strafford and threaten parliament with dissolution. Many hitherto reluctant MPs were thus persuaded – and perhaps intimidated – into voting 204 to 59 to attaint Strafford though many in both Houses stayed away. Fearing for his own safety and that of the queen, Charles gave his assent to the attainder. Consequently, on 12 May on Tower Hill, in front of a crowd estimated to number 100,000, Strafford was executed. His execution was important both as an illustration of attitudes in 1641 and in the consequences it was to have. It showed to what extent many MPs hated and mistrusted Strafford. The anti-Strafford demonstrations were the first indication of the attitudes of people outside the political nation and it showed how weak and isolated Charles was. Moreover, it made a future settlement between king and parliament both easier and harder. It was easier because parliament was not as solidly anti-government as it had been before. It was harder because the execution made the two sides more suspicious of each other.

Alongside their aim of removing those connected with Personal Rule, MPs now tried to restrain the royal prerogative, though before the summer of 1641 little had been done. There were only two restrictions upon the royal prerogative and even they were not all that they seemed. One was the Triennial Act,

The execution of Strafford, 12 May 1641. Charles had promised Strafford that he would never assent to his execution. The eventual sacrifice of Strafford thus ensured that his ghost was at Charles's shoulder for the rest of his life.

passed in February 1641. It followed the example of the Scottish Triennial Act of 1640 in that the king was obliged to call a parliament at least once every three years. If he failed to do so then parliament would meet anyway. The other was what is sometimes called the Act Against Forcible Dissolution, passed on 10 May. Intimidated by crowds outside his Whitehall apartments, and anxious to counter fears that he might dissolve the parliament, Charles assented to a bill which ensured that the dissolution of parliament could not occur without its own consent. This act applied only to the current parliament. It was not a permanent limitation on the royal prerogative.

In the summer of 1641, MPs deprived Charles of the means of Personal Rule. The various financial levies, which were of dubious legality, were scrapped. In June tonnage and poundage were abolished, impositions could be levied only with parliamentary consent. In August ship money, knighthood fines and forest laws were declared illegal. (In this first session MPs agreed to the levy of six subsidies plus an additional poll tax to pay for the cost of the armies in the north.) The machinery of Personal Rule was also abolished. The **Court of High Commission** and Star Chamber were outlawed, the latter in particular because of its role in enforcing Laudianism. The judicial powers of the Council of the North and the **Council of the Marches** were suppressed.

The **Court of High Commission** was a court that heard ecclesiastical disputes and could impose fines or imprisonment.

The **Council of the Marches** acted as an extension of the privy council and was based in Ludlow. It exercised legal and administrative power in a region remote from Westminster.

Identify the main pieces of reforming legislation enacted by the Long Parliament by the summer of 1641.

In August 1641 Charles and the Scots agreed on peace terms. The Scottish army withdrew from England and the English army began to disband. Charles decided to go to Scotland. Some MPs urged him not to go but he ignored them. The English parliament was adjourned in early September. MPs and peers went home for what they believed was a well-earned rest. By the early autumn of 1641, the immediate crisis seemed to have passed. When parliament reassembled in late October the situation soon became many times worse.

Division, rebellion and civil war, October 1641 to August 1642

During this period, three factors in particular were working to polarise opinion within the English political nation and generally destabilise the political situation.

Firstly, there was a deepening mistrust of Charles. Many MPs felt he could not be trusted to govern according to the legislation to which he had given his consent. After all, Charles had ignored the terms of the Petition of Right of 1628. Even more worrying was the revelation of evidence that implicated Charles in a number of schemes that envisaged the use of either English, Scottish or Irish forces against parliament in 1641, for example the First Army Plot. During his three-month stay in Scotland, Charles had apparently conspired in a scheme to arrest the leading Covenanters, Argyll and Hamilton, in the so-called Incident of October 1641. Such news did nothing to allay suspicions about Charles.

Secondly, this distrust of Charles encouraged Pym and his supporters to insist that the royal prerogative must be *reformed*, not simply *restrained*. In particular, they asserted that Charles should be obliged to surround himself with ministers of whom parliament approved. As early as December 1640, there were reports that negotiations were taking place for Bedford to become lord treasurer and for Pym to become the chancellor of the exchequer. Bedford was the hinge around which this so-called 'bridging scheme' was expected to swing and his death on 9 May 1641 led to the collapse of any such agreement. There was no one acceptable to both king and MPs who could take his place. For many, however, the demand that the king should appoint as ministers only those approved by parliament amounted to a breach in the traditional constitution. Increasingly uneasy about the aims and the methods of the group led by Pym, many of the political nation began to lend their support to Charles.

This last development was reinforced by the third factor – religion. MPs could agree to dismantle the Laudian reforms (as they did on 1 September) because they believed that they were evidence of a popish plot. They could not agree to abolish episcopacy in all its 'roots and branches', as demanded by the Scots and by petitions from the English counties. The **iconoclasm** that began in 1640 to 1641 resulted in counter-petitions to keep the episcopacy. This showed Charles that his position was far from lost. Indeed, it seemed possible that Charles would be able, at some point, to dissolve the Long Parliament with its assent. But then came an event which made the situation many times more complicated and difficult to solve, the Irish Rebellion.

On 22 October the Catholics of Ulster rebelled. Encouraged by the success of the Scots' religious demands and fearful of the advance of radical Puritanism in England, their revolt resulted in the death of perhaps 3,000 Protestants. Before long, as they were joined by the Old English, the revolt spread across most of Ireland. To MPs in the Long Parliament this was hard evidence of a popish plot. It was made worse by the claim (probably false) of one of the rebel leaders that Charles had authorised them to take up arms. Meanwhile, rumours swept London that as many as 20,000 Protestants had been killed. In English political circles, there was no question but that an army had to be raised in order to put down the Irish. The key question was about who would lead such a force. Could Charles be trusted to do so? The immediate and most important political consequence of the Irish Rebellion was that it focused attention on the monarch's military authority, a key aspect of his prerogative that Charles had resolved never to relinquish. It also ensured that parliament would have to remain sitting in order to raise funds for the proposed military expedition. Moreover, fears about Irish Catholics crossing the Irish Sea and massacring English Protestants added to the tensions of the time.

At the same time as news of the rebellion reached London, another factor complicated the crisis. In November, Pym introduced into the Commons the Grand Remonstrance. This was a lengthy, one-sided account of Charles's reign, upon which opposition MPs had been working for many weeks. Alleging that the 'evils under which we have now many years suffered . . . are fomented and cherished by a corrupt and ill-affected party', the Remonstrance reiterated the demand that the king employ only ministers approved by parliament. Pym found it hard to gain parliamentary approval for the Grand Remonstrance but the Commons approved it by 159 votes to 148 on 22 November. Three days later, the king returned from Scotland.

The Commons' decision to publish the Grand Remonstrance before the king had formally responded to its contents heightened the already charged atmosphere on the streets of London. 'I did not dream that we should remonstrate downwards, tell stories to the people, and talk of the king as of a third person,' lamented Dering. Driven in part by the effects of a worsening economic recession, large crowds began to appear outside parliament and

Iconoclasm is the deliberate destruction of all religious images. From 1641 the extreme Puritans carried out a programme of destruction in many parish churches and cathedrals, smashing stained glass windows, statues and wood carvings and whitewashing wall paintings. Many medieval religious books were also destroyed because of the pictures they contained.

Describe how the Irish Rebellion raised the political tension in England.

Perhaps 3,000 Protestants were killed in the Irish Rebellion of 1641, though rumour placed it at 20,000. This series of pictures shows the Protestant version of events.

demanded the exclusion of bishops from the Lords. On 27 December there was fighting between these demonstrators and the London militia. The crowd prevented the bishops from taking their seats in the Lords. Meanwhile, Charles could no more hope for support from the City of London because, on 21 December, it had elected a new common council (governing body) which encouraged the mob in its demonstrations of support for Pym.

Charles, acting with an increasing sense of panic, now made three crucial errors:

- In December he appointed Colonel Lunsford to the Tower of London. Lunsford was a convicted felon and, therefore, to the supporters of Pym it appeared as though the king was planning a coup. Although Charles quickly replaced Lunsford, the damage was done.
- On 4 January Charles entered the Commons with an armed force in order to arrest Pym, Holles, Haselrig, Strode and Hampden – members of the Commons – and Lord Mandeville, whom he regarded as the leaders of his opposition. However, these men had been tipped off and escaped. In a moment of high drama in the Commons' chamber, Charles exclaimed, 'I see that the birds are flown.'

- On 10 January he left London, fearing for the safety of Henrietta Maria. This meant that London and its immense resources henceforth belonged to parliament.

By early 1642 there were two issues which separated Charles and his opponents. Firstly, his opponents argued that it was necessary to reform the royal prerogative rather than simply restrain it. This they believed essential in order to secure the gains they had made over the past year or so, to stop Charles using military force to restore Personal Rule. Control of the militia was the key issue. Charles had made it plain that he was not prepared to yield. Political deadlock followed. The second issue was religious. On one side, Charles would never assent to the abolition of episcopacy, which most MPs saw as necessary to receive support from the Scots. On the other side, many MPs saw Charles as intent on introducing not just an anti-Calvinist church but a papist one.

Identify the two main issues which blocked the chances of settlement between Charles and parliament by early 1642.

The gap between the two sides was so great that a settlement was out of the question. Both sides began to prepare for war. For a number of reasons this was a big step, especially for parliamentarians who were challenging God-given royal authority. Firstly, they needed the authority to raise forces. On 5 March parliament passed the Militia Ordinance. Passed by the two Houses but not the king, the ordinance gave authority to lords lieutenant and deputy lieutenants in the counties to raise local militia to serve within the county. Charles replied with the Commission of Array, a medieval device, which he issued to individuals or groups of individuals in the counties. Though both devices were controversial, the Commission of Array probably aroused more suspicion about its author's intention than did the Militia Ordinance. Secondly, the two sides needed money. Both appealed for subscriptions from individuals but this did not raise a great deal. Parliament then used part of £400,000 that had been approved for crushing the Irish Rebellion to raise forces in England. Thirdly, the two sides had to win the support of as many men as possible. They issued statements attacking their opponent and putting their own case. Perhaps the most important was parliament's Nineteen Propositions of June 1642. The document began by blaming all the present troubles on the 'subtle insinuations, mischievous practices and evil counsels of men disaffected to God's true religion, your Majesty's honour and safety and the public peace and prosperity of your people'. Thus, the first three propositions stated the need for the king's ministers to be approved by parliament. Two concerned the royal family, three religion and most of the rest the desire to avoid persecution by the king should a settlement be reached. Within three weeks, the king had rejected them. In a carefully reasoned case, he argued that the propositions would upset the balance between king, Lords and Commons of the current 'regulated monarchy'; that 'this splendid and

By what means did each side set about raising an army?

What was the document known as the Nineteen Propositions and what was its main purpose?

Charles raises his standard at Nottingham on 22 August 1642. It was an ill omen that it blew down during that night.

Jack Cade led a Kentish revolt in 1450. At one point, Cade's men entered the capital and executed unpopular courtiers.

Wat Tyler led the Kentish section of the Peasants' Revolt in 1381 and orchestrated a march on London.

excellently distinguished form of government' would 'end in a dark, equal chaos of confusion, and the long line of our many noble ancestors in a **Jack Cade** or a **Wat Tyler**'. With one side fearing absolutism, the other anarchy, the differences of perception were too great to be bridged.

On 22 August Charles raised his standard at Nottingham. The English Civil Wars had begun.

Historical interpretation: the origins of the Civil Wars

There are few, if any, subjects that have provoked as much argument among historians as the origins of the English Civil Wars. It is worth outlining the four main schools of thought which have developed over the past 150 years because the debate can be properly understood only by referring to these schools and their leading historians. They are as follows.

Whig

The Whig interpretation of history explains the English Civil Wars as part of the onward march towards parliamentary government. The Stuarts blocked progress towards that goal. The parliamentarians demolished their opposition and thus ensured the triumph of that uniquely successful device, the English constitution. The school prevailed from the early nineteenth to the early twentieth century. The leading Whig historians are Macaulay, Gardiner and Trevelyan.

Marxist

The Marxists see the events of the 1640s and 1650s as the English Revolution, as a time when the gentry and the middle classes removed the last vestiges of feudalism from the political and economic system, and laid the foundations for the bourgeois capitalist society of the eighteenth and nineteenth centuries. For Marxists, economic forces and relations are the driving force of history. The English Revolution was England's bourgeois (or middle-class) revolution. The great Marxist historian is Christopher Hill, who, in the mid and late twentieth century, led the way in developing Marxist ideas of the seventeenth century.

Revisionist

This is a catch-all term for those historians who reject both Whig and Marxist versions of the English Civil Wars, which means almost all modern historians of the period. If they do have anything in common, it is that they emphasise short-term and/or particular causes, whether political or religious, rather than the long-term and more general social and economic factors preferred by the Marxists.

Revisionist historians have sought the origins of the Civil Wars not only in the period immediately prior to its outbreak but also by viewing events from their British perspective. Observing that Scotland and Ireland rebelled before England, Conrad Russell has articulated a three-kingdom 'billiard ball' explanation for the outbreak of conflict in England. Nevertheless, Russell's argument that rebellions in Scotland and Ireland were necessary preconditions for the same process in England has met with criticism. John Morrill, for example, believes that 'at times Russell seems to let the Scottish tail wag the English dog' and that, at least in religious matters, since 'there was by 1640 a "coiled spring" of godly zeal' in England, rebellion in that nation was not necessarily dependent upon Scottish actions.

Both Russell and Morrill are revisionist historians, which shows that there is no single revisionist explanation of the outbreak of civil war in 1642.

Post-revisionist

A few historians of the period label themselves 'post-revisionist'. Building on the revisionists' analyses, they are attempting to develop a coherent account of the origins of the Civil Wars which makes connections between

Outline the main arguments put forward about the English Civil War by the various schools of historians.

political and/or religious conflicts and longer term social factors, usually by emphasising cultural factors. For a detailed account of this developing school of thought read the introductory essay, 'After revisionism', by Richard Cust and Ann Hughes, in *Conflict in early Stuart England* (1989).

Why civil war?

The notion that crown and parliament had been on a collision course for several decades before 1642 has been discredited by revisionist historians. Similarly it is not possible to argue convincingly that social and economic developments created circumstances in which civil war became unavoidable. After all, England suffered no major rebellion beyond the middle of the sixteenth century, no peer was tried for treason during the years 1601 to 1639 and, unlike the rest of Europe, tax collectors needed no royal protection. Moreover, from the 1570s the incidence of riot declined decade by decade, so why, within two years of the collapse of the Personal Rule, did civil war break out in England?

It is generally agreed that in order for any war to occur and to be sustained, three particular conditions are necessary:

- the existence of opposing sides;
- an absence – or failure – of negotiated settlement between these sides;
- the existence of ideological differences over which to fight.

Each one needs to be considered more carefully.

The formation of opposing sides

The essential precondition for a civil war was absent in England in 1640. Two 'sides' did not exist because in 1640 the greatest part of the political nation was united against Charles's government. However, after the Long Parliament first met in November 1640, a royal 'party' began to emerge and for three main reasons:

- Distaste over the methods and policies of Pym. An increasingly large number of MPs came to regard the methods of John Pym and his group as distasteful. For instance, many became concerned at the process used to dispatch Strafford. Disaffection also came from the fact that the Grand Remonstrance was designed as an appeal to the people. There was a further haemorrhaging of support from Pym to the king because of growing doubts about Pym's sincerity. Having supported Pym in his quest to dismantle the machinery of the Personal Rule, increasing numbers of MPs were unable to share Pym's belief that it was necessary not only to restrain but also to reform the established prerogative of the crown, an ambition which earned him the nickname 'King Pym'. His arguments persuaded an increasing number of the political nation to lend their support to Charles. Particularly divisive was Pym's demand that parliament acquire some influence over the appointment of crown ministers. By the end of 1641 Pym was insisting that parliament would not help Charles suppress the Irish Rebellion unless he conceded the right to nominate royal councillors, a central theme of the Grand Remonstrance. Many MPs balked at such an invasion of the crown pre-rogative, as the vote on the Grand Remonstrance showed. These developments caused the emergence of constitutional royalism. People like Edward Hyde, Viscount Falkland and Sir John Culpepper believed that the Church of England should be preserved from 'root and branch' reform and that the king had conceded enough.

- The actions of the king. Charles also gained support by his own positive actions. For instance:
  - He apparently demonstrated a royal desire to conciliate by giving his assent to all the reforming legislation of the first session of the Long Parliament.
  - He diminished the impact of accusations of a popish plot by marrying his daughter, Mary, to the Protestant **William of Orange** on 2 May 1641. He also appointed and promoted bishops most of whom were opponents of Laud.
  - His responses to demands for reform, especially his measured rejection of the Grand Remonstrance on 23 December 1641, gave the impression that he was more reasonable than Pym.

- The presence of the Scots in English affairs. The presence of the Scots in English politics and their insistence that the episcopacy be abolished aroused resentment in England. Indeed, political divisions were deepened and crystallised by opposition MPs' determination to abolish episcopacy 'root and branch', not least because those with property feared that the abolition of bishops would lead to a general breakdown in law and order. For this reason, as Conrad Russell has argued, 'the Royalist party was an anti-Scottish party before it was a Royalist party.'

William of Orange (1626–50) ruled as captain-general and *stadholder* of Holland for three years from 1647 to 1650.

The combination of these three factors may, in time, perhaps have led to the isolation of 'King Pym' and his junto. However, this was prevented from occurring because the king became implicated in a number of schemes which envisaged the use of force against the English and Scottish parliaments. This involvement provided Pym with an irreducible minimum level of support.

The failure of negotiation
The formation of sides meant only that conflict became possible, not that

it was necessarily probable. Differences could yet be resolved by negotiation and a lasting settlement established. However, for a number of reasons the attainment of a negotiated settlement proved elusive in 1641:

- The death of Bedford on 9 May 1641, the key figure in the 'bridging scheme' of appointments, diminished the possibility of a lasting compromise between Charles I and his opponents.
- The implication of the king in a number of plots, which involved the use of force against parliament, made many suspicious that he intended concessions to his opponents to be short-lived. In order to make sure that these concessions would continue, Pym was obliged to make more radical demands. Thus political attitudes polarised. This division was exacerbated by religious issues. A negotiated settlement became harder to achieve. The king's determination not to yield some aspects of government, such as the episcopacy and his right to act as the commander-in-chief of the army, made it even more remote.
- Since Pym owed his influence over the king to the Scots, it was absolutely necessary to his self-preservation that he keep their support. The most effective way to do this was by implementing some of the war aims of the Covenanters, especially those designed to emasculate Charles's authority in England, in particular the abolition of bishops. Yet on this very point, Charles was as immovable as had been his father: 'No bishop, no king'. Charles could no more relinquish bishops than Pym's group could relinquish the Scots.

An ideological issue over which to fight

The presence of two parties and the absence of a negotiated settlement meant that a resort to force was increasingly likely, though not yet wholly probable. However, for two reasons in particular, the Irish Rebellion significantly advanced the prospects of civil war in England:

- Any possibility of dissolving the Long Parliament was now removed because it was necessary for Charles to keep parliament sitting in order that it provide supply to furnish an army to send to Ireland.
- The Irish Rebellion posed with acute urgency the question of the king's military authority, the issue over which king and parliament were to go to war in 1642. In this way, events in Ireland caused opinion amongst members of the English political nation to become more polarised. A significant proportion of the political nation distrusted the king sufficiently to refuse him control of an army to put down the rebellious Irish, an established aspect of the royal prerogative, which Charles was prepared to fight for rather than yield.

The only way in which a clash between the two sides might yet have been avoided was if either became strong enough to impose some sort of dictated settlement. Pym tried to achieve this objective by appealing to the people in the form of the Grand Remonstrance, Charles by his attempt of 4 January 1642 to remove those he perceived as orchestrators of the opposition.

The possibility of civil war seemed increasingly likely from 1641. The terms '**Roundhead**' and '**Cavalier**' became terms of abuse that the two sides, which were already beginning to form, shouted at each other. Once Charles left London and began to rally support in the midlands and the north, while parliament looked to London, it became very difficult to imagine political and religious differences being resolved peacefully. In the summer of 1642 the English found themselves having to respond to a situation of which none had personal experience – civil war. How they responded was to have a great effect on the history of England in the next few years and far beyond.

Roundhead was a term of abuse heaped upon the parliamentarians. It derived from the fact that many of them wore their hair very short.

Cavalier was a term of abuse levelled against the royalists. It was derived from *cavaliero* or *caballero*, the name for a Spanish trooper – the traditional oppressor of Protestants and the national enemy.

Summary questions

1 (a) Identify and explain any *two* disputes which divided Charles I and parliament from 1640 to 1642.

   (b) Compare the importance of at least *three* causes of the outbreak of the English Civil War in 1642.

2 At what point did a civil war in England become inevitable? Explain your answer.

3 To what extent does a knowledge of events in Scotland and Ireland from 1637 to 1642 help to explain the descent into civil war in England?

7

The First Civil War, 1642–46

Focus questions

◆ Who were the royalists and parliamentarians?

◆ How did the parliamentarians gain the upper hand?

◆ Why did the royalists lose the First Civil War?

Significant dates

1642   *22 August* Charles raises his standard at Nottingham.
        23 October The Battle of Edgehill takes place.
        13 November The Battle of Turnham Green takes place.

1643   *February–April* Peace talks are held at Oxford.
        24 February Parliament introduces weekly (later monthly) assessment.
        22 July Parliament introduces excise duty.
        15 September The Cessation Treaty is agreed.
        20 September The First Battle of Newbury takes place.
        25 September Parliament and the Scots Covenanters sign the Solemn
        League and Covenant.
        8 December John Pym dies.

1644   *25 January* Fairfax overwhelms 2,500 Irish troops at Nantwich.
        2 July The Battle of Marston Moor takes place.
        27 October The Second Battle of Newbury takes place.

1645   *January–February* Peace talks are held at Uxbridge.
        17 February The New Model Army Ordinance is issued.
        3 April The Self-Denying Ordinance is issued.
        14 June The Battle of Naseby takes place.
        10 July The Battle of Langport takes place.
        25 August A second Cessation Treaty is signed.
        13 September The Battle of Philiphaugh takes place.

1646   *5 May* Charles I surrenders to the Scots.

Overview

The First Civil War lasted for four years. After a few months, neither side was
able to gain a clear advantage, even though the king probably had the slight
upper hand. Allies were sought. Parliament found the Scots, who, in 1644, sent

into England a second army in four years. The king was able to gain the physical support of the Irish, whose army had never been of the same standard as that of the Scots'. Moreover, as the war entered its third year, parliament organised itself more effectively, raising large sums of money and setting up the New Model Army, a unified national army, controlled and paid from Westminster rather than the counties. The longer the war lasted, the more the royalists struggled in comparison. By 1645 the royalist war effort was facing collapse. The following year Charles surrendered – but to the Scots rather than parliament. What had brought about the dramatic change in his fortunes over the previous three or four years?

Taking sides

Hard choices

'Few wars can have broken out as untidily as the English Civil War,' writes Anthony Fletcher in *The outbreak of the English Civil War* (1981). People had not been expecting war much before 1642. There was no great military tradition in England; the navy was its main form of defence. Above all, in the towns and counties of England men – and more particularly the **gentry** – had to make some hard choices. They were faced with competing claims on their loyalty, with two sides each asserting the right to raise men in the form of the county trained bands. Parliament had the Militia **Ordinance**, the king the Commission of Array. How did the counties respond? By October, out of 42 English counties, 24 had accepted parliament's ordinance and 11 the king's commission, while 7 had avoided making any choice. Most of the pro-parliamentary group was in the south and east of the country, the royalists in the west and north. This is the basis of the common argument about the geographical division of England in 1642: south-east England, along with London, chose parliament while the north and west plumped for Charles.

It was not so simple. During the past 30 years or so, local communities have been much studied. The pattern of choices was much more complex than allowed for by either Whig or Marxist historians. Local factors were the key to explaining why people decided for king or parliament. Alan Everitt, in *The local community and the Great Rebellion* (1969), compared two adjoining counties, Northamptonshire and Leicestershire. The gentry of Leicestershire were divided into two rival (and Puritan) groups. They concentrated on local rivalries and thus avoided making a national choice until 1645. Northamptonshire chose for parliament in 1642 because the leading royalist families left to support the king, leaving the Puritans to rally the county behind Pym. Some counties tried to avoid getting drawn in. John Morrill, in *Revolt in the provinces* (1999), says he has found attempts to form neutrality pacts in

The **gentry** made up the social group immediately below the level of the peerage or the nobility. Their income from land freed them from dependence on others and gave them the leisure to become involved in government. The total number of English gentry grew from around 5,000 in 1540 to about 15,000 by 1640.

Ordinances were legislative measures drawn up and passed by parliament but which failed to receive the royal assent. They were broadly equivalent in their way to royal proclamations.

22 English counties and many towns. He goes on to maintain that 'side-taking for the great majority was contingent'. Local circumstances decided whom they chose to support, if anyone. For a sizeable minority, however, choice was less arbitrary. Morrill believes that 'it was the men who felt most strongly about religion who began the war'. Marxist historians would argue religious beliefs were the expression of more fundamental economic and social interests and that social class was the key to explaining how England divided in 1642. Most of the gentry, the 'middling sort', the vast majority of whom were Puritans, identified with parliament. Most of the aristocracy – and some of the gentry – supported Charles. As with so much about the Civil Wars, the historical debate on this subject will continue.

What factors have historians suggested were important in the taking of sides in 1642?

The two sides in 1642

There was no permanent – or standing – army in England in 1642, no national army. The counties raised trained bands that did not traditionally operate outside their county boundaries. Both sides used the trained bands that they came to control as the basis for field armies that might fight outside their counties. Both sides relied on volunteers. In order to counter the effects of localism they also formed regional associations, armies composed of a number of different county bands. The most significant of these was to be parliament's Eastern Association, led by the earl of Manchester. These devices resulted in the appearance in the field of armies that were large for the time, on occasion numbering 15,000 to 20,000 men. Yet, they were not a constant feature of the Civil Wars. As Ian Gentles, in *The New Model Army in England, Ireland and Scotland 1645–1653* (1992), has observed, 'the armies of both sides were like mushrooms, shooting up almost overnight, and then disappearing even more quickly'.

The armies of both sides were composed of infantry, cavalry and artillery. The infantry were divided into units of pikemen and musketeers, the former flanked by the latter when in battle formation. Though both groups carried swords, the principle weapon of the pikemen was a pike, a pole of up to 5.5 metres in length, topped with a steel spike. The musketeers were equipped with matchlock muskets, in which ignition of the powder charge was achieved by placing a burning length of 'match' (combustible cord) into some refined gunpowder placed on the priming pan. These weapons were notoriously slow to load and inaccurate, though they could inflict horrible injury and death. The cavalry of both sides was generally of the **harquebusier** style. This heavily armoured cavalry, though well protected, was dangerously cumbersome. Indeed, Sir Arthur Haselrig's regiment of 'lobsters' probably suffered defeat at Roundway Down in 1643 because their ponderous condition made them unable to respond to a flank attack. The dragoons were the mounted infantry,

A **harquebusier** was a soldier armed with a harquebus or arquebus, which was an early type of portable gun, usually supported on a tripod or trestle or some other device.

Robert Devereux, earl of Essex (1591–1646), was forced in 1613 into a humiliating annulment of his marriage to Frances Howard on the grounds of impotence. Experienced in fighting in the Palatinate in 1620, he then served with the Dutch for short periods in 1623 and 1624. In 1639 he was appointed lieutenant-general of horse for the Scots campaign but was superseded by the earl of Holland. In 1640 he declined to serve. He was appointed lord chamberlain and general of the militia south of the Trent by Charles I in 1641, though so deeply attached was Essex to parliament's cause that Charles was forced to remove him from

An engraving of a musketeer showing his matchlock musket and the bandolier draped across his shoulder. From this hang half a dozen cartouches known as the 'Twelve Apostles'. Each carries a charge of about one half ounce of powder.

the generalship. He fought at Edgehill in 1642 and without significant result at Newbury in 1643. His greatest success was his relief of Gloucester in 1643; his greatest failure his defeat at Lostwithiel in 1645. He was forced to resign his command in 1645.

Oliver Cromwell (1599–1658) was a consummate cavalry commander who played a key role at Marston Moor. He was excepted from the terms of the Self-Denying Ordinance (see p. 99) and appointed lieutenant-general of horse in the New Model Army. He was central to the defeat of the royalists in the Second Civil War and came to believe in the necessity of executing Charles I. He became lord protector in 1653 and declined the offer of the crown in 1657.

What were the main components of the Civil War armies?

Who were the leading personnel on each side?

soldiers who rode into battle and then dismounted to fight on foot. Finally, both sides employed artillery, usually cannon though mortars were also used. The former, in particular, could be highly destructive, though they seem to have played a major role only in the First Battle of Newbury in 1643 and at Langport in 1645.

Parliament chose as its leader **Robert Devereux, earl of Essex**. He had had some military experience in the Thirty Years' War but he was conservative by nature and pessimistic about parliament's chances of victory. He took with him into battle the sheet in which he would be buried if he were killed – just in case. As we shall see before too long, he was replaced with a more effective lord general. The royalist commander-in-chief was Charles I. He was not without considerable personal courage and leadership skills in battle. However, he possessed a poor judgement of human character and, as king, he could not be replaced. The most talented of Charles's generals was his nephew, Prince Rupert. As a dashing cavalry commander, Rupert acquired a formidable reputation. Yet, unlike **Oliver Cromwell**, he was not always able to maintain the coherence and direction of his cavalry charge, as was the case at Edgehill in 1642 and Naseby in 1645.

What were the two sides fighting for?

The most complete public statement of parliament's aims is usually taken to be the Nineteen Propositions of June 1642 while the best statement of royalists' aims is the king's reply to those propositions. It is worth considering both documents in order to show how close the two sides were. The Nineteen Propositions revealed that MPs still saw the crown as the lynchpin of government; the king's reply confirmed that he saw parliament as having an important role in national government. Both accepted the traditional constitution. Even on religious matters, the two sides were not that far apart, at least if these two documents are taken at face value. Both wanted a reformed church. The expressed difference came over parliamentary approval of the king's ministers, the sticking point in negotiations since the summer of 1641. The vast majority of the political nation chose to believe that this had not been resolved because Charles had surrounded himself with 'evil counsel'. Thus, they were prepared to fight the king on behalf of the crown. Only when they could blame no one but Charles would some MPs and, more importantly, some soldiers move against the monarchy.

The main stages of the First Civil War
Royalist ascendancy, 1642–43

The royalist strategy at the start of the war was to advance towards London with the aim of entering the capital. Raising the royal standard at Nottingham on 22 August 1642 attracted such little support that the king had to postpone his advance on London until he had sufficient troops. He headed west, to Wales and the Marches, which proved to be 'the nursery of the King's infantry'. He was then able to move south east towards London. At Edgehill, in Warwickshire, Essex's army confronted him and the first major battle of the Civil Wars took place. The battle is usually reckoned to be a draw. The royalists failed to take advantage of what was probably a winning position when Prince Rupert allowed his cavalry to leave the battlefield in order to pursue fleeing parliamentarians. Nevertheless, when Essex withdrew towards Warwick on the morning after the battle, the way to London remained open. However, instead of ordering an immediate descent upon the capital, Charles chose to set up a garrison and base at Oxford. This proved to be a strategic error. Essex had time to reach London before Charles did. The royalist advance was halted at Turnham Green, several miles outside the city, because Charles declined to engage Essex's army, strengthened by trained bands of London, a total force of 20,000. The king retreated to Oxford for the winter.

The shock of the clash of arms provoked calls for peace. Negotiations took place at Oxford from 1 February to 14 April 1643. One of the reasons why the Treaty of Oxford failed was because the Commons, determined to maintain their links with the Scots, insisted that Charles agree to the immediate abolition of bishops and archbishops. Another reason was that the king could still realistically expect to defeat his opponents militarily.

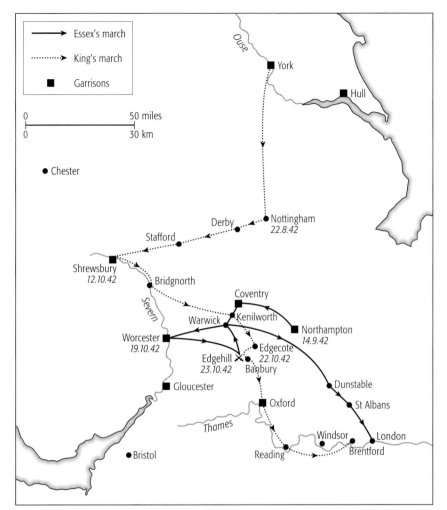

The movements of Essex, parliament's lord general, and the king in late 1642 are shown. Both sides were proved wrong in their general expectation that the war would be brought to a conclusion quickly and in one decisive battle. Edgehill, the only major battle fought in 1642, proved highly indecisive.

By mid 1643 it seemed that royal expectations were being fulfilled. In the north of England, **William Cavendish, marquis of Newcastle**, had achieved much. Not only had he consolidated his hold over the northern coalfields around Newcastle but also he advanced south, taking considerable parts of east and north Yorkshire, north Lincolnshire and the important town of Newark. At the Battle of Adwalton Moor on 29 June, he defeated the **Fairfaxes**, father and son, and thus took control of much of west Yorkshire. There were limits to his success. He was prevented from advancing further south by the actions of Oliver Cromwell and because Hull remained parliamentarian. Since the navy's allegiance was to parliament, Hull could be supplied and thus pose a threat to the marquis of Newcastle from the rear.

William Cavendish, marquis of Newcastle, (1593–1676) was Charles I's commander-in-chief in the counties of northern England from 1642 until 1644 when, after Marston Moor, he resigned his command and went into exile. On his return after the Restoration Charles II awarded him a dukedom.

Sir Thomas Fairfax (1612–71) acquired some military experience in the Thirty Years' War and fought for parliament in the north of England as second-in-command to his father, **Ferdinando Fairfax**. His forces were badly mauled at Marston Moor in 1644. As lord general of the New Model Army, he defeated the royalist forces at Naseby and Langport. He became increasingly concerned by the radicals and failed to appear at the king's trial. He resigned his command in 1650.

The extent of the territories held by the king and parliament at the end of 1643

Sir Ralph Hopton
(1596–1651) was the leading royalist commander in the West Country. He was temporarily blinded and half paralysed when one of his ammunition wagons blew up after the Battle of Lansdown in 1643. He finally surrendered at Torrington in 1646 and went into exile. He was famous for his description of the Civil Wars as 'this war without an enemy'.

Sir William Waller
(1597–1668) was the architect of a series of important parliamentarian triumphs in the south and south west in the early part of the war, which earned him the nickname William the Conqueror. However, he was defeated decisively at Roundway Down in 1643 and removed from military command in 1645 according to the terms of the Self–Denying Ordinance.

More impressive was royalist progress in the south west. **Sir Ralph Hopton** had expanded royalist influence from Devon and Cornwall eastwards into much of Wiltshire and Dorset. This had been achieved, firstly, by inflicting serious damage upon the forces of **Sir William Waller** at Lansdown on 5 July 1643. Secondly, with the aid of Prince Maurice, Rupert's brother, Hopton soundly defeated Waller at Roundway Down on 13 July. Finally, on 26 July, Rupert captured Bristol, providing the royalists with not only a port but also the resources of England's second largest city.

These successes, however, were soon offset. Essex and his army left London in order to lift the siege of Gloucester, which they did on 8 September. Essex found his return to London blocked by the king's army at Newbury. The outcome of the battle fought there, on 20 September, was, in effect, a draw. Most importantly, Essex continued towards London. Though the king had gained territory in both the north and the south west, he had not yet threatened parliament's control of London.

Draw up a list of the main battles fought during the period 1642–43.

Allies and divisions, 1643–44

After a year of civil war, both sides tried to improve supplies of money and men and to gain the support of allies outside England. The king was keen to drive home his successes on the field, parliament to avoid total defeat. The alliances formed in 1643 fundamentally affected the course of the rest of the war.

In terms of finance, parliament took more drastic measures than did the king. Charles relied on traditional forms of revenue such as wardships, the sale of titles and loans, especially from the continent. He avoided increasing taxation until parliament had led the way. In 1643 parliament introduced several new taxes, including the weekly (later monthly) assessment, a direct tax levied by means of the ship-money system, and the excise, a tax on many basic goods. In addition, sequestration meant the seizure of the estates of those who had voluntarily contributed to the royalist cause. These devices were all very effective, especially the assessment, a land tax roughly equivalent to a parliamentary subsidy every fortnight. Kent, for example, was paying more each month in assessments than it had for an entire year of ship money. Despite the fact that these 'illegal taxes' aroused bitter resentment, they increased the incidence with which parliament paid its troops, a development which in turn perhaps persuaded communities to support parliament simply because it appeared to be the winning side.

In terms of manpower, parliament introduced impressment for one of its armies in August 1643. All men aged between 18 and 50 were liable for military service, though parliament tried to ensure that the policy was carefully administered to avoid provoking too much opposition.

In terms of allies, Charles looked to Ireland. The marquis of Ormonde, the commander of the king's forces in Ireland, successfully concluded a one-year ceasefire, or Cessation Treaty, in September 1643 with the Irish Confederates, a union of the Gaelic Irish and Old English. During the next nine months, a total of around 22,000 troops made their way from Ireland to England, Scotland and Wales. However, because these troops came across in piecemeal fashion, they were militarily ineffective. Indeed, Fairfax easily overwhelmed a force of 2,500 Irish troops at the Battle of Nantwich, in Cheshire, in January 1644. Some who were captured changed sides and thereafter fought for parliament. Many others were stationed in Welsh garrisons and consequently took little part in any fighting. Yet, the cessation also did political damage to the king's

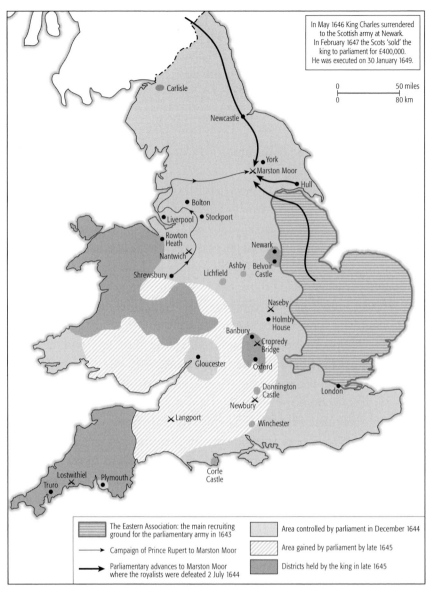

In May 1646 King Charles surrendered to the Scottish army at Newark. In February 1647 the Scots 'sold' the king to parliament for £400,000. He was executed on 30 January 1649.

| 0 | 50 miles |
| 0 | 80 km |

Carlisle

Newcastle

York
Marston Moor
Hull

Bolton
Liverpool • Stockport
Rowton Heath
Nantwich
Shrewsbury

Newark
Ashby
Belvoir Castle
Lichfield

Naseby
Holmby House
Banbury
Cropredy Bridge
Gloucester
Oxford
Donnington Castle
Newbury
London
Langport
Winchester

Lostwithiel Plymouth
Truro
Corfe Castle

The Eastern Association: the main recruiting ground for the parliamentary army in 1643

Campaign of Prince Rupert to Marston Moor

Parliamentary advances to Marston Moor where the royalists were defeated 2 July 1644

Area controlled by parliament in December 1644

Area gained by parliament by late 1645

Districts held by the king in late 1645

The course of the Civil War, 1644–46

cause because it seemed that Charles was willing to do a deal with the Catholics. In this sense, it was a propaganda disaster.

Pym looked to Scotland. In September 1643, parliament signed the Solemn League and Covenant with the Scots Covenanters. The two sides agreed that parliament would impose 'the reformation of religion' in England and Ireland 'according to the word of God and the example of the best reformed churches', a term which was soon to cause many problems between parliament and the Scots. In return, the Scots would provide an army of 21,500 men to fight for parliament. Parliament was to pay £30,000 per month to offset the costs of the

What were the Cessation Treaty and Solemn League and Covenant?

Scottish army. This force crossed into England in January 1644, under the command of the earl of Leven, and rapidly pushed Newcastle's army back to York. Then, on 2 July, they were instrumental in securing a parliamentarian victory at Marston Moor, the largest battle of the Civil Wars with some 44,000 men taking part. Spiritually stimulated by his experience of this victory, in which he had played an important part, Cromwell considered that it was God who had made the royalists 'as stubble to our swords'. The defeat at Marston Moor meant that the king lost control, not only of the city of York, but of the whole of the north of England. It was also the first time that Rupert had been defeated. Broken, Newcastle slipped into exile.

Before the Scots army entered England, Pym had died from cancer in December 1643. Much of parliament's new methods of 1643 were credited to Pym. He saw the need to fight the war effectively if parliament was not to lose. He was acceptable to the two parliamentary groups of the time, the peace and the war parties, and thus helped to keep parliament united. When his wartime strategies are added to his leadership of parliament from 1640 to 1642, it can be seen that Pym had accomplished much.

Despite the setbacks in the north for the royalists, three factors in particular suggested that all was not lost for the royalists. Firstly, Charles enjoyed victories over Waller at Cropredy Bridge on 29 June 1644 and then over Essex himself at Lostwithiel on 2 September 1644. Secondly, Scottish royalist forces, led by Montrose, defeated a Covenanting army at Tippermuir on 1 September. This was the first in a spectacular run of six successive victories that was only ended by defeat at Philiphaugh a year later. Above all, parliament was unable to follow up the victory of Marston Moor. Its leaders were increasingly divided. Understanding these divisions requires some knowledge of the main parliamentary groupings. In order to make sense of the various factions at Westminster, historians have devised the terms Political Presbyterian and Political Independents. The Political Independents – men like Cromwell and Sir Arthur Haselrig – wanted to defeat the king decisively and then impose harsh terms upon him. The Political Presbyterians – typified by Essex, Manchester and Denzil Holles – were reluctant to pursue the war to a military conclusion and, instead, sought a compromise settlement. Generally speaking, these political positions were mirrored by one of two religious outlooks. Thus, most Political Independents were also Religious Independents – that is, in broad terms they sought 'liberty to tender consciences', or toleration (except to Catholics). Equally, most Political Presbyterians can also be classed as Religious Presbyterians. Firmly believing that religious toleration would lead to the breakdown of law and order, they became the natural allies of the Scots because the latter sought to impose a national (Presbyterian) church in England. It was possible, however, to be a political Independent and a religious Presbyterian.

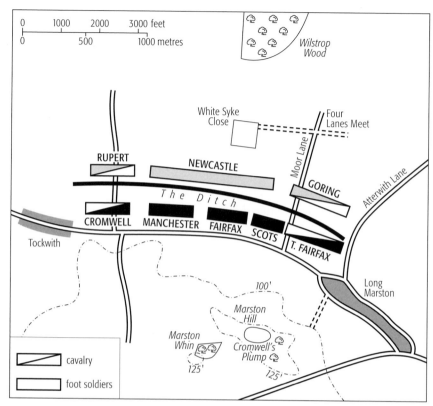

The Battle of Marston Moor, 2 July 1644. This was the largest battle of the Civil Wars. The allied forces were made up of Manchester, the Scots and a northern force under the Fairfaxes and numbered at least 27,000. The total number of royalists was about 17,000. Initially, the royalists had the advantage but divisions within their high command contributed to a parliamentarian victory. Perhaps 4,000 men were killed. From then on, the king lost control of the north of England.

These divisions explain why the Second Battle of Newbury, on 27 October 1644, proved indecisive, even though parliament outnumbered the king's army by more than two to one. The battle resulted from an attempt by parliament to stop Charles's army returning to royalist headquarters at Oxford. Cautious tactics by Manchester and the Eastern Association meant that Charles slipped through the net. It resulted in the famous row between Manchester and Cromwell. Manchester, the leader, exclaimed, 'if we beat the King ninety and nine times yet he is King still '. . . but if the King beat us once we shall all be hanged.' To which Cromwell, his subordinate, replied, 'My Lord, if this be so, why did we take up arms at first? This is against fighting hereafter, if so, let us make peace, be it never so base.' The quarrel was soon to have significant consequences. At the end of 1644, however, it must have seemed to Charles that, despite the setback which his cause had suffered, for parliament now controlled 70 per cent of England as opposed to 40 per cent at the start of the year, he might yet win what was now becoming a war of attrition.

Give three reasons to explain why, despite the parliamentarian victory at Marston Moor, the war continued beyond 1644.

Parliament ascendant, 1645–46

Charles could not have anticipated, in late 1644, the reforming zeal which swept Westminster in the aftermath of the debacle of the Second Battle of Newbury. It followed another attempt to settle the conflict. The English Presbyterians and the Scots agreed on terms to be put to Charles in what became known as the Uxbridge Propositions. Charles wasted little time in rejecting this set of proposals, which included the suggestion that he take the Covenant and introduce Presbyterianism. Parliament then passed two very significant reforms:

- In February 1645, an ordinance was issued creating the New Model Army. This created a single national army (though others remained) of 21,000 men, which was thought necessary to achieve the military victory the failure of negotiations at Uxbridge had shown to be necessary. It was to be well paid, the infantry receiving eightpence a day, the cavalry two shillings. Its commander was a young Yorkshireman, Sir Thomas Fairfax. Fairfax replaced Essex because Essex was reluctant to defeat the king decisively on the field of battle. Fairfax had war-winning qualities of inspiration, determination and energy. Oliver Cromwell, a rising figure in the Eastern Association, exhibited similar qualities. As a cavalryman, Cromwell is most famous for training his regiment to halt and regroup after a charge, a tactic for which they were rewarded with the nickname of Ironsides.

- In April, parliament passed the Self-Denying Ordinance. This stipulated that all MPs and peers had to resign any military commands and civil offices they might hold. Thus, peers such as Manchester and Essex were forced into retirement. Cromwell should also have stood down but he obtained an exception to the ordinance. He was needed to lead the cavalry of the New Model Army. He was appointed lieutenant-general and, as such, was second-in-command.

What were the main features of the New Model Army?

What was the Self-Denying Ordinance?

In June 1645 the New Model Army outnumbered, and then decisively defeated, the king's forces at Naseby, the last major battle of the First Civil War. A month later, the New Model Army defeated Charles's western army at Langport. Everywhere, the royalist cause was now collapsing. Bristol fell in September, a setback that resulted in the dismissal of Prince Rupert, and, later in the same month, a royalist force was defeated on Rowton Heath, while Charles, allegedly, watched from a tower on the wall of Chester. In Scotland, Montrose's run of victories came to an end at Philiphaugh.

Eventually, the king had no option but to surrender. He gave himself up to the Scots, rather than parliament, on 5 May 1646.

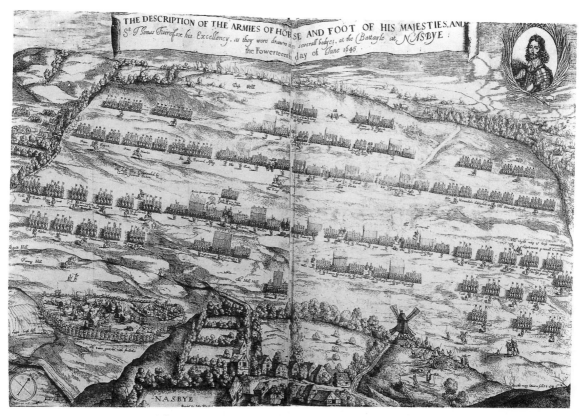

Robert Streater's map of the Battle of Naseby, 14 June 1645. The parliamentarian forces are at the bottom of the illustration, the royalists at the top. The parliamentarian baggage train, which Prince Rupert left the battle in order to besiege, is in the bottom left corner. Naseby proved the decisive battle of the Civil Wars and was the first occasion when the New Model Army demonstrated its military skill.

Why did the royalists lose the First Civil War?

In order to answer this question it is necessary to examine two particular themes set out below.

The weaknessnes of the royalists compared to the strengths of the parliamentarians

From the outset of hostilities the royalist cause suffered from a number of deficiencies.

Firstly, Charles, though personally brave, as he demonstrated at Naseby in 1645, was no war leader. He frequently ignored the advice of those more experienced in military affairs than himself and he failed to resolve the damaging feud between the leading members of his Council of War, Rupert and Digby. Charles failed to press home his advantages in 1642–43 before his opponents could organise their own war effort more effectively. A descent upon London directly after Edgehill in 1642, or before parliament's relief of Gloucester in 1643, might have won the war.

Charles also balked at the notion of promoting on merit rather than social status. All six of his regional commanders were grandees. Of these, only Newcastle enjoyed any significant success when he beat the Fairfaxes at Adwalton Moor in 1643.

The royalist war effort, moreover, was fatally hamstrung by Charles's belief that there was no need to depart from known laws and ancient institutions. Some of these institutions, however, were so ancient that their authority was legally dubious. 'The commission of array', noted Clarendon, 'was a thing not heard of before . . . and so was received with jealousy, and easily discredited by the glosses and suggestions of the Houses.' John Morrill has concluded that it amounted to 'a dreadful blunder'. Only in 1644 did Charles at last copy his opponents by instituting an excise tax, but, even then, only after it had received the assent of the royalist parliament sitting at Oxford.

Secondly, the royalists lacked foreign assistance. The king's attempts to secure foreign aid were misjudged. Henrietta Maria was sent to France in order to acquire material support but her mission was a failure, in large part because France was engaged in the Thirty Years' War. The decision to conclude a one-year truce in September 1643 with the Irish Confederates proved disastrous, both in military and propaganda terms. Despite this, Charles persevered in his efforts to recruit troops from Ireland. When news of an ultimately abortive second Cessation Treaty of 25 August 1645 leaked out its effect was to bolster parliament's cause because many were horrified at the king's apparent willingness to grant concessions to the Catholics in return for arms.

Thirdly, the royalists were at a severe disadvantage because they controlled less wealthy territories, such as the north and south-west of England. Moreover, since some of these areas were the centre of fighting, the consequent deprivation resulted in an inability to pay taxes, convincing John Morrill that 'financial thrombosis [ultimately] killed the Royalist cause'. Troops who were paid only infrequently sought free quarter. This, in turn, brought about, in the last year of the war, the Clubmen movement. These were rural insurrectionaries determined to protect themselves from plundering soldiers. Since most of the Club risings occurred in royalist territory they did a great deal to dislocate Charles's war effort.

However, parliament's victory is explained not only by the deficiencies of the royalist cause, but also by the fact that parliament benefited from circumstances and a political vision not enjoyed by its opponents.

Firstly, parliament's war machine was more effective than the royalists'. 'They [parliament] were not tied to a law', commented Lord Wharton in 1643, 'for these were times of necessity and imminent danger.' Thus, in order to defeat their opponents, parliament breached almost every clause of the Petition of Right. Above all, as a consequence of the New Model Army and the

Self-Denying Ordinance, parliament reshaped its military high command and created a professional army. Some historians have attempted to play down the impact of the New Model Army by pointing out that its victories at Naseby and Langport were practically inevitable because it was significantly superior in numbers. Nevertheless, in the context of the time, it was 'new' in that promotion was on the basis of military expertise, it was regularly paid and its members were driven by a Calvinistic Puritanism which, according to Ian Gentles, 'endowed them with a holy ruthlessness'.

Secondly, parliament had foreign assistance. Parliament's ally, the Scots, were important in the defeat of the royalist forces at Marston Moor in 1644 and, unlike the Cessation Treaty, the Solemn League and Covenant was not a propaganda disaster (though it did induce political and religious divisions within parliament).

Thirdly, Parliament benefited from the allegiance of much of the richer parts of England, the south, the east and, most importantly, London. Possession of the capital was significant in a number of ways:

- It was a centre for propaganda.
- It was the economic and commercial hub of the nation and, therefore, hugely wealthy. For instance, 70 per cent of all customs duties were contributed by London and between one quarter and one third of the assessment received by the treasurers derived from the capital. The City continued to advance loans against future revenues. Almost three-quarters of all parliamentary revenues were anticipated in this way.
- The trained bands of London, especially significant at Turnham Green and in lifting the siege of Gloucester in 1643, were well drilled and well officered under the leadership of Philip Skippon.
- With a population of about 400,000 – roughly one tenth of the total population of England – London was a war-winning resource base. At least 6,000 of the initial recruits to Essex's army were from the ranks of the unemployed that wandered around the streets of the capital.

Furthermore, as Clarendon remarked, 'of unspeakable ill consequence to the King's affairs' was the defection of the ship-money fleet to parliament. Consisting of 18 men-of-war and 24 armed merchantmen, it made difficult the passage of munitions from Europe to the royalists. It also meant that parliamentary outposts, even those deep in royalist territory, like Hull and Plymouth, could be victualled by sea.

Finally, not only did parliament possess the greater resources but also the vision of John Pym ensured that it was able to exploit them effectively. Pym was also instrumental in containing the growing religious divisions within parliament. The concern about the breakdown in law and order associated with the attack upon episcopacy had resulted in a backlash against religious

An engraving of parliament triumphant over its foes. The leading royalist personnel are drowning, while the English Ark sails to safety. The king is not to be found in this picture because it was not against him that the war had been waged but against his evil councillors.

radicalism, the effect of which inevitably bolstered support for the king, since he was the natural leader of such a movement. In order to stem this process, Pym established the Westminster Assembly on 12 June 1643, thereby, for the time being, effectively shunting the religious issue off stage and blunting the polarisation of allegiances caused by the debate over religion. As Derek Hirst has remarked in *England in conflict 1603–1660* (1999):

> Pym hoped with this to meet various urgent needs. These were to satisfy Covenanter zeal; to give substance at last to parliament's familiar protestations of godly goals; to gain a final victory against the Arminians and, not least, to provide a stable core for an English church that might check the growing ferment in London.

The strengths of the royalists compared to the weaknesses of the parliamentarians

The notion that a royalist victory was most likely if the war were of short duration is also supported by a comparison of parliamentarian weaknesses with royalist strengths.

Firstly, parliament had to create executive machinery from scratch whereas the king could rely upon the fact that he was a divinely ordained authority who possessed an established position in the seventeenth-century constitution. This circumstance – on paper at least – imbued institutions like the royalist parliament at Oxford with an authority greater than that of the Houses at Westminster.

Secondly, unlike the supporters of the king whose main aim was to take London, the parliamentarians were not united in pursuit of a particular objective. Indeed, there emerged two distinct groups in parliament, the peace and war parties, latterly the Political Presbyterians and Political Independents respectively. Until the passage of the Self-Denying Ordinance in 1645, the divisions within parliament and its forces were great and growing, not only between commanders like Manchester and Cromwell but also between the Religious Independents and the Scots.

Unfortunately for the king, the achievement of Pym was largely to overcome the first of these weaknesses of parliament while the reforming ordinances of 1645 – the Self-Denying and New Model Ordinances – removed the second. Thus, after the early months of 1645, it is hard to avoid the conclusion that it was only a matter of time before the king was defeated.

The consequences of the First Civil War

It is worth emphasising that there were relatively few set-piece battles. Rather, the ebb and flow of military fortune over these years was marked more by skirmishes, sieges and small engagements than by the outcome of a single battle. Even after the Battle of Naseby, in June 1645, it was almost a year before the king surrendered, yet the effects of this fighting in terms of numbers killed was staggering. Charles Carlton has estimated that during the First Civil War a total of 62,000 soldiers (English and Scots combined) were killed. Of these, 28,000 had been fighting for parliament and 34,000 for the king. Indeed, Carlton has reckoned that the total of English war dead, killed by either direct or indirect action for the whole period of the Civil Wars, amounts to 190,000, the equivalent of 3.7 per cent of the population.

This was the background against which the political nation sought to reach an agreement with the defeated king.

Summary questions

1 (a) Identify and explain any *two* problems which caused serious difficulties in the royalist prosecution of the war.

   (b) Compare the importance of at least *three* factors which help to explain why parliament was ultimately successful in the First Civil War.

2 How far would you agree that, before the formation of the New Model Army, the royalists seemed likely to win the First Civil War?

8

The road to regicide, 1646–49

Focus questions

◆ Why did it prove impossible to achieve a negotiated settlement after the First Civil War?

◆ Why was Charles I executed?

Significant dates

1646   *July*   The Newcastle Propositions are presented to Charles I.
     October   Parliament passes the ordinance abolishing episcopacy.

1647   *30 January*   The Scots hand over Charles I to parliament.
     25 May   Parliament orders the army to disband.
     4 June   The king is kidnapped by the army.
     14 June   The Declaration of the Army is issued.
     23 July   The Heads of the Proposals are presented to Charles I.
     26 July   Parliament is invaded by a crowd in support of Presbyterian leaders.
     6 August   The army occupies London.
     28 October   The Agreement of the People is issued.
     28 October–5 November   The Putney Debates on the Agreement of the People are held.
     11 November   Charles I escapes from Hampton Court to the Isle of Wight.
     15 November   Cromwell puts down a mutiny at Corkbush Field.
     24 December   Parliament presents the Four Bills to Charles I.
     26 December   Charles I concludes the Engagement with the Scots.

1648   *3 January*   The Vote of No Addresses is passed.
     March–July   Various risings, directed mostly at parliamentarian 'tyranny', occur.
     29 April   An army prayer meeting is held at Windsor Castle.
     17–19 August   The Battle of Preston takes place.
     24 August   The Vote of No Addresses is repealed.
     18 September–27 November   The Treaty of Newport is concluded.
     20 November   The Remonstrance of the Army is presented to parliament.
     5 December   The Commons vote by 129 to 83 to continue negotiations with Charles I.
     6 December   Pride's Purge takes place.
     14 December–13 January   The Whitehall Debates on the Agreement of the People are held.

1649   *6 January* The Rump establishes a High Court of Justice.
        20 January The trial of Charles I opens in Westminster Hall.
        30 January Charles I is executed.

Overview

The 33 months from May 1646 to January 1649 are among the most dramatic and most significant in English history. At the start, parliament and the king were seeking a political settlement to England's problems. By January 1649 a parliament, dominated by the English army, arranged a show trial of the king. As a result of this, he was publicly executed. Events between these dates were complex and confusing. At the risk of simplifying, it is possible to identify five distinct periods:

- May 1646–March 1647: attempts at a political settlement between king and parliament;
- April–August 1647: conflict between parliament and the army;
- August–December 1647: conflict within the army;
- January–August 1648: rebellion and war;
- September–January 1649: the English Revolution.

The first relatively quiet period gave no hint of what was to come. The second saw England on the verge of anarchy as the army mutinied against civilian rule and Londoners revolted against the intervention of the army. Even the army was divided. The most famous example of these various tensions was the Putney Debates hosted by the General Council of the Army in late 1647. As Robert Ashton points out in *The English Civil War 1640–9* (1978), the pattern of events in 1648 is 'strikingly similar' to those of 1647 'though with an even fiercer intensity'. In early 1648 there were various county revolts against army rule; in the summer, for the third time in eight years, a Scottish army invaded England, though this time in support of the king. Once the Scottish threat had been defeated, the English once more argued over the political and religious settlement of the country. The army leadership lost patience with the political leaders. It excluded from parliament all who were unsympathetic to the army and its aims. Then it brought Charles I to trial before executing him a few weeks later. With the old order overthrown, the army could then impose its own political settlement on England.

The search for a settlement, 1646–47

The Newcastle Propositions

In the immediate aftermath of the First Civil War, no one could yet contemplate the formation of a lasting settlement without the person of the king.

Within a few weeks of the end of the war, parliament presented Charles with what were known as the Newcastle Propositions. The Political Presbyterians were behind these terms, which were much more detailed than the Nineteen Propositions of 1642. The most significant proposals were:

- parliaments: the Triennial Act to be maintained;
- officers of state: parliament to nominate 13 ministers;
- militia: parliament to control it for 20 years;
- the church: episcopacy to be abolished and a Presbyterian Church to be established for three years;
- 58 royalists to be excluded from general pardon.

Charles played for time. His first reply, which came within a few weeks, said that he needed more time to consider such an important and complex issue. Charles believed that by prevaricating he could yet win the peace. He was expecting his victors to divide, allowing him to rule once more. Certainly the political landscape during the years 1646–47 seemed to justify such a policy. The alliance that had won the war soon began to fall apart.

What were the main features of the Newcastle Propositions?

The main divisions in the anti-royalist alliance

Parliament and the Scots

Parliament and the Scots were on the brink of war as early as 1646. This was the consequence of arguments over who guarded the king and religion. Differences over religion were the more pointed. According to the Solemn League and Covenant of 1643, the Scots had expected parliament to establish in England a Presbyterian Church according to the Scottish version. However, parliament recognised that the formation of such a national church would alienate many in England. It had no choice but to establish an unhappy compromise. The result, effected by ordinances on 19 and 26 August 1645, was, as the Scottish observer Robert Ballie lamented, 'a lame **Erastian Presbytery**'.

Parliament and the New Model Army

Relations between the New Model Army and parliament became increasingly antagonistic in 1646–47 and for two reasons. One was that the political and religious settlement with the king being sought by the Presbyterians made many soldiers uneasy. They thought that as they had played a leading part in defeating Charles, they should have a say in the peace settlement. The other reason was their future as soldiers. A large army was no longer needed. Many soldiers would have to be paid off. All soldiers needed to be paid the backlog of their wages. In 1646 these problems rumbled on and, in 1647, they exploded.

An **Erastian Presbytery** was a church in which bishops had been abolished, but where the jurisdiction of the church was still subordinate to the state. This did not satisfy the Scottish Presbyterians who wished the church to be completely independent.

The Scots and the New Model Army

Serious differences also emerged between the Scots and the army, especially over religion. Many soldiers believed they were fighting for liberty to tender consciences, in other words religious freedom. The national Presbyterian Church desired by the Scots would result in religious uniformity. Cromwell was alleged to have said that he would draw his sword against the Scots as readily as against any in the king's army.

Further differences

To make matters worse, there were differences *within* each of the elements of the victorious coalition:

- The Scots. In Scotland, there was a growing reaction against the Covenanters, which was encouraged by the defeat of Covenanting forces in Ireland in June 1646. Not only was there a growing anti-Covenanting group but the royalist Scots were still a presence. In 1648 these divisions were to have an important effect on events in England.
- Parliament. Once Charles had been defeated, the differences between the Independents and the Presbyterians began to grow. In 1646 the Presbyterians were the dominant group in parliament. They wanted to settle with the king as soon as possible. As the king delayed his response, so the position of the Presbyterians was weakened. Recruiter elections (now called by-elections) in 1646–47 saw several Independents returned to Westminster. However, the Presbyterian position was strengthened in January 1647 when the Scots agreed to leave England once they had been paid £400,000. Their departure removed a potentially unsettling force from the English scene. It also meant that Charles was handed over to parliament's care. He was brought south to Holdenby (or Holmby) House in Northamptonshire. By the spring of 1647 the Presbyterian leaders felt strong enough to deal with the problem of the English army. Their actions set in motion a very significant six months in the history of the Civil Wars.

> Identify the main lines of division amongst the victorious elements of the First Civil War.

Parliament versus the army, April–June 1647

A crisis resulted from parliament's plans for the New Model Army. Some 12,400 men would be sent to Ireland and another 6,400 would stay in England. Other soldiers would be dismissed. There was no mention of arrears of pay, no indemnity against prosecution for actions undertaken while in military service. First the officers and then the ordinary soldiers began to complain. The response of parliament was to offer eight weeks' arrears of pay – the infantry were owed 18 weeks' pay, the cavalry 43 weeks' – at the same time as it ordered the army to disband. On 29 May the army refused. Events then moved fast. A few days later a force of 500 soldiers led by Cornet Joyce rode to

A meeting of the General Council of the Army, which was created in June 1647, in response to rank and file agitation. The Council met to discuss political issues such as the army's grievances against parliament, the impeachment of the 11 Presbyterian MPs and the Leveller Agreement of the People.

Holdenby House and took control of Charles I away from the parliamentary guard. Charles was taken to the army's headquarters at Newmarket. The army set up its own General Council of Officers. As parliament looked to London to provide forces with which to challenge what was in effect an army mutiny, the army marched towards London. On 14 June the General Council of the Army issued a Declaration of the Army, in which it declared it was not 'a mere mercenary army' and called for the Long Parliament to be purged. When the army demanded the impeachment of 11 leading Presbyterians (including Denzil Holles), a civil war among the victors seemed possible. It did not happen because the Eleven Members fled the capital. However, after demonstrators loyal to the Presbyterian leaders invaded parliament on 26 July, the Eleven Members returned. With tension mounting, 60 leading Independent MPs took refuge with the army. Ten days later, the army occupied London and reinstated the Independent MPs.

What did parliament intend to do with the army in early 1647?

The army divided, July–December 1647

By the late summer of 1647, the army also suffered from internal divisions between the rank and file and the **grandees**, as the generals were known. One difference was the fear of the soldiers that the grandees would soften the army's position in order to conclude a settlement with Charles. Divisions were made worse by the election of **Agitators** by the rank and file. These Agitators did not agitate in the modern sense. They represented the ordinary soldiers. Some of the Agitators did belong to or sympathised with the ideas of the various radical groups which were emerging at the time, the best known of which were the Levellers (see pages 186–88).

The Heads of the Proposals

The Agitators watched carefully in July 1647 as the grandees submitted to their royal prisoner their own set of proposals for a settlement, a document known as the Heads of the Proposals. Its main terms were as follows:

- parliaments: Triennial Act to be repealed in favour of biennial parliaments;
- officers of state: parliament to nominate ministers for ten years;
- militia: parliament to control it for ten years;
- the church: bishops to remain but with limited power and religious toleration should be established;
- seven royalists excluded from general pardon.

It is important to compare these terms with those of the Newcastle Propositions which, in September 1647, Charles dismissed in favour of the Heads of the Proposals. At this stage, his strategy of divide and rule seemed to be working.

The Agreement of the People

In October the Levellers, with whom the Agitators were linked, came up with their own set of proposals, the Agreement of the People. This brief document was much more radical than the two that preceded it. It argued that parliament was sovereign in all but five areas. These included religious matters and the ability to exempt individuals from the law of the land. In such cases, the people were to be sovereign. Without explicitly saying so, the Agreement of the People was arguing for a democratic republic.

It was this Agreement which precipitated division within the army. It was discussed by the General Council of Officers in a series of debates held at Putney between 28 October and 5 November 1647. The most heated argument centred upon the franchise, the Levellers advocating universal male suffrage. However, **Henry Ireton**, speaking for the grandees (including Cromwell), insisted that the franchise should be restricted to those with 'a permanent fixed interest in the kingdom'. In other words, the vote should only

'Grandees' was a scornful term that was used particularly by the Levellers and Agitators when referring to senior army officers.

Agitators were representatives of the soldiers. They were elected from each regiment in the army in order to present their demands through the officers to parliament.

What do you understand by the terms: 'grandees' and 'Agitators'?

Henry Ireton (1611–51) was an accomplished soldier and, by 1648, a driving force in the English Revolution. He was largely responsible for the Heads of the Proposals. A son-in-law of Cromwell, he died in Ireland in 1651.

go to those who possessed property; otherwise there would be 'a disturbance to a good constitution of the kingdom'.

A few weeks later there was an army rendezvous at Corkbush Field near Ware. Some of the soldiers wore in their hats copies of the Agreement of the People to which they had added the slogan 'England's Freedom, Soldiers' Rights'. Two regiments should not have been there. Cromwell acted swiftly. He had the ringleaders arrested and one of them shot. Army unity was restored. For Cromwell, that unity was essential given the problems the army was now facing.

Charles I's escape

The most immediate problem was that Charles had escaped from army control, reaching the Isle of Wight where he became the guest of the governor of Carisbrooke Castle. The whole incident remains mysterious. Though he left a note saying he feared for his life, Charles's motives remain obscure. And there is a theory that Cromwell knew of Charles's plan to escape the restraints of the army. Once on the island he was approached by envoys from parliament and the Scots. Parliament's proposals took the form of the Four Bills. They would give parliament control of the militia for 20 years, annul all the king's proclamations against parliament, cancel peerages conferred since the start of the Civil Wars and grant parliament the right to adjourn to whichever place in England it chose. They also included many elements of the Newcastle Propositions. Charles quickly rejected these bills, but not before he signed the Engagement with the Scots on 26 December. He agreed to introduce Presbyterianism into England for three years in return for the military support of the anti-Covenanting Scottish faction. A week later parliament passed the Vote of No Addresses forbidding further negotiations with Charles.

Why was there no negotiated settlement from 1646 to 1647?

Three explanations are possible:
- Firstly, there was no settlement because the king was offered terms that his conscience would not allow him to accept. This impasse could have been broken only by the unthinkable: a settlement without the king. Even in defeat, the king was intransigent. Believing that he had made his concessions in 1641, and haunted by the ghost of Strafford, he was not prepared to yield yet more of his prerogative. He was wedded and glued to the preservation of his friends, his crown and, above all, his church. Indeed, his letters from this time suggest that he had already resolved upon martyrdom.
- Secondly, the king's intransigence was hardened because of a growing

Which group produced the Agreement of the People and what was its main argument?

What was the main difference of opinion that emerged during the Putney Debates between the grandees and some of the rank and file?

What were the main terms of the Engagement?

County committees
were set up by both sides to deal with matters as diverse as military forces, sequestration and taxation.

resentment at what was perceived as parliamentarian tyranny. The continued levy of the excise and assessment taxes and the heavy-handed actions of the **county committees** caused particular resentment. David Underdown, in *Pride's Purge: politics in the Puritan Revolution* (1971), has described this period as exhibiting 'a widespread yearning for the good old days . . . even at the cost of some crucial elements in the programme for which parliament had gone to war'.

- Finally, the nature of the victorious coalition meant that there was remarkably little agreement among the victors about peace terms. It was extremely difficult for any single faction to produce terms to which a majority of its wartime allies was prepared to give support, especially those terms that related to religious issues. For instance, although the creation of a fully Presbyterian Church in England would have won the support of the Presbyterians and the Scots, it would have alienated the army and the Independents.

Rebellion and war, 1648

While the Scots prepared to invade England once more, parts of England rebelled against army rule. In Kent, Essex, south-west England and south Wales, people protested against their economic circumstances. Bad harvests had increased prices to their highest level in a hundred years while taxation remained at wartime levels and central government was as interfering as at the height of war. They wanted the traditional order to return and the king to be released. They were against the new tyranny and not necessarily for the old monarchy. Many had supported parliament during the First Civil War. These county revolts did not succeed mainly because they were unco-ordinated. The army was able to pick them off one by one.

The Second Civil War between proper armies was short and, for Charles, not so sweet. The Scottish army was easily beaten in a running battle at Preston on 17–19 August. It was not just the battle-hardened efficiency of the New Model Army which explains its victory but also the weakness of the royalist cause. The lack of support in the English counties for Charles has already been mentioned. To make matters worse, the Engagement proved highly divisive in Scotland. The hard-line Covenanters under the leadership of Argyll were unable to support an agreement that instituted a Presbyterian Church in England for only three years. Consequently, the Scottish military effort was seriously weakened even before it eventually reached England. Then the effectiveness of the Scottish invasion was further undermined by the military ineptitude of **James Hamilton**, the leading Engager, who raised and led the force into England. By the end of August, Charles's attempt to regain the initiative had come to nothing.

James Hamilton, 1st duke of Hamilton
(1606–49), was Charles's leading Scottish adviser during the Prayer Book crisis. He fell out with Charles in the early part of the Civil Wars. He refused the Covenant in 1643 and joined the king at Oxford where, on grounds that he could not be trusted, he was imprisoned until 1646. As a consequence of his defeat at Preston, he was condemned and executed.

Many soldiers, increasingly influenced by sectarian preachers, now believed that Charles, by attempting to overturn the verdict of the First Civil War, was going against the word of God. As early as April 1648, in a prayer meeting at Windsor, the army resolved 'to call Charles Stuart, that man of blood, to an account for that blood he had shed, and mischief he had done'.

Parliament, however, made one final attempt to settle with Charles. On 24 August MPs repealed the Vote of No Addresses and reopened negotiations with Charles at Newport. As Charles continued with his usual tactic of prevarication, the army grandees formulated their position, which they presented to parliament as a Remonstrance on 20 November. It described Charles as 'the capital and grand author of all our troubles' and demanded that he be brought to justice so that the bloodshed he was guilty of could be avenged. The army leaders were not prepared to accept continued talks with 'that man of blood'. As in August 1647, the army moved towards London. This time, the Political Presbyterians did not have the London crowd to help them. Extraordinarily, parliament made no attempt to appease the army. Indeed, MPs inflamed the situation by pointedly ignoring the Remonstrance and voting, on 5 December, that Charles's answers at Newport were sufficient for further negotiation to take place.

> Give two reasons for the failure of the Scottish invasion in 1648.

The English Revolution, 1648–49

On 6 December, with Colonel Pride standing at the entrance to the Commons, the army decided which MPs should be allowed into the chamber. Of the 507 MPs, 45 were arrested and 186 were secluded. A further 86 withdrew in protest and another 80 or so stayed away during December and January but returned in February 1649. Parliament had been 'cleansed' in what became known as Pride's Purge.

The assumption is often made that once parliament was purged the execution of Charles was just a matter of time. To kill the king after a public trial might not, however, have been the intention behind the purge. David Underdown, in the classic work on the subject, *Pride's Purge* (1971), argues that the army leaders, rather than purging the parliament, wanted to dissolve it before calling a new election. Independent MPs persuaded them that cleansing was preferable to closing down. The purge clearly asserted the superior power of the army. That power would be used against Charles, 'that man of blood'. What exactly they would do, however, remained a subject of debate for several weeks. Charles could have been deposed and sent into exile. Then either the monarchy could have been abolished or one of his sons made king. Perhaps Charles's third son, Henry, duke of Gloucester who, born in 1639, was young enough to be manipulated by the enemies of his father. Charles could have

A contemporary print showing the execution of Charles I, 30 January 1649. Various details demonstrate the artist's distaste at the execution of a king.

been tried and imprisoned. He could have been kept prisoner without trial. The monarchy could have been abolished without killing Charles. These possibilities were all considered. The army leaders decided on a public trial in order to make a public and legal case for getting rid of the king. They decided to have him executed because, as long as he lived, Charles would be a focus for all groups opposed to the new order. Charles had to be killed in order to bring the bloodshed to an end.

Thus the remaining 70 MPs established a High Court of Justice in which to try Charles. The House of Lords refused to support the move but the House of Commons claimed the authority to speak for the English people. To hear the case, 135 commissioners were appointed, including 29 army officers, Cromwell among them. On the first day of the trial, 68 turned up. Charles refused to recognise the court. After a week, the court pronounced Charles to be guilty of 'divers high crimes and treasons'. Charles's death warrant was signed by 59 commissioners. Charles I was publicly executed outside the Banqueting House of the Whitehall Palace on 30 January 1649.

What is the event known as Pride's Purge?

Why was Charles I tried and executed?

Why was Charles I put on trial?

The decision to put the king on trial was the consequence of the army's determination publicly to legitimise its desire to execute the monarch. If Charles could be made to confess to treason, then the regicide would be justified, an act of necessity. However, there were two main problems with trying the king. Firstly, the statutory definition of treason meant that it was absurd to charge the king with that offence. That problem was overcome by redefining treason. Thus, on 1 January 1649 parliament declared that 'it is treason in the King of England . . . to levy war against the Parliament and Kingdom of England'. Secondly, the success of the trial, in terms of winning people over to the soldiers' point of view, was dependent upon the king pleading guilty to the charge. However, his refusal to do so not only won him much support (only 59 of the 135 commissioners of the High Court signed the king's death warrant) but also served to highlight the illegal nature of the court.

Why was Charles executed?

Long-term causes

Recent research has criticised the Whig interpretation that earlier events were leading inevitably to the regicide. Republicanism did not exist as an ideological force driving events towards 30 January 1649. Instead, doctrines of non-resistance and passive obedience were widely respected, while disorder and rebellion were regarded as sinful. In 1643 Henry Marten was expelled from the Commons for arguing the case for a republic. Moreover, the repeal of the Vote of No Addresses, on 24 August 1648, provides evidence of a continuing desire to reach a settlement with the king, despite his instigation of the Second Civil War.

There was certainly no popular demand for Charles to be tried and executed. After Charles had been executed, some of the crowd rushed forward to collect pocketfuls of earth from below the scaffold and others to dip their handkerchiefs in the royal blood. One observer recorded that as the axe fell there was 'such a groan as I never heard before, and desire I may never hear again'. It is inconceivable that the trial and the subsequent execution of Charles I would have occurred if the army had refrained from purging parliament on 6 December 1648. So why did the army purge parliament? There are several key explanations.

- The actions of Charles. The king's decision to foment a Second Civil War did much to harden opinion against him. This was vividly evident when, on 1 May 1648, the army resolved 'to call Charles Stuart, that man of blood, to an account for that blood he had shed, and mischief he had done to his utmost against the Lord's cause and people in these poor nations'. Moreover, the fact that Charles had been negotiating with parliament at the same time as he had been shaping a deal with the Scots persuaded many MPs, at least temporarily, that here was a duplicitous king who could not be trusted to abide by the terms of any settlement. 'Men who would have been willing to come to terms with him [thus] despaired of any constitutional

An allegorical picture of 1649. As the king is thrown overboard, lightning strikes the House of Commons. Discord and anarchy then break out amongst the citizens.

arrangement in which he was to be a factor', observes S. R. Gardiner, 'and men who had long been alienated from him were irritated into active hostility.'

- The impact of radical groups in London. It was unlikely that the army would have been able to effect the coup d'état of 6 December, and then go on to organise the trial and execution of the king, without at least the passive acceptance of religious and political radicals in London. In particular, the Levellers seem to have enjoyed substantial popular backing, some of their petitions – demanding, amongst other things, the sovereignty of parliament over the king – collecting as many as 40,000 signatures. The army grandees reopened discussions in the Whitehall Debates about a second version of the Agreement of the People, which the Levellers had helped draft. The Levellers did not openly support either the trial or the execution but neither did they oppose them.
- The leadership and impetus provided by Ireton and Cromwell. Henry

Ireton was largely responsible for building and maintaining the radical coalition that was necessary to ensure the execution of the king. The author of various manifestos of the New Model Army, including the Remonstrance of 1648, Ireton had grown determined to bring the king to trial and ultimately to execute him. In place of the increasingly diffident person of the Lord General Fairfax, who, through illness, real or imagined, was frequently absent from key meetings, Ireton eventually enjoyed the wholehearted support of his father-in-law, Oliver Cromwell.

The established view about Cromwell and regicide is that he remained reluctant and uncertain about killing the king until late in December 1648. John Morrill has recently questioned this view. He has argued that Cromwell was convinced of the need to remove the king from much earlier in 1648. The resolve and determination of Cromwell and Ireton did much to facilitate the trial and execution of the king. Moreover, the resolve of the two men was based, in part, upon their religious beliefs.

- The belief in Providence – in God's will. Cromwell's resolve to kill the king had been shaped by his conviction that he was submitting to God's will, evidence for which was taken to be the victories of the New Model Army. After the Battle of Preston, Cromwell informed the speaker that he considered the royalist defeat as 'nothing but the hand of God' and concluded that 'wherever anything in this world is exalted, or exalts itself, God will pull it down'. Thus, Cromwell justified the trial and execution of the king by arguing that 'the Providence of God hath cast this upon us [and] I cannot but submit to Providence'. To Cromwell and others like him, it had become clear that, since Charles was not prepared to make concessions in order to reach a settlement, then a settlement must be had without him. It was God's will.

Identify the arguments which have been put forward to explain
- why Charles was put on trial;
- why he was executed.

Personal Rule and civil war, 1629–49: a summary

The 20 years from 1629 to 1649 were a period of great and dramatic change in government of England. In 1629 the king had decided to rule without parliament until it came to its senses. In 1649 a parliament controlled by army leaders decided to rule without the king because they believed that, with Charles as king, England would never be at peace. Eleven years of ordered government in England during the 1630s had been followed by nine years of political and military conflict. This resulted in the overturning of the traditional political and religious order. There had been rebellions against royal authority in Scotland and Ireland as well as England. 'No bishop, no king' had, by 1649, become reality. The anarchy feared by supporters of the crown all but occurred in 1647–48. Moreover, the fears of despotism, identified by parliamentarians such as Pym in 1629 and 1640, had proved well founded except in one fundamental respect – the despotism was parliamentarian not monarchical. It is worth trying to explain how these extraordinary changes had occurred as well as mentioning one or two important features of the period which have not yet been considered.

As to explanation, when covering both the outbreak of civil war and the execution of Charles I, both long-term and short-term causes were identified. (These can also be called conditional and contingent factors.) In both cases, recent studies have preferred to emphasise the importance of short-term or contingent factors – though they never dismiss the long-term or conditional. Certainly there is little evidence of groups planning civil war or regicide more than a few weeks ahead of their happening. All sides wanted a settlement, both in 1640–41 and 1646–47, but they wanted it on their own terms. They feared what would happen if they gave way. Thus the way they interpreted – or rather misinterpreted – their opponents' words and actions helps explain why events developed as they did. In 1640–41 Pym and his supporters believed that the royalists were part of a conspiracy to return England to Rome. In 1647–48 Charles and his supporters believed that the Independents in parliament and the army would destroy the hierarchy in church and state that ensured order and stability. These beliefs were built on factors that included traditional beliefs of family and social groups, as well as the more immediate influences of personal experience and changing circumstances.

There can be little doubt that the British context of the English Civil War was most significant. Charles's attempts to rule all three kingdoms in similar ways helped to cause rebellions in Ireland and Scotland. These made it necessary to call the English parliament in 1640. The Scottish dimension remained significant throughout the 1640s, as evidenced by the intervention of the Scottish army on no less than three occasions in eight years.

Scotland was important because of the pressure it put on the English Puritans to introduce Presbyterianism; Ireland because it helped heighten Puritan fears of a papist onslaught. The religious attitudes and values of the time are also most important in explaining the key developments of the 1640s. Religious beliefs were central to people's lives. Events were understood in terms of religion in general and the Bible in particular. For the Puritans the Bible was the word of God. As Calvinists, they believed in predestination. Many parliamentarians, therefore, began to see the events of the 1640s, and especially the unexpected success of what was essentially a rebellion against the crown, as evidence that they had been chosen to create the Godly society in England. Cromwell's belief in Providence is just one example of this belief. This sense of righteousness helps explain the determination of a few to get rid of Charles at all costs. He was in the way of a better life for all Englishmen.

If religion gave these leaders the justification to make war and execute the king, the rise of the army gave them the means to impose their will. They could not afford to lose the First Civil War and in creating the army to ensure their victory they created a military force which soon became a political one. For the soldiers, even more than the politicians, quickly developed a strong sense of their own righteousness. As the politicians tried to reach a settlement the soldiers became increasingly impatient. No less than seven different sets of proposals were put to Charles in the seven years from 1642 to 1648. There was no evidence in 1648 that a settlement was any closer than it had been in 1642. More likely was that the military conflicts and social unrest of recent years would continue. The army officers concluded that a settlement would have to be imposed.

Leading the grandees in reaching this conclusion was one man, Henry Ireton. Son-in-law of Oliver Cromwell, he is often overlooked, in part, because he died in 1651, aged 40. Appointed commissary-general of the horse in the New Model Army in 1645 and also elected as an MP, he came to play a leading role in drafting both the Heads of the Proposals and the Remonstrance of the Army. By November 1648 he was in London, involved in preparations for Pride's Purge. Cromwell, by contrast, was still in the north (it is unclear whether out of military necessity or political convenience) and did not return to London until the evening of the day of Pride's Purge. It was Ireton who led the Whitehall Debates and who decided that Charles had to be tried and executed. Cromwell took longer to be convinced – there is a story that in December 1648 he made one last attempt to reach a settlement with Charles – but after that he became as resolute on getting rid of Charles as his son-in-law was.

In 1649 Cromwell was second-in-command of the army and Sir Thomas Fairfax still its leader. However, Fairfax was no politician and he was increasingly disenchanted with the direction of events at the end of 1648, refusing to join the court that tried Charles. Cromwell was both soldier and politician. Though he had been a relatively insignificant MP in the 1628 parliament and in the early days of the Long Parliament, he became a national figure as a result of the skills of military leadership he revealed, first in the Eastern Association and then in the New Model Army. By 1645 he was so indispensable that he was exempted from the terms of the Self-Denying Ordinance. His membership of both parliament and the army gave him a unique opportunity to act as a contact between the two, a role which added to his importance in 1647–48. He could also act quickly and effectively to deal with threats to his authority, as shown by his controlled ruthlessness at Corkbush Field. By 1649 he was emerging as the dominant figure in parliament and the army. In the 1650s that dominance was to become even greater.

Summary questions

1   (a) Identify and explain any *two* reasons why the king and parliament fought the Second Civil War in 1648.

(b) Compare the importance of at least *three* causes of the execution of Charles I in 1649.

2   Explain why it proved impossible to produce a lasting settlement after the First Civil War.

3   At what point did the execution of Charles I become inevitable? Explain your answer.

The Interregnum, 1649–60

10 The Rump and the Nominated Assembly, 1649–53

Focus questions

◆ What problems faced the Rump of the Long Parliament?

◆ What, if anything, did the Nominated Assembly achieve?

Significant dates

1649	**5 February** Charles II is proclaimed king of Great Britain and Ireland at Edinburgh.
	17 March The act abolishing monarchy is passed.
	19 March The act abolishing the House of Lords is passed.
	14–15 May A Leveller rebellion is put down at Burford.
	19 May The act declaring England a Commonwealth is passed.
	2 August The Battle of Rathmines takes place.
	15 August–28 May 1650 Cromwell is in Ireland.
	11 September Drogheda falls.
	11 October Wexford falls.
1650	**2 January** The Engagement Act is passed.
	10 May The Adultery Act is passed.
	June Charles II lands in Scotland.
	28 June Cromwell is appointed lord general in place of Fairfax.
	22 July–August 1651 Cromwell leads the English army in Scotland.
	9 August The Blasphemy Act is passed.
	3 September The Battle of Dunbar takes place.
	27 September The Toleration Act is passed.
1651	**1 January** Charles II is crowned king by the Scots.
	July–August Charles II invades England.
	3 September The Battle of Worcester takes place. Charles II flees to the Continent (**15 October**).
	9 October The Navigation Act is passed.
1652	**January** The Hale Commission on law reform is appointed.
	19 May The First Anglo-Dutch War begins.
1653	**20 April** Cromwell dissolves the Rump Parliament.
	4 July The Nominated Assembly convenes.
	12 December The Nominated Assembly returns power to Cromwell.

Overview

The position of the **Rump Parliament** in 1649 was far from strong. It faced opposition from most political and religious groups in England, from Scotland and Ireland and from the monarchs of Europe. It also faced the expectations of the devout Puritans that it would introduce a Godly society. The MPs themselves were divided and lacked an obvious political leader. The Rump Parliament was seen as the army's creation. At least, initially, the army's support was the one factor working in the Rump's favour as the army could use its power to defeat the Rump's enemies. In 1649 it crushed the Levellers before dealing with the Irish. It turned to crush the Scots in 1650 and, a year later, defeated a Scottish invasion force led by Charles II. Only then was the Rump's position really secure. The army then turned its attention to the Rump. The soldiers had expected it to introduce radical reforms before dissolving itself but neither of these things happened. In April 1653 the army lost patience. Cromwell, accompanied by 20 or 30 musketeers, entered the Commons and expelled the Rump of the Long Parliament.

Influenced by millenarian ideas, Cromwell decided to implement the scheme of the **Fifth Monarchist, Thomas Harrison**. The resulting assembly, hand-picked by the army leadership, was intended, in Cromwell's words, to be a 'door to usher in things that God hath promised and prophesied of'. It was not and the record of the assembly proved disappointing. In a state of near collapse it returned its power to Cromwell on 12 December 1653.

The republic established, 1649

Having got rid of the king, the Rump had to devise a new system of government. It had no blueprint for doing so. MPs did not readily agree on the form of the new government, especially as, from February 1649, MPs who had been excluded by Pride's Purge were given the chance to return to parliament. Between 100 and 140 did so over the next few months. They outnumbered the 70 or so revolutionaries who had seen through the trial and execution of Charles. The Rump moved cautiously. As the monarch had been dispatched, the monarchy had to go to. The abolition of the monarchy, moreover, would require the abolition of that other hereditary element, the House of Lords. Not until March 1649 was the necessary legislation passed. It was another two months, moreover, before the Rump declared England to be 'a Commonwealth and Free State' to be governed by the supreme authority of the nation, 'the representatives of the people in Parliament and by such as they appoint'.

They decided to create a council of state to replace the privy council. This was to be elected annually by the Rump Parliament and to consist of 41

The **Rump Parliament** was the name given to the Long Parliament after it had been purged on 6 December 1648.

A **Fifth Monarchist** was a member of a millenarian sect, perhaps numbering 10,000 at the peak of their influence, that emerged in the wake of the execution of Charles I. Fifth Monarchists believed that the four great empires of Babylon, Persia, Greece and Rome would shortly be followed by the Fifth Monarchy. During this time, King Christ would rule on earth with his saints for 1,000 years culminating in the Day of Judgement.

Thomas Harrison (1606–60) was an effective soldier who fought with the New Model Army. He signed the death warrant of Charles I. During the Protectorate he was reprimanded by Cromwell for his relations with religious radicals and was imprisoned from 1655 to 1656 and again from 1658 to 1659. He was exempted from the 1660 Act of Indemnity and executed that same year.

individuals. The first council included 34 MPs and 5 peers, 14 of who were regicides. Cromwell was a member; Ireton was not. Only 19 of the 41 took the Engagement, an oath indicating that the subscriber would be 'true and faithful to the Commonwealth of England, as it is now established'. This was neither a government of revolutionaries, nor was it rule by the army. The army was too busy defeating the Commonwealth's enemies.

What was the council of state?

Enemies within and without, 1649–51

The list of groups and countries opposed to the new republic was a long one. Royalists had no love for the new republic while Presbyterians had little. A moderate Oath of Engagement was gradually introduced in order to help identify the Rump's most determined opponents as well as develop some form of commitment to the regime. Even the army could not be relied on in 1649, mainly because the soldiers were still owed large sums of back pay. Eventually, in 1650, the Rump got round to paying the arrears. But this was not before some regiments had mutinied in protest at their conditions. In April and May, the army dealt quickly and effectively with two separate incidents. In London one soldier, Robert Lockyer, was shot and, in the churchyard of Burford, in Oxfordshire, Fairfax and Cromwell had three mutineers shot. A related Leveller-inspired rising, also in Oxfordshire, resulted in its Leveller leader, William Thompson, also being shot.

The Levellers

It was the Levellers who posed the first direct challenge to the Rump. For various reasons, they had kept quiet in late 1648 and early 1649. In part, this was because they were hoping that parliament would accept the revised Agreement of the People and thus that the Rump would be dissolved and new, more democratic elections held. When it was obvious that the Rump was there to stay, at least in the short term, the Levellers felt betrayed. John Lilburne returned to London and published *England's new chains discovered* in February 1649. **Richard Overton**'s *The hunting of the foxes* followed soon after. Lilburne and Overton, together with two other civilian Levellers, were soon imprisoned in the Tower of London, from whence a third version of the Agreement of the People was issued in May. The defeat of the Leveller groups in the army greatly weakened the Leveller cause. The Rump then brought Lilburne to trial on the charge of treason. He was acquitted by the jury. The other three were released once they agreed to take the Oath of Engagement. By 1649 the Leveller cause was being outflanked by more radical left-wing groups such as the True Levellers or Diggers and by religious sects such as the Fifth Monarchists, Muggletonians, Ranters and Quakers (see pages 190–91). These

Richard Overton (?–1663) was imprisoned in the Tower along with other leaders of the Levellers for his share in the authorship of *England's new chains discovered*. He fled to the continent in 1655, where he obtained a commission from Charles II.

groups were too fragmented and too inward looking to prove any effective threat to the regime. Their existence helped make the Rump more conservative than it might otherwise have been.

The Irish

A yet greater threat to the republic came from Ireland, which had been in revolt since 1641. Ireland was part of the English state and yet anti-English forces controlled almost all of the country. There appeared to be every likelihood that **Charles Stuart** would put himself at the head of the rebellious forces. Thus, as well as needing to reassert English authority over Ireland, it was a matter of some urgency to stop Charles Stuart from using Ireland against England. In the summer of 1649, therefore, Cromwell and Ireton, with 20,000 troops, were sent to Ireland. Helped by the fact that the Irish royalists had been defeated by a force loyal to the Rump at Rathmines on 2 August, before he had arrived, Cromwell had effectively quelled the rebellion by the end of the year. In the process, he had ordered the killing of some 3,000 at Drogheda, including 1,000 civilians, and 2,000 at Wexford, where some were put to death in cold blood. Cromwell regarded this slaughter as 'a righteous judgement of God upon these barbarous wretches who have imbrued their hands in so much innocent blood'. The action against Drogheda and Wexford remains controversial to this day. Cromwell's critics argue he exceeded the rules of war and allowed acts of atrocity to take place, mainly because he saw the Irish as sub-human. His defenders argue, firstly, that Cromwell did keep to the rules of war of the time and, secondly, that the actions at Drogheda and Wexford brought the war in Ireland to a rapid end, thus avoiding greater casualties elsewhere. By the time he left Ireland to Ireton (who died there of a fever a few months later), the great part of Ireland was under English control once more.

Charles Stuart (1630–85) was the second son of Charles I and Henrietta Maria. He withdrew to the continent in 1646. Proclaimed king in Edinburgh on 5 February 1649, he became practically a prisoner in the hands of Argyll and the Presbyterian party. Having been defeated at Worcester on 3 September 1651, he escaped his pursuers by hiding in an oak tree. He spent the 1650s in exile on the continent. He was restored as king in 1660.

The Scots

A more serious threat now came from Scotland. The Scots were furious that the English had executed their king. They soon proclaimed Charles Stuart as King Charles II. In June 1650 he arrived in Scotland. In return for agreeing to erect a fully Presbyterian Church in England, Charles would be provided with an army to invade England. The English saw Scotland as different from Ireland, not least in that it was Protestant whereas the other was Catholic. Nevertheless, the English acted quickly to contain the threat posed by an independent Scotland. Rather than wait until the Scots invaded England, Cromwell led a force of 15,000 into Scotland. At Dunbar, on 3 September 1650, he won a great victory, even though outnumbered two to one. Of the Scots, 3,000 were killed while only 20 English died. It confirmed Cromwell's belief that Providence was on his side. Finally, the Scots did invade England. Cromwell chased after them and, at Worcester, exactly one year later defeated the Scots in a hard-fought battle. Charles II escaped to the continent, hiding in an oak tree on the way to the south coast. The Rump announced the union of England and Scotland that James I had wanted but could not achieve.

By late 1651 not only had the threats to the Rump been defeated but England had also asserted its control over all parts of the British Isles. The army could now concentrate on English affairs once more.

Identify the threats that the Rump had to overcome.

Domestic policy

New legislation

In England, the Rump moved more cautiously in all areas of policy than had been expected by the army who had helped save parliament from dissolution in 1648–49.

It passed various acts dealing with religious matters in the spring and summer of 1650 that were intended to advance the quest for a moral and Godly reformation. They included:

- an Act for the Propagation of the Gospel in Wales, Ireland and parts of England;
- an Act for Better Observation of the Lord's Day, Days of Thanksgiving and Humiliation;
- an Act for Suppressing the Detestable Sins of Incest, Adultery and Fornication;
- an Act against the Detestable Sins of Profane Swearing and Cursing;
- an Act against Atheistical, Blasphemous and Execrable Opinions, Derogatory to the Honour and Destructive to Human Society (about 50 people were executed according to its terms).

The Toleration Act of September 1650 abolished the need for people to attend church so long as they went to some form of religious service each week. Nothing was done about either the Presbyterian structure, introduced in the mid 1640s, or the longstanding grievance of church tithes.

The reformers had expected that the law would be less punitive towards and more accessible to ordinary people. An Act for the Relief of Poor Debtors, in September 1649, did end imprisonment for debtors who possessed less than £5. In addition, over a year later, in December 1651, the Rump agreed to set up a commission under Sir Matthew Hale to discuss the whole issue of law reform.

Growing opposition from the army

These acts did little to satisfy the army. Much of the legislation that seemed to further a moral and Godly reformation was intended more to curb the radical sects such as the Ranters and the Quakers. The Toleration Act was a misnomer because, as Blair Worden has remarked, 'it gave with one hand and took with the other'. As for the Hale Commission on law reform, even though it met three times a week until July 1652, not one of its recommendations was implemented.

The army had reason to be dissatisfied with the Rump, not only because of the limited nature of the legislation but also because fewer acts were being passed. From 125 in 1649, the number had fallen to only 51 in 1652. The army began to see the Rump as corrupt and self-serving. The main example of the Rump's selfishness was its failure to move to dissolve itself, despite an act of 14 November 1651, which stipulated that it would happen by 3 November 1654 at the latest. Relations between the two became increasingly strained until they broke down completely.

Taxation

The final aspect of the Rump's domestic policy that needs to be considered is its taxation policy. The circumstances with which it had to cope meant that it had to maintain high levels of taxation. Having to fight the Irish, the Scots and, from May 1652, the Dutch meant that the army and the navy had to be maintained at levels that inflicted a substantial cost upon the taxpayer. In December 1652 the Rump raised the monthly assessment from £90,000 to £120,000, a sum which, calculated on an annual basis, was equivalent to roughly 24 pre-war parliamentary subsidies. Popular resentment at the absence of any peace dividend translated itself into resentment of the regime in general. Life under a monarchy had been a cheaper option.

For what reasons was the army dissatisfied with the Rump?

Foreign policy

Why did England find itself at war with the Dutch in 1652? It was certainly the opposite of what the Rump had intended in 1651. After the United Provinces, a strongly Protestant state, had recognised the Commonwealth in early 1651, the Rump sent a mission to the Netherlands with a view to a union of the two states. The Dutch dismissed the idea. The Rump then passed the Navigation Act, which stated that non-English ships could enter English ports only if they carried goods from their own country. This hit the Dutch hard because their fleet carried more goods from other countries than from their own. The royalist sympathies of its sailors meant that the Dutch fleet refused the English demand that they salute the flag on English ships. There was a clash of fleets in the Channel – an event which started a two-year long war. The first battle went to the Dutch but the English won the second and third, at Portland and the Gabbard, in 1653. War was continuing when the Rump came to an end.

What was the Navigation Act?

The dissolution of the Rump

On 20 April 1653, his patience exhausted, Cromwell and 30 soldiers entered the House of Commons and sent MPs packing. 'You have sat too long here for any good you have been doing lately,' he told his cowed listeners. 'Corrupt, unjust persons', he went on, 'scandalous to the profession of the Gospel. How can you be a Parliament for God's people? Depart I say, and let us have done with you. In the name of God, go!'

'If Mr Pym were alive again', Dorothy Osborne wrote in a note to her lover, 'I wonder what he would think of these proceedings, and whether this would appear as great a breach of the privilege of Parliament as the demanding of the 5 Members.'

There are key moments in Cromwell's career where no evidence exists to form a definitive conclusion as to his involvement and/or opinion of an event. Did he approve of the army kidnapping the king from Holdenby House on 4 June 1647? Did he deliberately facilitate the escape of Charles from Hampton Court on 11 November 1647 in order to heal the divisions in the army revealed by the Putney Debates? Was he purposefully absent from London during Pride's Purge so that he would not be associated with an act of violence against a freely elected parliament? For historians, perhaps the most frustrating of these events is that of 20 April 1653. The problem is that the bill that parliament was discussing at the time was destroyed, apparently by Cromwell himself. Thus it is impossible to determine the exact reason why he expelled the Rump.

Nevertheless, historians have deduced from reports and letters of contemporaries that, on 20 April, the Rumpers were discussing a bill for a new representative (that is, a new parliament) and that they had agreed to dissolve themselves in November 1653. It seems likely that the details of this bill provided for an immediate dissolution and for fresh elections to occur without the army imposing any qualifications on those who could stand. Clearly, aware of the disaffection that had built up towards the army and the associated high taxation, Cromwell must have feared the result of these elections. They would return Presbyterians and royalists, groups that had no interest in furthering a moral and Godly reformation and were actively hostile to liberty to tender consciences. According to this interpretation, Cromwell, therefore, dissolved the Rump to prevent the proposed elections from happening, an action that can be seen as that of a tyrant.

On the other hand, if the Rumpers had been preparing to hold recruiter elections, thereby perpetuating their own power, then Cromwell's action is more that of a liberator. The problem with this interpretation is that it is the explanation that Cromwell himself offered a few days later. He might have hoped that the Rump would dissolve itself and then that there would be fresh

A Dutch print showing Cromwell dissolving the Rump Parliament on 20 April 1653. The writing on the wall says 'This House to let.'

elections overseen by a temporary council of MPs and army officers. These would have ensured the election of a parliament that would have advanced the Godly cause. However, if it became apparent that the Rump would not go along with these plans, then Cromwell had to act.

It is most unlikely that we shall ever know what exactly caused Cromwell to act against the Rump in the way that he did. The action against the Rump on 20 April certainly highlighted the dominance over English politics of the army in general and Cromwell in particular. Events of the past four years had strengthened the position of both.

The Nominated Assembly, 1653

In the immediate aftermath of the dissolution of the Rump, Cromwell and the army moved quickly towards constructing a new constitution. Although presented with the opportunity to install a military dictatorship, Cromwell declined to do so. He rejected the accusation that he had stifled the 'liberty of the people' by declaring that 'it is only suspended, 'tis a sword taken out of a mad man's hand till he recover his senses.' There were two plans. The practical one came from **John Lambert**, who wanted an army-led council of state to rule and a parliament eventually to be elected. The more idealistic one came from Major-General Harrison who wanted an assembly of the Godly. He wanted an assembly of 70 to be nominated, based on the precedent of the

What arguments have been put forward to explain why Cromwell dissolved the Rump?

John Lambert
(1619–83) took up arms for parliament at the beginning of the Civil War. He assisted Ireton in drawing up the Heads of the Proposals in 1647. He fought in the Second Civil War and took part in the Battles of Dunbar and Worcester. Author of the Instrument of Government, he clashed with Cromwell in 1657 and was forced into retirement. He made a last-ditch effort to sustain the republic as it collapsed in 1660, an act for which he was tried for high treason and condemned to death. In fact, he was imprisoned on Guernsey from 1664 until his death in 1683.

Jewish **Sanhedrin** in Jerusalem. Cromwell agreed to elements of both. On 29 April the lord general nominated a new council of state composed of just ten men instead of the previous 41. Seven were military men, three civilians. A Nominated Assembly was established, composed of 140 Godly men chosen by the army officers. It included six representatives of Ireland and five of Scotland, which helped make it the first British assembly.

The Nominated Assembly first met on 4 July 1653. It was addressed by Cromwell who told the members that 'truly God hath called you to this work . . . We are at a threshold.' Cromwell saw the assembly as the chance to bring about the Godly society. The assembly became the focus of radical hopes, which the Rump had never fulfilled. Yet the members of the assembly were never told what this work might be and never presented with a programme of reform. They were expected to know what to do. It seems that Cromwell expected them to act as a temporary surrogate for a parliament elected by the people. To this end he anticipated that they would institute reforms designed to win people over to Godly forms of behaviour and an acceptance of liberty to tender consciences. Once this had been accomplished, then the Nominated Assembly would dissolve itself and free elections could take place in the expectation that the electorate could then be relied upon not to elect Presbyterians and royalists.

Members of the assembly soon called it a parliament, even though it was not elected. It is sometimes called the Little Parliament, but more often the Barebones Parliament after one of its more colourful characters, Praise-God Barebone, a London leather seller and religious radical (authors have variously described him as a Fifth Monarchist, a Baptist and an Independent). However he held no position of authority within the assembly. The label helps perpetuate the view of the assembly that it was composed of religious radicals, often from lower social classes, idealistic and not a little dangerous. In fact, the parliament contained relatively few religious radicals. Moreover, recent research has demonstrated the inaccuracy of Clarendon's assertion that 'much the major part of [the members] consisted of inferior persons, of no quality or name, artificers of the meanest trades, known only by their gifts in praying and teaching'. It is now clear that at least four-fifths ranked as gentlemen, indicating, as David L. Smith has remarked, that 'the Assembly thus marked a shift of power within the gentry rather than away from the gentry'.

Even though the moderates were in the majority, they often lost out to the more radical minority which attended more regularly. The assembly still managed to pass some useful practical reforms including:

- the establishment of the idea of civil marriages, to be performed by a justice of the peace rather than a cleric;
- the compulsory registration of births, marriages and deaths;

- the relief of impoverished creditors and debtors;
- protection for lunatics and their estates;
- sterner measures against thieves and highwaymen.

By the end of 1653 the parliament that had passed more than 30 laws was preparing many more bills. However, the more conscientious radical members were sufficiently well organised to push through a number of measures that alarmed the moderate majority. When, on 10 December, the radicals managed to overturn a committee's report in favour of retaining tithes, the moderates became alarmed. Both self-interest (many of them benefited from **impropriated tithes**) and a desire not to jeopardise the social hierarchy caused the moderates to act. Early in the morning, on 12 December, while the radicals were attending a prayer meeting, the moderates voted to return to Cromwell the powers which they received from him. The experiment in Godly government was over.

The Nominated Assembly had been designed to 'win the people to the interest of Jesus Christ and the love of godliness'. Therefore, its failure was a defining moment for Cromwell. He at once lamented that its collapse was the result of his own 'weakness and folly' but consoled himself that if it had been allowed to continue to sit it would have 'brought the confusion of all things'. He now turned away from reform to 'healing and settling'. Thus the end of the Nominated Assembly was also an important moment in the English Revolution. Stable government became as important as Godly government.

Tithes originally amounted to one-tenth of agricultural produce produced by each parishioner and were paid to the parish church for the support of the priest. By the early seventeenth century, tithes had been commuted into cash payments and many of these had been acquired by laymen. The latter were known as **impropriated tithes**.

What were the two main choices facing Cromwell after the dissolution of the Rump?
Who chose those who sat in the Nominated Assembly?
What was the social background of those who sat in the Nominated Assembly?

Summary questions

1   (a) Identify and explain any *two* problems which caused serious difficulties for the Rump during the period 1649–53.

   (b) Compare the success of the Rump in dealing with at least *three* problems it encountered.

2   Why did the Rump find it so difficult to produce stable government?

11

The Protectorate, 1653–59

Focus questions

◆ What were Cromwell's aims?

◆ Why did Cromwell decline the crown?

◆ How successful was Cromwell as lord protector?

Significant dates

1653   *16 December* The Instrument of Government is introduced and Cromwell installed as lord protector.

1654   *March* The 'triers', a national body to vet all new clergy, is established.
August The 'ejectors', local bodies to expel inadequate teachers and ministers, are set up.
September–January 1655 The First Protectorate Parliament is in session.
12 September MPs are obliged to agree to the Recognition.

1655   *March* Penruddock's Rising breaks out.
August Major-generals are appointed in England and Wales.

1656   *September–June 1657* The first session of the Second Protectorate Parliament is held.
December The Nayler case occurs.

1657   *January* Cromwell abandons rule by the major-generals.
February The Humble Petition and Advice is proposed.
8 May Cromwell accepts the Humble Petition and Advice without the crown.
26 June Cromwell is re-installed as lord protector.

1658   *January–February* The second session of the Second Protectorate Parliament is held.
3 September Oliver Cromwell dies and is succeeded by his son, Richard Cromwell.

1659   *January–April* The Third Protectorate Parliament is in session.
22 April Parliament is dissolved by order of the General Council of Officers.
7 May The Rump Parliament is recalled.
24 May Richard Cromwell resigns as lord protector.

Overview

For the first time in its history, for just over the five years from December 1653 to May 1659, Britain had a written or codified constitution. This was, firstly, the Instrument of Government and then, from 1657, the Humble Petition and Advice. The Instrument, the product of the General Council of Officers, did restore civilian rule and, in particular, elected parliaments. It also introduced a head of state, the lord protector, for whom Cromwell was the obvious choice. Thus, Britain edged edged towards a more balanced or mixed system of government with which it was more familiar.

However, the five and a half years of the Protectorate were to see several changes to that system. The first attempt at some kind of parliamentary government was altered in early 1655 when Cromwell introduced rule by the major-generals, a kind of military Godly rule. That experiment was also abandoned after 18 months, with another parliament being elected. That parliament offered the crown to Oliver Cromwell in the Humble Petition and Advice. Cromwell rejected the crown but accepted the other parts of the Humble Petition. It was this system that Richard Cromwell inherited on the death of his father in September 1658. The Protectorate outlived the lord protector by only a few months. In May 1659 it collapsed.

How successful was the Protectorate? How successful was the lord protector? We need first to understand the main features of the new constitution and the aims of Cromwell as lord protector.

Cromwell and the Protectorate

The Instrument of Government

There was not the debate and delay following the end of the Nominated Assembly that there had been earlier in the year following the end of the Rump Parliament. On 16 December 1653 the General Council of Officers approved the Instrument of Government, a written constitution devised in large part by Major-General John Lambert. Its main features were:

- The supreme legislative authority 'shall reside in one person and the people assembled in parliament', that person to be known as the lord protector.
- Oliver Cromwell would be lord protector for life, his successors to be chosen by parliament.
- The exercise of the 'chief magistracy . . . and government' shall 'be in the Lord Protector assisted with a council' of nor more than 21 and no less than 13 individuals. The Instrument named 15 who were to sit for life. Subsequent vacancies were to be filled by parliament.

- A single-chamber parliament would meet for at least five months every three years and was to be composed of 400 English MPs, 30 Scottish and 30 Irish. The first parliament was to meet on 3 September 1654 and, until then, the lord protector could issue ordinances with the force of law.
- An army of 10,000 horse and 20,000 foot would be paid for by a 'constant yearly revenue'. There was also the provision of a further £200,000 a year to cover the cost of civil government.
- Religious toleration would be provided except for those who 'hold forth and practice licentiousness' and the Catholics.

In total, these measures were designed to ensure that the executive and legislature would interact through a series of checks and balances. Sovereignty was shared, in marked contrast to the Rump Parliament. Cromwell later protested that the terms of the Instrument had 'hemmed him in as though a child in swaddling clouts'. However, the Instrument would result in a more balanced, more representative system than the Rump had been – if it could be made to work. It possessed three major deficiencies:

- there was no provision for amendment;
- there was no machinery for the adjudication of disputes;
- provisions for religious toleration contrasted with the sentiment of most of the political nation.

Overcoming these weaknesses and gaining support for the Instrument, which had been imposed on the English, not approved by them, set a great challenge for the council and above all the lord protector. What was he hoping to achieve?

Cromwell's aims as lord protector

As might be expected, it is not possible to identify specific aims for Cromwell as lord protector during his four and three-quarter years in office. Most historians have identified two broad aims.

To 'heal and settle' the nation

'That which I judge to be the end of your meeting, the great end . . . [is] healing and settling,' Cromwell told the First Protectorate Parliament. Similarly, in April 1657, he told a parliamentary delegation, 'I am hugely taken with the word Settlement, with the thing and with the notion of it.' After the disappointment of the Rump Parliament and the collapse of the Nominated Assembly, Cromwell turned away from Godly reforms, which would always involve the minority imposing on the majority, to achieving some kind of settlement that concentrated on winning the support of the majority of the political nation. Introducing the more balanced constitution of the Protectorate and restoring parliament were moves that were intended to heal and settle. Even his acceptance of the post of lord protector was part of those moves.

'Just and righteous reformation'

Cromwell could, however, never completely abandon his desire for reform. Since Cromwell never defined what he meant by 'just and righteous reformation', frequently referring to it as the 'cause', it is open to various interpretations. Nevertheless, it is certain that Cromwell perceived two aspects to this 'reformation', social and religious:

- A social reformation. Cromwell was particularly concerned to provide social justice, such as reform of education and improvements to the law. When he addressed the First Protectorate Parliament he was keen to point out that he 'desired to reform the laws . . . and to consider how the laws might be made plain and short, and less chargeable to the people, how to lessen expense, for the good of the nation'.

  Establishing **ejectors** in 1654 to improve the quality of schoolteachers was an example of gradual social reform.

In August 1654 commissioners known as **ejectors** were appointed in each county to expel 'scandalous, ignorant and insufficient ministers and schoolmasters'.

- A religious reformation. In common with other radical Protestants, Cromwell wanted to further the Reformation, which had begun in the sixteenth century. He believed that this process could only occur 'by subduing those corruptions and lusts and evils that are [in our hearts]'. Only when this inner reformation – a 'reformation of manners' – had occurred would the country gain God's blessing. Thus, it was necessary to outlaw drunkenness, swearing, adultery, blasphemy, sexual immorality and Sabbath-breaking. Once God's blessing had been received, then it would be easier to achieve what was undoubtedly Cromwell's ultimate goal, toleration of all Protestant groups. Yet, it also follows from this that it was necessary to bring together 'the several sorts of godliness in this nation'. In other words, a Godly commonwealth would not only come about through a moral reformation but also by Protestant unity. That is one reason why he established the system of ejectors in early 1654, to improve the quality of the clergy.

What were the two main aims of Cromwell?

Rule by ordinance, 1654

The first parliament was not due to meet until September 1654, which gave Cromwell nine months in which he had the authority to rule by ordinance. He was certainly busy, issuing 82 ordinances before parliament met. This period and these ordinances reveal much about Cromwell's concerns:

- He was concerned with order, which could not be taken for granted. Establishing the Protectorate had, if anything, added to his opponents those republicans who saw the new system as too close to the old order they had helped to bring down and who believed Cromwell had betrayed their cause.

Many were to be found in the army though spread thinly between regiments in England, Scotland and Ireland. Most were demoted, expelled or allowed to retire quietly. The Fifth Monarchist and creator of the Nominated Assembly, Harrison, was dismissed from the army. Lilburne, who had returned from Rump-imposed exile in 1653 only to be arrested, tried and acquitted yet again – though this time kept in prison – was exiled to the Channel Islands. The radical menace was thus contained. The royalists were another matter. They were a problem in Scotland from 1653 until 1655. They became a threat in England in 1655, with consequences to be explained later.

- He wanted to broaden the basis of support for the new regime. Thus, he abandoned the Rump's Oath of Engagement; all that was required was an Oath of Loyalty to the lord protector. In the counties, the landed gentry were given greater autonomy. In London, the City bankers were conciliated.
- He was concerned about finance. There were more ordinances on finance than on any other subject. Most reformed the existing system of tax collection, making it more efficient.
- He wanted to achieve religious reform. He wanted a broad Protestant church. The **triers** included Presbyterians as well as Independents and Baptists. He claimed of the triers and ejectors that 'there hath not been such a service to England since the Christian religion was perfect in England'. However, his avoidance of any grand national scheme, such as compulsory church attendance, saw the Protestant churches lose out to the radical sects on one side and to the episcopalians on the other. The reality of religious reform was less than Cromwell had hoped for.

In addition, in the first months of the Protectorate, Cromwell was also involved in developing foreign policy in Europe and beyond. He had much to contend with, even before he met his first parliament.

The First Protectorate Parliament

One reason for the delay in calling parliament was the need to redraw the constituency boundaries. This had to be done in order to provide for the 400 MPs allowed for England and Wales in the Instrument of Government, of whom two-thirds would be county members, a considerable redistribution from former parliaments. The election of 1654 was the first in 14 years. Though there were no clear groupings, many opponents of the Protectorate had been elected. They questioned the legitimacy of the Instrument of Government. Thus, on 12 September, Cromwell responded by listing what he considered to be the 'four fundamentals' of government:

- Government should be carried out jointly by a single person and parliament.
- Parliaments should not perpetuate themselves.

In March 1654 a national body of **triers** was set up to examine all new clergy before allowing them to preach.

What did Cromwell achieve during his rule by ordinance?

- There should be liberty of conscience.
- Control of the militia should be shared between the executive and the legislature.

Cromwell obliged members to take the Recognition, an oath of loyalty to the first of these 'fundamentals'. However, the Recognition forced the withdrawal of about 100 MPs, many of them – the **Commonwealthsmen** – protesting that the notion of government 'by a single person' smacked too much of monarchy and was therefore a betrayal of republican ideals. Despite this purge, the remaining members proved little more co-operative, continuing to question the Instrument and refusing to confirm the ordinances which had been issued during the first nine months of the Protectorate. Therefore, Cromwell dissolved parliament at the first constitutional opportunity, on 22 January 1655, after five lunar months instead of after five calendar months. The latter would have taken the parliament to 5 February. He had saved himself a fortnight of further frustration.

Commonwealthsmen were full-blown republicans such as Henry Marten, Edmund Ludlow and Sir Arthur Haselrig. They lamented the demise of the Rump and resented rule by a single person in the form of the lord protector.

What was the Recognition?

Rule by the major-generals, 1655–56

To the sense of frustration that had overtaken Cromwell during the First Protectorate Parliament was now added an element of alarm brought about by two events in particular.

Penruddock's Rising

Firstly, in March 1655, a royalist rebellion occurred in Wiltshire, led by John Penruddock, the only instance where a planned nationwide rebellion on behalf of Charles II actually occurred. It was an ineffectual affair, easily put down by John Desborough who had been appointed major-general of the west for this purpose. Nevertheless, since the sense of assurance received from his victories in the Civil Wars had evaporated of late, Cromwell seized rather desperately on the defeat of Penruddock, regarding it as a sign of 'the hand of God going along with us'.

Defeat by the Spanish

Secondly, in April 1655, Cromwell learned that the fleet which had been despatched the previous December to protect the religious rights of English merchants in Spanish ports on the Caribbean – the so-called Western Design – had been turned back by the Spanish. The impact of its failure upon Cromwell was dramatic. He interpreted it as God's rebuke because 'we have provoked the Lord [by our sins]'. It was therefore more urgent than ever, or so Cromwell believed, that 'all manner of vice may be thoroughly discountenanced and severely punished; and that such a form of government may be exercised that virtue and godliness may receive due encouragement'.

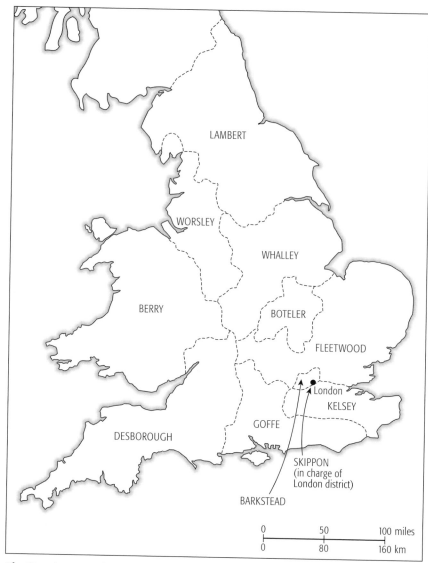

The 11 major-generals and the regions over which they presided. Cromwell appointed the major-generals in late 1655. He later claimed that they had been 'justifiable as to necessity [and] more effectual towards the discountenancing of vice and settling religion than anything done these fifty years'.

Further Godly reform

From these two episodes Cromwell concluded that not only was the security of the republic under threat but also that it was jeopardised because of the absence of 'reformation'. The objectives of his change of approach therefore combined the maintenance of order with another attempt at Godly reform. In August 1655 England and Wales were divided into ten (later eleven) regions, each of which was ruled by a major-general. Each was to raise a local militia, which, together, would total 6,000 horse, paid for by the **decimation tax** on

Decimation tax was a 10 per cent income tax on all former royalists. Its legality was widely challenged as contrary to the Rump's 1652 Act of Oblivion.

the estates of royalists. In October they received their instructions that, amongst other things, they:

- 'endeavour the suppressing [of] all tumults, insurrections, rebellions or other unlawful assemblies';
- 'shall endeavour . . . that the laws against drunkenness, blaspheming and taking of the name of God in vain, by swearing and cursing, plays and interludes, and profaning the Lord's Day, and such like wickedness and abominations, be put in more effectual execution than they have been hitherto'.

Most of the major-generals were conscientious in carrying out their responsibilities, though their impact varied considerably. They maintained order. They might have reduced wickedness and abomination. They had great trouble in raising the decimation tax. Several were not helped by their low social status, which turned the landed gentry against them.

Not surprisingly, the major-generals were unpopular. Therefore, when Cromwell was obliged to call parliament in order to obtain supply for the war against Spain (see page 152) the elections in the summer of 1656 were dominated by the cry 'No swordsmen! No decimators!' Ultimately, on 27 January 1657, the Second Protectorate Parliament rejected a continuation of the decimation tax. Cromwell accepted its decision. Rule by the major-generals was a short-lived innovation and only partly successful.

Identify the two events that are fundamental in explaining why Cromwell resorted to rule through the major-generals. What was the decimation tax? What was the main purpose of the major-generals?

The Second Protectorate Parliament

The election results seem to have been similar to those of 1654. However, the council of state tried to avoid a rerun of the first parliament by excluding 100 known republicans. Another 50 MPs stayed away. The remaining 'rump' proved much more co-operative than had its purged predecessor, passing reform measures that ranged from schemes intended to set the poor to work to the ending of indecent fashions among women. The first session of the Second Protectorate Parliament (17 September 1656 to 26 June 1657) witnessed two significant events in addition to ending the rule of the major-generals.

The Nayler case

The first was a vicious attack upon the Quaker James Nayler. James Nayler was a Quaker leader who, in October 1656, entered Bristol riding an ass with women throwing foliage at his feet, a deliberate attempt to re-enact Jesus Christ's entry into Jerusalem. He was duly arrested and brought to London where MPs voted on 8 December that he was guilty of 'horrid blasphemy'. He was sentenced to be branded, bored through the tongue, flogged twice and then imprisoned for life. Fearful of the Quaker emphasis upon the concept of the 'inner light' (see page 190), MPs believed Nayler's mutilation necessary for

In 1657 the Quaker James Nayler was found guilty by parliament of 'horrid blasphemy'. Fearful that the Quakers were encouraging a breakdown in political order, parliament ordered Nayler to be branded, bored through the tongue, flogged twice and then imprisoned for life.

the preservation of order, hierarchy and property. The Nayler incident illustrates two key features of the Protectorate. The first was the continued absence of parliamentary support for toleration. The second was that, in a dispute over the Instrument, there was no body to arbitrate between lord protector and parliament. As Derek Hirst has observed, 'when the Protector faced a parliament trying to regain powers the Instrument had sought to curtail there was, as one member pointed out, "No judge upon earth" between them.'

The Humble Petition and Advice, 1657

The second significant development was the Humble Petition and Advice. On 23 February 1657 the Civilian Cromwellians introduced a proposal for revising the constitution. This group was a conservative faction in parliament, acting under the influence of Lord Broghill and enjoying the broad support of a House purged of its republicans. The Civilian Cromwellian's main proposal was that Cromwell become king. Their action was precipitated by a number of factors:

- The conservative opposition to the regime of the major-generals.
- The discovery of assassination plots that were designed to remove the protector focused attention upon the provisions for his successor. Although the Instrument had put in place arrangements for an elective succession, in practice the protector-in-waiting was the strongest man in the army, Lambert. This was an unappealing prospect to many MPs. Thus, in order to ensure that events would not fall into 'blood and confusion' upon the death of Cromwell, there was political support to remove the uncertainties of an elective succession.

- An appreciation that the weaknesses of the Instrument (see page 134) were sufficient to induce a constitutional crisis. The Swedish envoy of the time noted, moreover, that 'this country has always been accustomed to be ruled by a king, and all their English statutes and ancient laws are founded on that.'

On 31 March Cromwell was presented with the new constitution, the Humble Petition and Advice. The main reforms to the Instrument of Government were:

- Cromwell was to take the title of king and to nominate his successor.
- It provided for a 'privy council' of no more than 21 to be chosen by the lord protector and 'approved' by parliament.
- Parliament was to have an 'Other House' of between 40–70 members nominated by Cromwell and approved by the Commons.
- Cromwell was to receive £1.3 million per annum, of which £1 million was allocated to the armed forces.
- The religious provisions of the Humble Petition provided for tougher measures against 'blasphemies'.

With its proposal for a second chamber of parliament, for a privy council and for Cromwell to become king, the Humble Petition and Advice marked a further step towards the return of the old constitution.

Cromwell prevaricated for weeks, his health failing as his indecision mounted. Eventually, almost two months later, on 25 May, he accepted a revised version of the Humble Petition and Advice that retained the title of lord protector rather than king.

Why did Cromwell decline the crown? Three arguments are usually put forward. Firstly, he feared the army's reaction. It is true that Lambert's original version of the Instrument of Government had proposed giving Cromwell the title of king, but a monarch enthroned by the army would always be different in kind to one enthroned by the gentry. Cromwell was concerned about how the army would react if he were now to take the title of king offered by civilians. It became apparent that the three great grandees, John Lambert, **Charles Fleetwood** and John Desborough, would withdraw their support from Cromwell if he did so. Of even greater concern to the lord protector was the prospect of a large part of the army, under the leadership of the disaffected grandees, making common cause with the civilian republicans, the Commonwealthsmen. Such an alliance would probably result in another civil war.

However, on 27 February 1657, Cromwell had met with the officers and probably won many of them over to the notion that he should accept the crown. He told them that 'by the proceedings of this [Second Protectorate] Parliament, you see that they [the Commons] stand in need of a check or

Charles Fleetwood (1618–92) was not particularly successful on the battlefield but he was an adept administrator. In 1652 he married, as his second wife, Cromwell's daughter Bridget, the widow of Henry Ireton. He was lord deputy in Ireland in 1654 and, having been removed from that position, was major-general of the eastern counties from 1655 to 1656. He sat in the Other House in 1657. Appointed commander-in-chief of the army in 1659, he was central in the removal of Richard Cromwell. Politically he was out of his depth, often, in times of stress, breaking into tears.

balancing power, for the case of James Nayler might happen to be your case. By the same law and reason they punished Nayler, they might punish an Independent or Anabaptist . . . This Instrument of Government will not do your work.' In other words, in return for giving up their scruples about the title of king the soldiers could secure religious toleration. The evidence for and against is evenly balanced.

Secondly, he feared giving too much influence to the civilian Cromwellians. Cromwell was perhaps concerned that, by accepting the crown from a civilian faction, he would be obliged to give influence to civilian advisors, a development that, in turn, would inhibit his quest for religious toleration.

Thirdly, there was the fear of incurring the wrath of God. Cromwell was disturbed that his acceptance of the title of king would perhaps be interpreted as a sign of his own self-advancement, ambition and sin of pride, all things which he sought to eradicate according to his quest for a moral and Godly reformation. Above all, the title of king was a thing which God had judged against in the civil wars. 'Truly the providence of God has laid this title [monarchy] aside,' Cromwell said in April 1657. 'He hath blasted the title [and] I would not seek to set up that that providence hath destroyed and laid in the dust.'

He did, however, accept a revised version of the Humble Petition and Advice. This meant that Britain now had a constitution that had been approved by an elected parliament, even though around a third of its members had been excluded. On 26 June Cromwell was installed as the lord protector once more. He wore purple and ermine and carried the sword of state. He was king in all but name.

The second session of the Second Protectorate Parliament lasted for only two weeks, in January and early February 1658. This was because the Commonwealthsmen, having been excluded from the first session of parliament according to the terms of the Instrument, now returned. The Humble Petition and Advice meant that Cromwell could not stop them. In addition, several of the leaders of the parliament had been appointed to the Other House. In making these appointments, Cromwell lost some effective parliamentarians. Under the determined leadership of Sir Arthur Haselrig, the Commonwealthsmen prevented the smooth running of parliament. They were particularly annoyed about the existence of the Other House. They also seemed to be making common cause with the disaffected elements in the army. This threatened the collapse of the whole Protectorate. It was to prevent this from happening that Cromwell dissolved parliament on 4 February.

Cromwell had only seven months to live. In that time, there was continued evidence of royalist plots, even if contained – thanks to **John Thurloe**'s spy system. Public finances were close to collapse and the government was being

---

Identify the three main events that occurred during the Second Protectorate Parliament.

John Thurloe, whom Cromwell inherited from the Long Parliament, was an excellent secretary of state who created a highly efficient spy system. This was extremely useful for Cromwell's conduct of foreign policy.

refused loans by the City of London. Cromwell seemed worn out by the uneven, unending political struggle. He died on 3 September 1658, the anniversary of his great victories at Dunbar and Worcester. He was 58 years old. Ralph Joselin noted, 'Cromwell died, people not much minding it.'

Identify three reasons why Cromwell declined the title of king. Why was the second session of the Second Protectorate Parliament so short-lived?

An assessment of Cromwell

It is important to consider Cromwell and, in particular, his methods, his aims and his achievements. In 1654 Cromwell told MPs that 'Jesus Christ will have a time to set up his reign in our hearts.' However, the fragmentation of the political nation (see pages 144–45), combined with the fact that Cromwell, already in his mid-fifties, was running out of time, meant that it was not enough to 'wait and hope'. The lord protector came to realise that change had to be forced. This is the reason for the commissions of triers and ejectors and the major-generals.

During the Putney Debates in 1647, Cromwell had let it be known that he was not 'wedded and glued to forms of government'. This is borne out by the five different constitutional experiments in the nine years during which he dominated English politics: the Rump, the Nominated Assembly, the Instrument of Government, the major-generals and the Humble Petition and Advice.

Not only was Cromwell unconcerned about worldly forms of government, as long as they facilitated progress towards divine ends but also, on occasion, he did not wince at employing heavy-handed and sometimes legally dubious

An engraving showing the Commonwealth ruling with a standing army. This is an example of royalist propaganda against the republican governments of the 1650s. For much of the 1650s, the standing army numbered some 50,000 men and this, combined with a navy of nearly 300 vessels, absorbed 90 per cent of the government's revenue.

tactics. The best example of this tendency was the expulsion of the Rump. He let it be known in 1654 that he believed that 'necessity hath no law'. He also made clear his opinion that there could be occasions when 'the Supreme Magistrate' should not be 'tied up to the ordinary rules'. This sentiment came to the fore in the frustration that Cromwell felt during, and immediately after, the First Protectorate Parliament. It would be difficult to assert that the Recognition, which Cromwell backed and probably even initiated, was in accordance with the Instrument of Government.

On the other hand, Cromwell could have acted in a yet more heavy-handed fashion. As lord general of an army which (stationed in all three kingdoms) totalled 53,000 by the end of 1654, he could have dispensed completely with civilian assemblies and ruled by the sword alone. Yet, when opportunities to establish this form of government occurred – in the immediate aftermath of the dissolution of the Rump or when the Nominated Assembly surrendered its powers – Cromwell looked elsewhere. His method was not that of a dictator. When the Second Protectorate Parliament voted against the decimation tax, he accepted its decision and its consequences.

Cromwell, moreover, provided no political lead for the MPs assembled in his parliaments. Instead, perceiving his role on these occasions as no more than that of the 'good constable to keep the peace of the parish', he failed to present a political programme. Indeed, Hugh Trevor-Roper has argued that Cromwell's failure fully to achieve his aims has two causes. One was his refusal to adopt the tactics of parliamentary management. The other was, as he suggests in 'Oliver Cromwell and his parliaments', in Ivan Roots (ed.), *Oliver Cromwell, a profile* (1973), errors of political judgement, such as the elevation in 1657 of leading government spokesmen from the Commons to the Other House. Perhaps in some ways Cromwell was no politician.

So, how far did Cromwell achieve his aims?

In the quest to 'heal and settle' the nation, he failed. Indeed, by the time of his death he was assailed, or had been, by a number of different groups who felt alienated from the republic by his actions:

- The Levellers. They had felt betrayed by Cromwell's refusal to implement the Agreement of the People. 'O Cromwell, O Ireton,' lamented Richard Overton in March 1649, 'was there ever a generation of men so apostate, so false and so perjured as these?'
- The Commonwealthsmen. Firm believers in republican government according to the Rump, they became consistent opponents of Cromwell after he expelled the Rump in 1653 and even more so when he was elevated to the position of lord protector.
- The Fifth Monarchists. Harrison and his supporters distanced themselves from Cromwell during the Nominated Assembly. Cromwell later said that

he regarded the demand that government occur by a select elite of Godly men until the reign of King Jesus in person as 'the mistaken notion of the Fifth Monarchy [Men]'.

- The civilian Cromwellians. When Cromwell turned down the crown, some of the faction who had been instrumental in drawing up the Humble Petition and Advice withdrew in disgust.

Though these groups opposed Cromwell's rule and the Protectorate, however, most, by themselves, were small in size. Furthermore, they would never all work together. Finally, all governments create enemies and opposition. Perhaps more surprising is the fact that Cromwell's revolutionary rule created so few enemies – at least enemies who could make themselves heard and their presence felt.

Identify those groups alienated by Cromwell.

Cromwell's failure to 'heal and settle' was due in part to the fact that his other aim, to effect a Godly reformation, took priority. Constitutional forms were to serve this greater end and, if Godly reform was not implemented by one form of government then another had to be tried, even if this meant disaffecting support.

How far, therefore, did Cromwell achieve a Godly reformation? He was no more successful in this than in healing and settling. The attempt to implement a 'reformation of manners' was generally resented. In addition, liberty for all Protestants was not provided. On the other hand, Cromwell's understanding of toleration should not be equated with the modern meaning of that word. For all his talk of liberty of conscience, there were clearly prescribed limits to Cromwellian toleration. For instance, Cromwell never believed that Catholics should be granted liberty of conscience. He often asserted that toleration would not be granted to those whose religious practices disrupted the peace and challenged magistracy. With this in mind, Cromwell was generally successful during the 1650s in extending liberty to a variety of groups that had hitherto been suppressed. Not the least of these were the Jews.

However, the political cost of this success jeopardised the whole republican experiment. This was because religious toleration had seen the emergence of groups, such as the Quakers, whose language and ideas threatened the interests of the property-owning class. Thus, they caused a reaction against toleration, evidenced by the parliamentary attack upon James Nayler. Such circumstances were one reason why Cromwell had to maintain a large standing army, the bastion of toleration. However, the immense cost of the army, in turn, alienated yet more support from the republic.

'He sings sweetly that sings a song of reconciliation betwixt these two interests [i.e. of settlement and reformation],' Cromwell told a parliamentary committee on 21 April 1657. Yet, given the nature of things in the middle of

Two representations of Cromwell illustrating the extent to which he polarised opinion. One shows him as the victor over faction; the other shows him as a military dictator in league with the Devil.

the seventeenth century, these 'interests' were probably mutually exclusive. If he had stood down the army and thus reduced taxation levels, Cromwell may have progressed towards healing and settling the nation. However, the conservative reaction induced by the emergence of radical groups after the collapse of the national church, meant that Cromwell was dependent on the soldiers to enforce religious liberty. In this sense, as Christopher Hill has remarked, in the last resort Cromwell was 'sitting on bayonets'. Cromwell could have achieved either of his two main aims only at the expense of the other. Arguably therefore, by attempting to implement both, he achieved neither.

The Protectorate after Oliver Cromwell

There is a danger in equating the Protectorate with Oliver Cromwell, in imagining that his death meant the demise of the Protectorate. In one sense it did, in another it did not. The Protectorate continued after 3 September 1658. Oliver Cromwell nominated his eldest son, Richard, to succeed him – or at least it was assumed that he did. The transfer of power was swift and smooth. Up until this time, 32-year-old Richard had lived the quiet life of the country gentry in Hampshire, though he had sat as an MP in 1654 and 1656. He was not identified with any one group and thus was initially acceptable to all. His great weakness was his lack of political experience, which made it very difficult to understand the complex reality of national politics. His position was worse than that of a hereditary prince who is prepared for the job from birth. As leader of the army in Ireland, his younger brother, Henry, might have been a better choice, since he had acquired knowledge and experience in government, as well as being acceptable to the soldiers. In response to pressure from the army, Richard appointed Charles Fleetwood, his brother-in-law, as commander-in-chief under the lord protector. Fleetwood's home, Wallingford House, became the label for the group of grandees who wanted to preserve the position of the army and their leadership of it.

A new parliament was called for January 1659, the third of the Protectorate, but chosen on the pre-Protectorate franchise. It was needed to help address the serious financial problem the lord protector faced. The parliament was not that awkward, despite the best efforts of the Commonwealthsmen. When in April 1659 the state of the national finances became clear, Richard Cromwell sided with parliament against the army's General Council of Officers, which he tried to dissolve. Perhaps he was expecting officers such as Fleetwood to support him. He was wrong. The General Council of Officers became united and stood firm, insisting that the Protectorate parliament be dissolved. Eventually, on 22 April, it got its way. Richard's authority was destroyed. A month later he resigned and eventually left the country. By then the Protectorate had already collapsed, to be replaced by the Rump Parliament so desired by the Commonwealthsmen such as Haselrig. Richard Cromwell became known as 'Tumbledown Dick', a harsh label and not really deserved. He was an inexperienced man placed in an impossible situation, a situation that rapidly went from bad to worse.

Why did Richard call a Third Protectorate Parliament?

Summary questions

1 (a) Identify and explain any *two* problems which caused Cromwell serious difficulties during the period from 1655 to 1658.

(b) Compare the importance of at least *three* threats to the stability of Cromwell's regime.

2 What were Cromwell's aims and by what methods did he attempt to fulfil them?

3 Why was Cromwell offered the crown and why did he not set up a House of Cromwell?

12 Cromwell's foreign policy, 1653–58

Focus questions

◆ What was Cromwell's priority in foreign policy: religion, trade or security?

◆ Was Cromwell's foreign policy traditional or forward-looking?

◆ Was Cromwell's active, aggressive foreign policy really necessary?

Significant dates

1652	*May*	The First Anglo-Dutch War begins.
1653	*31 July*	Monck defeats the Dutch at the Battle of Texel.
1654	*5 April*	The Treaty of Westminster ends the Anglo-Dutch War.
	July	A commercial agreement is made with Portugal.
	December	Cromwell undertakes the Western Design.
1655	*April–May*	The Western Design fails.
	October	An Anglo-French commercial treaty is signed.
1656	*February*	War breaks out with Spain in Europe.
1657	*March*	An Anglo-French military treaty is signed.
1658	*14 June*	The Battle of the Dunes takes place and England gains Dunkirk.

Overview

Cromwell's foreign policy merits separate consideration, apart from the complexities of domestic politics. In just five years, he made England a major player in European affairs, for the first time in many decades. His foreign policy had a greater range than that achieved by any previous English monarch. The English army made its presence felt on the continent, while the English navy influenced events in the Mediterranean, the Baltic and the Caribbean. The main historical issues have centred around Cromwell's motivations and his priorities. Were they essentially religious or more economic? Linked with that is the question of whether his foreign policy was backward-looking, concerned with fighting wars which were no longer important to

England's best interests, or whether it anticipated England's future interests. Some historians believe that Cromwell laid the foundations for the English commercial and naval successes of the eighteenth century. Finally, some historians question whether England really needed to be involved – and often expensively involved – in so many different issues of foreign policy. Studying Cromwell's foreign policy and his motivation might also make his domestic policies and their priorities easier to understand. Certainly there are useful links between the two.

The context of Cromwell's foreign policy

There were two slightly different contexts to Cromwell's foreign policy, the long-term and the short-term. Under Elizabeth I, England had emerged as a leading Protestant state, eventually standing up to the power of the Spanish Habsburgs. The Stuarts had not maintained that position. James I wanted to be a peacemaker. Charles I, after the embarrassments of the brief wars with Spain and France in the 1620s, avoided a positive role thereafter, despite the Thirty Years' War reaching a critical stage in the 1630s. The remembered glories of Elizabethan foreign policy exercised a powerful influence on the Puritan revolutionaries of the 1640s and 1650s.

By the 1650s the Thirty Years' War was over. Disputes continued, however, in two areas. One was the Spanish Netherlands, where Spain and France were still at war. Many Englishmen wanted Cromwell to return to the traditions of an anti-Catholic, anti-Spanish policy. Both powers sought England's support. If anything, in the early 1650s, relations had been better with Spain than with France. Cromwell had three choices: to ally with France, to ally with Spain or to remain neutral, as the Stuarts had done for all but a brief and regrettable period in the 1620s. It took 18 months for Cromwell finally to make up his mind.

The other area was the Baltic. England had great material interest in this region as it was the main source of naval supplies. This meant that England could not afford to see the area dominated by just one power, as Sweden was threatening to do. Cromwell also hoped for an alliance of the Protestant states of the area against Catholic powers such as Poland and Austria. The two aims could not be reconciled.

> What were the main choices that Cromwell faced in foreign policy?

The Anglo-Dutch War, 1652–54

The war against the Dutch had broken out under the Rump. Cromwell, who had never been keen on the war against fellow Protestants, wanted to bring it to an early end – as did the Dutch after their defeat by Monck at the Battle of Texel in 1653.

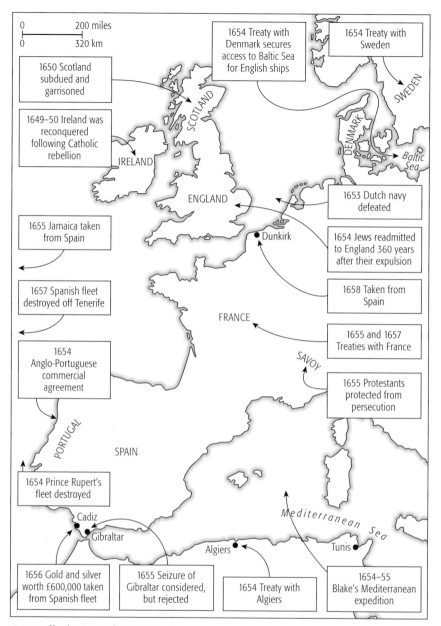

Cromwell's foreign policy, 1649–58

The Treaty of Westminster, signed in April 1654, gave England most of what it wanted. The treaty provided some economic benefits, such as compensation for injuries done to English merchants in the East Indies and in the Baltic. England's security was enhanced because the Dutch agreed not to shelter Charles II and his family. In addition, simply ending a war with a fellow Protestant state furthered England's religious interests. Cromwell was, however, criticised for a peace that conceded too much to the Dutch.

He had agreed to peace so that he could now concentrate on other aims of foreign policy, aims that ideally involved the co-operation of the Dutch. He saw them as natural allies against the Spanish. They refused to join England in an anti-Spanish crusade despite the peace. For the Dutch, England remained a rival in trade in several parts of the globe. In the summer of 1654, moreover, England signed a trade treaty with Portugal, a Catholic power, which gave the English trading rights in the Portuguese empire. This development was bound to hit Dutch trading interests.

What was the main reason for Cromwell concluding the Anglo-Dutch War in 1654? Why were the Dutch antagonised by England's trade treaty with Portugal?

From the Dutch War to the Spanish War, 1654–55

Identifying a coherent strategy to Cromwell's foreign policy in the 21 months between the end of the war with the Dutch and the start of the war with Spain in Europe is almost impossible. The policy was certainly a very active one and conducted on at least four different fronts.

Cromwell sought to construct a Protestant league in Northern Europe in order to take on the Habsburgs. Thus, in the spring and autumn of 1654, England signed treaties with Sweden and Denmark, though attempts to fashion an alliance with the Dutch came to nothing. Yet, Cromwell's ambition was, perhaps, misguided. He seems to have regarded Charles X of Sweden as a latter-day **Gustavus Adolphus**, when in fact his ambitions were dynastic and territorial, not religious and idealistic. Moreover, there was intense rivalry between Sweden on the one hand and Denmark and the Dutch on the other. Nevertheless, the lord protector did secure English access to the naval supplies of the Baltic.

In Italy, Cromwell wanted to help the Vaudois, the Protestant subjects of Savoy, who were persecuted by its ruler with the help of French troops. He appealed to Protestant powers to join together on behalf of the Vaudois. He provided financial aid, including £2,000 of his own money, and diplomatic support. The most effective help was the Treaty of Pignerol with France, signed in October 1655.

In the western Mediterranean, the English fleet led by Robert Blake, which had been sent there in 1653, bombarded Tunis. In June 1654, a treaty with Algiers was signed which opened up the area to English traders and released English prisoners.

The success of this expedition helped Cromwell to decide in favour of an expedition against Spanish colonies in the West Indies, the so-called Western Design. Some see this as a throwback to the exploits of Elizabethans such as Sir Francis Drake while others argue it was importantly different. The motives were twofold: to establish a foothold in the West Indies at the expense of the Spanish and then to gain the benefit of a greater share of the trade with the Americas. Cromwell's intention was to keep the conflict confined to the New

Gustavus Adolphus (ruled 1611–32) was the great Protestant warrior king of Sweden who successfully pushed back the Catholic forces in the Thirty Years' War and sought to establish a union of Protestant nations. He was killed at the battle of Lützen fighting against the imperial troops.

World. At this stage, in late 1654, he was not planning to go to war with Spain in Europe. However, he did attack Spain 'beyond the line', on the other side of the Atlantic, in what might be seen as halfway to a full war.

The fleet sailed in December 1654, aiming to attack San Domingo in Hispaniola. However, the expedition proved disastrous. The quality of the troops was poor and the leadership divided. The only compensation was the seizure of Jamaica, less important at the time than it was to become later. The failure of the Western Design in 1655 was the only significant failure of Cromwell's foreign policy.

Identify the four main ways in which Cromwell pursued an active foreign policy during the period 1654 to 1655.

War with Spain, 1656–58

A consequence of the Western Design was that relations with Spain became very bad. English merchants lost access to Spanish trade, from which their Dutch rivals benefited. As relations with Spain deteriorated, England responded to French approaches for an alliance. In October 1655 the two states signed a defensive treaty, mainly commercial, though the French also agreed not to support the Stuarts. Eighteen months later, in March 1657, over a year after war had broken out between England and Spain, England and France signed an offensive alliance. Cromwell agreed to provide 6,000 men and a fleet to join 20,000 French troops for a campaign against Spain in Flanders. The English army arrived on the continent in late 1657, playing an important part in the Battle of the Dunes the following June, as a result of which Britain gained Dunkirk.

Why did England form an alliance with France?

The land war against Spain followed a naval war that had been going on since early 1656 when Blake was sent to attack the Spanish navy. In September 1656 the Spanish treasure fleet was destroyed (though not by Blake). In April 1657 Blake did ensure that all 16 ships of a Spanish fleet were destroyed at Santa Cruz in the Canaries.

Cromwell's foreign policy: an assessment

Three questions can be asked about Cromwell's foreign policy: how Protestant was it, how traditional and how necessary.

How Protestant was Cromwell's foreign policy?

Three pieces of evidence suggest that Cromwell did put religious interests before national and commercial concerns. Firstly, it seems that Cromwell's hopes of forming an Anglo-Dutch Protestant crusade against European Catholicism led him to agree to a peace settlement in 1654 that was less harsh than the military circumstances warranted. The English had captured more than 1,400 ships, including 120 men-of-war. A harsher peace would have inhibited the commercial success of England's traditional rival in trade. Secondly, Cromwell's attempts to form a Protestant alliance in the Baltic permitted Sweden to dominate that area and thus pose a threat to what was the main source of England's naval supplies. Thirdly, an obsession with defeating Catholic Spain seemingly led Cromwell further to damage England's trading interests. A consequence of the Western Design was that English mercantile interests declined since merchants could not continue their trade with Spain, which went to the Dutch. In addition, war with Spain resulted in alliances with Spain's enemy, France. Slingsby Bethel believed that the subsequent formation of the Anglo-French agreements in 1655 and 1657 made France, a growing trade rival to England, 'too great for Christendom'.

However, this interpretation of Cromwell's foreign policy has been criticised by historians, among them Michael Roberts in 'Cromwell and the Baltic', *Essays in Swedish history* (1967). They have argued that considerations of trade and security also played a part in shaping foreign policy. Trade was not consistently sacrificed in order to advance the Protestant cause. Recognising that the Dutch continued to threaten English access to trade in the Baltic, Cromwell ensured that the 1651 Navigation Act was implemented beyond 1654. Indeed, in 1655, 60 Dutch ships were seized for contravening its terms. Also, Cromwell did not ignore the question of national security, the greatest threat to which was posed by the exiled House of Stuart. Thus, the 1654 Treaty of Westminster obliged the Dutch to refuse any help to Charles II and exclude from power the pro-Stuart House of Orange. Cromwell's declaration of support for Charles X was also motivated by security in that Charles X's enemy, Jan Casimir of Poland, sympathised with Charles II. Moreover, the formation of an alliance with France denied Charles II the opportunity of using that country as a launch pad for invasion. Consequently, Charles II was forced into an agreement with Spain on 2 April 1656. In doing this, he damaged the Stuart cause because of its association with the Catholic **Black Legend**. To make matters worse for Charles, Spain proved singularly incapable of financing and equipping an invasion of England on his behalf.

Possessing an armed force of around 50,000 and the largest navy in Europe, Cromwell proceeded in such a way that the two great continental powers, France and Spain, outbid each other in order to win an alliance with the Protectorate. Thus, Spain's offer to return Calais if Cromwell would assist a Spanish offensive in Flanders was trumped by a French offer of the port of Dunkirk. John Thurloe considered that the eventual acquisition of Dunkirk meant that Cromwell 'carried the Keys of the Continent at his Girdle'. It certainly denied Charles II a potential invasion base and trade privateers a convenient port.

The **Black Legend** originated in the sixteenth century when exaggerated stories of Spanish brutality towards captured English seamen began to circulate around England. These stories were seized on by the English Protestants and became known as the Black Legend.

Thus, although Cromwellian foreign policy was in part fashioned by religious considerations, these were not pursued consistently at the expense of concerns of commerce and national security.

How traditional was Cromwell's foreign policy?

This issue overlaps with the Protestant issue but is significantly different. Cromwell's critics would argue that he fought the wrong opponents, as a result of having a traditional, Elizabethan view of the world. He fought Spain which, by the 1650s, was in decline because it was England's traditional enemy. He allied with France, the rising power of Europe and the country that would become England's great rival in the eighteenth century. He made peace with the United Provinces because he saw the Dutch as England's Protestant allies when, in fact, they were great trading rivals. Significantly, England was to go to war against the Dutch twice more under Charles II. It would have been far more appropriate, argue his critics, if Cromwell had allied with Spain and fought the French and the Dutch.

Defenders of Cromwell argue that his traditional view of the world was always tempered by a sound understanding of the realities of the 1650s. When the Dutch ignored his attempts at a closer alliance after the end of the war, he signed a treaty with Portugal that hurt the Dutch. The extension of the Navigation Act was clearly an anti-Dutch move. War against Spain brought the financial benefits when the Spanish treasure fleet was seized. An alliance with France led to the acquisition of Dunkirk and thus to greater control of the Channel. It also meant that Charles II had to turn to Spain for possible assistance, which weakened the Stuarts' position in England. Moreover, it is not realistic to have expected Cromwell to have anticipated the rise of France in the late seventeenth century. In the 1650s it was by no means apparent that France was set to emerge as a greater threat than Spain to England's interests.

Cromwell grew up in the first decades of the century, heavily influenced by the traditions of the Elizabethan era. In some respects, it is surprising that it took Cromwell so long – almost four years – to send an army against Spain in Europe.

How necessary was Cromwell's foreign policy?

This argument considers need against cost. Was the Western Design really necessary? What fundamental interests did it further? The same could be said of Blake's expedition to the Mediterranean. Though acquiring Dunkirk was an obvious success, did it really strengthen the position of England? Critics argued it would become a liability, that the actual line of defence was the English Channel. England's immediate need was for security. Even treaties that isolated the Stuarts did little to make England more secure. If France and the

Netherlands had continued to provide a base for Charles II, there was little likelihood of a serious threat to an England whose army had imposed its will on all parts of the British Isles.

The equipping of a large navy and the expeditionary force of 1657–58 was also expensive. Thus, Cromwell's ambitious foreign policy meant higher taxation or greater debt and all the domestic problems that each entailed. In addition, it was not that popular, especially with the all-important City of London. Finally, the failure of the Western Design, which came at the time of Penruddock's Rising, added to the problems of the Protectorate that could have been avoided. In this light, foreign policy undermined the Protectorate.

The Protectorate would have done better, this argument goes, had its foreign policy been less ambitious and less aggressive. However, it is unrealistic to suggest that the Protectorate leaders should have behaved differently. As Cromwell said in 1654, 'God has not brought us hither where we are but to consider the work we may do in the world as well as at home.' Though the foreign policy was expensive and unpopular, it developed English interests and resulted in an expertise that later generations could build on. As even Clarendon had to admit, 'Cromwell's greatness at home was a mere shadow of his greatness abroad.'

Summary questions

1 (a) Identify and explain any *two* foreign policy problems which England faced in the 1650s.

   (b) Compare the importance of at least *three* foreign threats faced by the regimes of the 1650s.

2 To what extent was Cromwell's foreign policy determined by religious rather than economic factors?

13

The Restoration

Focus questions

◆ Why was the monarchy restored in 1660?

◆ What exactly was restored in 1660?

Significant dates

1658   **3 September**   Oliver Cromwell dies; Richard Cromwell is made lord protector.

1659   **7 May**   The Rump Parliament is recalled by the General Council of Officers.
31 July–16 August   Booth's Rising occurs.
13 October   The army dissolves the Rump.
26 October   Monck, the leader of the army in Scotland, declares for the Rump.
3–13 December   The Portsmouth garrison, the navy and Irish army declare for the Rump.
26 December   The Rump is reinstated by elements of the army.

1660   **1 January**   Monck and his army enter England.
3 February   Monck's army arrives in London.
21 February   Those MPs 'purged' in December 1648 return to parliament.
16 March   The Long Parliament declares itself dissolved and calls for fresh elections.
4 April   Charles II issues the Declaration of Breda.
25 April–13 September   The first session of the Convention Parliament is held.
5 May   Parliament votes in favour of government by king, Lords and Commons.
25 May   Charles II lands at Dover.
29 May   Charles II enters London.

Overview

In May 1659 the Protectorate collapsed. A year later, the monarchy was restored. To many, there was an air of inevitability about this rapid transformation. Nevertheless, it is important to explain how and why this turn-about happened. It was certainly an unusual few months. There is a reversal of events as first the Rump is restored, then the Long Parliament and, eventually, the crown. The army, which had been such a powerful political force for the previous 13 years, seemed to melt away. This was because, yet again, another army entered England from Scotland, the fifth in 20 years. Charles II returned to England, not at the head of an invading army, as had seemed likely ever since 1651, but with a small band of soldiers and supporters.

It is also important to understand exactly what was restored in the settlement of 1660. How far was the clock turned back? Was it to 1642, 1640 or 1625? Did the Restoration apply equally to state and church government? How did the royalists treat the defeated republicans? There are many questions, the answers to which affect understanding not just of 1660 but of the two eventful decades that had led up to the Restoration.

The Rump restored and dismissed, 1659

Once the General Council of Officers had made Richard Cromwell dissolve the Third Protectorate Parliament it was able to recall the Rump, which had been dissolved by Cromwell and the army six years before. On 7 May, 42 of the 78 former Rump MPs who were eligible to do so retook their seats in the Commons. The wishes of the Commonwealthsmen such as Haselrig had been fulfilled. 'The good old cause' had returned.

If the army officers had expected the Rump MPs to be grateful, they received a rude awakening. The Rump had different priorities from the army. The civilian republicans refused to share power with their namesakes in the army. They asserted civilian control over the army and dominated the new council of state. The two groups came together to prevent various royalist risings planned for the summer of 1659. Only one in Cheshire, Booth's Rising, led by Sir George Booth, was of any importance and even that was soon defeated. A radical revolution seemed possible once more. This was because the return of the Rump had encouraged the revival of radical sects such as the Quakers and Fifth Monarchists. Royalists and Presbyterians had, moreover, suffered another setback. However, the republicans in parliament and the army could not work together. Each side tried to assert its political supremacy. Eventually, in October 1659, the Rump, led by the old warrior, Haselrig, took steps to control the army in ways that were reminiscent of Richard Cromwell's actions a few months before. Yet again, the army asserted its superior physical power and closed down the Rump.

George Monck
(1608–70) acquired military experience in the Thirty Years' War. He fought for the king in the First Civil War and was captured at the Battle of Nantwich in 1644. He was imprisoned in the Tower until 1646. From 1647 to 1649 he served parliament as a major-general in Ulster. He accompanied Cromwell on the Scottish campaign and fought at Dunbar. In 1651 he was appointed commander-in-chief in Scotland and completed the English conquest of Scotland during 1652. During the First Anglo-Dutch War, he acted successfully as an admiral. He supported Richard Cromwell and showed no sympathy with royalist intrigues. His actions in 1660 are not easily explained, especially since he was devoid of political ambition. He was created duke of Albermarle in 1660 by a grateful Charles II.

What form of government replaced the expelled Rump? Who was the leader of the army in Scotland and what form of government did he seem to support? When did this army descend into England?

The army divided, 1659

After deliberating for a fortnight, the General Council of Officers set up a Committee of Safety 'to secure the people's liberties as men and Christians, reform the law, provide for a godly preaching ministry, and settle the constitution without a single person or a House of Lords'. Headed by General Fleetwood, it was composed of army leaders and their civilian supporters. It was faced with an increasingly difficult situation, both at home and abroad.

The Committee of Safety had few, if any, friends to help it deal with these difficulties. In London, chaos grew steadily worse. There were protests against the army by the apprentices, merchants refused to pay taxes until a 'free' parliament was summoned and the law courts ceased to function. Much more significant was the opposition to the closure of the Rump expressed by the leader of the army in Scotland, General **George Monck**. He was an English soldier of many years' experience, a former royalist who had gained the trust of Cromwell, hard, successful and, until late 1659, non-political. He now took great care in preparing a united army to act to restore the Rump, even if it meant invading England. The council of state prepared a force under John Lambert, which was sent north to oppose Monck. The army was at war with itself.

The civilian republicans in England such as Haselrig, encouraged by the news from Scotland, looked to stimulate army mutinies elsewhere. The garrison at Portsmouth was first to declare for the Rump. The fleet soon followed suit, blockading the Thames. The army in Ireland was not far behind. Lambert's army in the north was weakened by lack of supplies and money. (Monck's army, by comparison, was well fed and well paid.) On the brink of renewed civil war, the Committee of Safety therefore dissolved itself. For more than a week, England had no official government at all. An element of the army then reinstated the Rump for the second time that year. The bad news from London forced Lambert to decide to turn south. As he did, his army disintegrated behind him and he found himself in the Tower. The one force that might have defended the army's interests had fallen apart. There was no civil war in the army. Monck was then able to enter England in January 1660, even though the return of the Rump meant that his original demand had already been met. He halted in York awaiting orders from the Rump politicians who no longer had an English army to oppose them. They asked him to come to London to help them restore order. He arrived there in early February.

The return of the Long Parliament

The Rump ordered Monck to shore up their support by restoring order in the City of London. Initially, Monck did its bidding but quickly changed his mind. He ignored orders and moved his troops into London rather than against the city. For ten days, he listened to the Rump on one side, London on the other. Then he acted to reverse Pride's Purge. He allowed those MPs secluded in 1648 to return to Westminster, though only on condition they restore a national church and dissolve parliament as quickly as possible. Their return over-whelmed the Rumpers. Monck was still worried that army regiments in England might use their power to restore the Rump once more but, by carefully dispersing the most troublesome regiments to different parts of the country, trouble was prevented. Lambert did escape from the Tower to make one desperate attempt to rally republican forces in April but the good old cause had become lost and forlorn. On 16 March the restored Long Parliament, after nearly 20 years, ended its own turbulent existence. The subsequent 'free elections' resulted in the Convention Parliament, so called because it convened itself.

Who was the principal opponent of Monck's decision to reverse Pride's Purge?

The Convention Parliament

The new parliament, which met on 25 April, included many royalists and Presbyterians and excluded most republicans and Commonwealthsmen. The question was no longer whether to restore Charles II but on what conditions. Since the dissolution of the Long Parliament, however, Monck had entered into secret negotiations with Charles. The outcome of these was that MPs received from Charles II the Declaration of Breda, a series of royal promises designed 'that those wounds which have so many years been kept bleeding may be bound up'. These were sufficient to persuade MPs to vote, on 5 May, that government should be by a king, Lords and Commons. Charles was therefore restored unconditionally. He was welcomed with enthusiastic celebration into London on 29 May, his 30th birthday. The Interregnum had ended.

What was the Declaration of Breda?

Why was the monarchy restored?

Historians have been unable to agree upon the moment from which the restoration of Charles II became inevitable. On the one hand, it has been argued that as the forms of government during the 1650s became more traditional a restoration became more likely. On the other hand, some historians have emphasised the importance of events from 1658 to 1660. They point to research on government in the localities, which demonstrates widespread acceptance of the republican regimes and to the smooth transition of power from Oliver to Richard. In turn, this latter group has identified a number of relevant factors, which can usefully be classified into two broad groups:

- the onset of conditions in England which pushed people towards demanding a restoration;
- actions by Charles II that resulted in pulling people towards supporting a restoration.

The 'push' explanation

As 1659 moved towards its end, the mounting breakdown in law and order and the prospect that England might descend into another period of civil war induced an intensely conservative reaction amongst the propertied classes. In the winter of 1659, with events made yet worse by a series of poor harvests after 1657, the City goldsmiths began moving out of the capital and news sheets spoke of 'shops shut, trade gone [causing] fears and jealousies [to] multiply'. Above all, the Quakers, whose emphasis upon the 'inner light' so alarmed the landed gentry, were visibly growing in number. In 1659 they were, perhaps, 60,000 strong.

These circumstances had been fomented by a number of developments since 1658:

- the collapse of the Protectorate;
- divisions between the Commonwealthsmen and the military republicans;
- divisions within the army, not only between the grandees such as Fleetwood and the rank and file but, also, between supporters of the restored Rump and those hostile to its return;
- divisions within the Commonwealthsmen, such as that between the factions headed by Haselrig and **Sir Henry Vane**.

Sir Henry Vane
(1613–62) was Puritan governor of Massachusetts from 1636 to 1637. On his return, he became the treasurer of the navy and, from 1640, an MP. He urged Strafford's impeachment and was opposed to episcopacy. In 1643 he negotiated the Solemn League and Covenant. As a republican, he criticised the Protectorate and opposed the Restoration. He was executed in 1662.

However, it is easy to exaggerate what one contemporary referred to as 'the great confusion in this kingdom'. Thus, noting that tax yields remained high, Derek Hirst concluded that 'until the summer [of 1659] the habitual acquiescence in face of authority had offered still a chance for a non-Stuart form of government to root itself'. Nevertheless, what was important in these circumstances was what contemporaries *thought* was occurring and, to most, it seemed that they were enduring 'great convulsions'.

Yet, the mere collapse of the republic did not make a restoration of the Stuarts inevitable. After all, there were alternatives available, such as the creation of a new Protectoral regime or the installation of King Monck. However, the *nature* of the collapse of the republic was anarchic. Therefore, to those owning property, it was a matter of some urgency that stable government be restored. The example suggested from history was that it should be a monarchy.

The 'pull' explanation

Despite the lamentable efforts of the **Sealed Knot**, Penruddock and Booth, there is no doubt that monarchy remained a popular option throughout the 1650s. After all, it was in recognition of this basic fact that Cromwell had been reluctant to hold free elections. Charles II played upon this sentiment in a way that mobilised considerable support in his favour. Acting upon a suggestion from Monck, Charles relocated his court from the hated Spanish Netherlands to the Protestant port of Breda. It was from there that he issued the Declaration of Breda, a brilliantly timed and carefully constructed document, drawn up under the influence of not only Monck but also Edward Hyde, Charles's leading counsellor. In the circumstances of April 1660, the Declaration created an irresistible demand for the restoration of the monarchy. It offered four things:

- a general pardon to all except those specifically exempted by parliament;
- a liberty to tender consciences;
- the resolution of disputes over land ownership to be decided by parliament;
- the payment of arrears of pay for the army.

These proposals showed that Charles intended to rule with parliament and would not be establishing a royal despotism. Charles was, therefore, invited to return, parliament having affirmed that he had been 'the most potent and undoubted king' of England, Scotland and Ireland ever since the moment of Charles I's execution. In this way, the Interregnum was deemed never to have existed.

> The **Sealed Knot** was a secret society operating in the 1650s, intent upon orchestrating the Restoration of Charles II.

> Identify those factors that pushed people into demanding a restoration and those factors that pulled people towards supporting a restoration.

What was restored in 1660?

It is useful to know the main features of the Restoration Settlement of 1660–62 if only to put into perspective the various attempts at settlement

The coronation procession of Charles II proceeds from the Tower of London to Whitehall on 22 April 1661.

made in the previous 20 years. Restoring monarchical government meant that only legislation that had received the royal assent was henceforth legitimate. At one stroke, all the parliamentary ordinances passed since 1642 became invalid. However, the reforms of 1641–42 had been approved by Charles I. This meant that many features of government which had allowed Personal Rule, such as the prerogative courts and taxes, were not restored in 1660.

If the monarchy had been restored so had parliament. It occupied an important place in the new settlement and two aspects of government in particular. One was finance. It was agreed that parliament would provide Charles II with an annual income of £1.2 million. This established the principle that parliament was the source of royal income, while the practice of providing insufficient funds for the king's government meant that the king would have to come back to and work with parliament. The other was religion. Charles II had promised liberty to tender consciences. The Cavalier Parliament, which in 1661 replaced the Convention Parliament, would have none of it. MPs wanted to restore uniformity of religious practice. Dissent was dangerous. Those clergy who refused to accept the new 1662 Book of Common Prayer were excluded and became non-conformists. The broad church, which had developed under Cromwell, became a narrow church under Charles II. Contrary to his own beliefs, the restored king grudgingly accepted parliament's wishes.

The right to control the militia and approve government ministers, rights which parliamentarians had argued long and hard for in the 1640s, were returned to the crown in 1660, with little debate. The experience of the later 1640s and later 1650s showed the value of strong government.

In general terms, the mixed system of government of crown-in-parliament had been restored with the balance tilted slightly more in favour of parliament than it had been before the Civil Wars began. With Charles II as king, a man who vowed 'never to go on my travels again', England had a ruler with a very different attitude to parliament than that of his father. To a great extent, he managed to accomplish the 'healing and settling' that Oliver Cromwell had desired as lord protector but had never achieved.

What were the main features of the Restoration Settlement?

14 The Interregnum, 1649–60: a summary

The 11 years of the Interregnum are the only period of republican government in English history. During that time, England had four different forms of government: a single-chamber republic; a government of the saints (the Nominated Assembly); a balanced republic and a quasi-monarchy. At the end of the period, the single-chamber republic returned briefly, the monarchy permanently. These many changes highlight the continual search for a stable settlement and the narrow base of support for three of those four different constitutions. It is important to highlight two key features of this important period of English history.

One is the importance of the army in two ways, military and political. Though the army's political role in the 1650s usually receives more attention, its military role should not be forgotten. In 1649–51 the victories of the army in Ireland and Scotland ensured the ascendancy of England in both countries. As well as being vital to the survival of the republic in the 1650s, this superiority marked an important stage in the development of the British state of the eighteenth century. The army also helped France defeat Spain in 1658, as a result of which England gained a temporary foothold on the continent. Nevertheless, the army's political role remains more significant. If the 1650s were the only period of republican rule in England, they were also the only period in its modern history of military rule. The army – or more precisely the army leadership – was the final arbiter of the system of government, although it rarely interfered in a government, once established. In this sense, England did not experience military rule in its complete form. However, the army leadership was prepared to end one form of government and introduce another, if it thought it necessary. This was the case in 1648, 1653 (twice) and 1659 (twice). The one exception came in 1657 when the Humble Petition and Advice was introduced.

The year 1659 is particularly important for an analysis of the role of the army. In the spring, it forced the end of the Protectorate and the return of the Rump. Disagreement over the Rump divided the army for the first time in 11 years. This division allowed the growth of popular opposition to army rule and, thanks to Monck's care and caution, the return of parliament and then the return of the crown. In one important sense, the monarchy was restored in 1660 because the army had split.

The unity of the army until 1659 is explained, in part, by the second important aspect of the Interregnum, the influence of Oliver Cromwell. By 1651 Cromwell had emerged as the predominant military and political leader of the republic. Before then, he had shared military leadership with Fairfax and the continuing wars meant he had insufficient time for political matters. As an MP as well as general, he remained acceptable to both the Rump Parliament and the army. His own ideas, a mixture of religious radicalism and social conservatism, received support from the soldiers and elements of the political nation. Though he usually tried to act as a bridge between the civil and the military institutions, in the last resort he sided with the army. He also acted ruthlessly to quell any division within the army, as in 1647 and 1649. Cromwell appreciated the importance to the republic of army unity and, in return, the army accepted the decisions of a man who had led them to great victories. His son Richard lacked both the insight of and respect given to his father. Thus, when Richard moved against the army, the army threw him out.

What did Cromwell do with the great power he had? His radical-Puritan side tried to achieve a more Godly society and he did try to make people live more Godly lives. He did not, however, try to impose a narrow view of religious practice and allowed the liberty to tender consciences that he preached. Admittedly, Catholics on one side and the more 'licentious' radical sects on the other were excluded from this inclusive community that Cromwell wanted to build. However, the breadth of Protestant practice that Cromwell allowed in the 1650s can be linked with the religious toleration of the next century. In the short term, however, the Cavalier Parliament imposed a narrow religious orthodoxy.

Cromwell's social conservatism caused him to seek to 'heal and settle'. This side of his beliefs came to the fore as the 1650s progressed. By 1657, with his acceptance of the Humble Petition and Advice, he had come a long way towards agreeing to a system of government that was the old monarchy in all but label. Though he found working with parliaments difficult, he was prepared to listen to them, as he did with the Humble Petition and Advice and with the vote against the decimation tax. Cromwell's abandonment of rule by the major-generals shows that he did want to gain the support of MPs and the gentry class they represented.

He was unable to do so to the extent needed to ensure the new republic was firmly based because he was unwilling to challenge the power of the army, for the political reasons already discussed. The army was also, of course, needed to defend the regime against possible threats, of which there were several, even after 1651. Maintaining the army required persisting with a high level of taxation which meant that, for many, the regime was unpopular as well as illegitimate. He left his son a large public debt to grapple with. Before 1658 Cromwell had not used his unique authority to permit the transition from wartime to peacetime government. Consequently, the Protectorate always suffered from a fundamental weakness. It was not just Richard Cromwell's fault that the Protectorate collapsed so quickly in 1659.

If Oliver Cromwell's freedom to rule England was always limited by the context within which he had to work, there were fewer restraints in making English foreign policy. In a short space of time, he made sure Protestant and/or English interests were furthered in many parts of Europe and the New World. There is something of a parallel with his religious policy in that this ambitious energetic policy won him few friends at the time, mainly because it seemed an expensive luxury. However, connections can be made between the expansion of English interests during the Protectorate and the establishment of Britain as an imperial power in the eighteenth century.

There is one broader point worth mentioning about the Interregnum. Its short-lived nature means that it is often dismissed as being an exception to the main themes of English history. However, it has informed the ideas and arguments of the English since that time. If the Interregnum, with its constitutional instability, its excessive taxation and its military rule, was the consequence of abolishing the monarchy, then maybe better not to abolish the monarchy. After 1660, and certainly after 1688, king and parliaments preferred to work together. In this way, if in no other, it can be argued that the Interregnum has been central to English history.

Summary questions

1 (a) Identify and explain any *two* issues which account for the political instability during the period 1658 to 1660.

   (b) Compare the importance of at least *three* developments in bringing about the Restoration.

2 To what extent do the actions of Edward Hyde and Charles II explain the Restoration?

Economy and society, 1603–60

15

Economic change

Focus questions

◆ What were the main features of the English economy in the early seventeenth century?
◆ How far was the period one of economic change?

Significant dates

1600	The East India Company is formed.
1604	Peace is made with Spain.
1607	The first successful English colony is established in Virginia, North America.
1620	The Pilgrim Fathers establish a colony in New England.
1646–69	There are a series of bad harvests, followed by high prices.
1651	A Navigation Act is passed.
1654	Cromwell embarks upon the Western Design.
1660	A further Navigation Act is passed.

Overview

The brief list of significant dates above gives the impression that little, if anything, happened in the economic history of England between 1603 and 1660. Such a view is misleading. There are two reasons why the list is so brief. Firstly, it is hard to specify a particular date for many important economic changes, most of which are often gradual and undramatic. In addition, in marked contrast to the political upheavals of the time, this period was one of gradual economic change. There were many small-scale, individual changes in how goods were produced and traded, in how people worked and in what they bought. These, taken together, created continuous economic change. Secondly, we know less about seventeenth-century economic history than we do about its political history. Accurate information about economic growth-rates, farming methods, even about how many people there were at the time, is just not available. The limited and marginal information that is available has to be used to make general statements about the early Stuart economy.

It is not possible, for example, to identify with any precision how and how far the economy grew between 1603 and 1660. We know there was a series of bad harvests in the 1590s and, again, in the late 1640s. Specifying exactly how the economy developed in between, however, is something we cannot do with any accuracy. Economic historians are happier placing the economic history of these 60 years in a longer period, the 200 years from 1550 to around 1750. Then it is possible to identify some clear contrasts. It is generally agreed that the 1650s and 1660s marked the end of one period and the start of another. The economic era which ended in the 1650s was one of unusually high rates of growth in population and prices but not in wages. The period after was one of static population growth, slowly falling prices and a rising standard of living. Thus Derek Hirst, in *Authority and conflict: England 1603–1658* (1986), writes that 'living conditions in the decades 1620–50 . . . have been called among the worst that England has experienced'. Some historians try to make a connection between these living conditions and the outbreak of civil war and revolution; others do not. What is less frequently considered are the consequences of the Civil Wars for the English economy. Was it coincidence that the 1650s saw a major change in the state of the economy? Before we consider that issue, we need to know more about the English economy of the time.

Population and prices

Population

A key factor in a country's economic development in the early modern period was the size of the population and whether there was enough food to go round. The margin between plenty and hardship was a thin one. A run of bad harvests could result in considerable suffering. There is evidence that the bad harvests of the 1590s caused famine in north-west England. An increase in the number of people could put more pressure on resources, especially if the increase was sustained for several decades. What was happening, therefore, to the population of England in the early seventeenth century?

The population was growing quite steadily and had been for some time. The best estimates available – the first census was, after all, in 1801 – suggest that, in 1600, there were around 4 million people in England, compared with around 3 million 50 years before. By the 1650s the figure had risen to just over 5 million, an increase of just over a quarter. This may not sound much but, in the context of early modern Europe, this was a considerable and sustained growth. The reasons for this long-term growth are not that easy to explain. Most historians now agree that it resulted from both a declining death rate and an occasional increase in the birth rate. The decline in the incidence of bubonic plague contributed greatly to the former; a decline in the age of

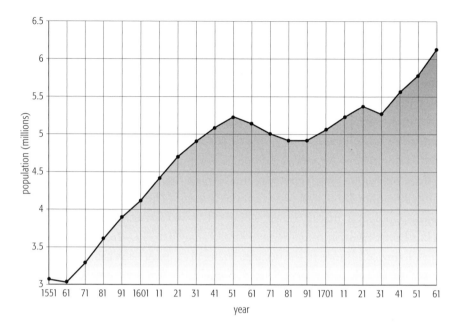

The population increase in England, 1551–1761
Source: E. A. Wrigley and R. S. Scholfield, *The population history of England 1541–1871: a reconstruction,* Cambridge (1989)

At what rate was population in England growing in the first half of the seventeenth century?
What explanations have been offered for this growth?

marriage and thus an increase in the number of years when women were 'officially sanctioned' to have children probably explains the latter. Some historians believe that the age of marriage fluctuated with the state of the economy. When times were hard, people put off getting married. If conditions improved, earlier marriage was possible. If the period from 1620 to 1650 was as bad as Hirst maintains and this hypothesis is valid, then marriages should have been postponed and the birth rate should have fallen. That might have happened. Our knowledge is too limited to be able to say with certainty.

Prices

The steady growth in the number of people put pressure on the country's resources. There were more mouths to feed, more bodies to house. It is now accepted that the increase in population is a major explanation for the increase in prices of the late sixteenth and early seventeenth centuries. The early modern period saw the sharpest rise in prices for many centuries. Historians used to see the increased supplies of gold and silver from the Americas as causing this inflation. Though they were a factor, they were less significant than the increased demand resulting from the growth in population. This growth in population also explains why the rate of increase in food prices was greater than for manufactured goods. The increased labour supply helped to reduce the costs of making things. Although even less is known about changing wage rates than about prices, wages lagged behind prices, making wage labourers worse off for most of this period. Had agriculture not managed to feed the extra population, the people would have been a lot worse off.

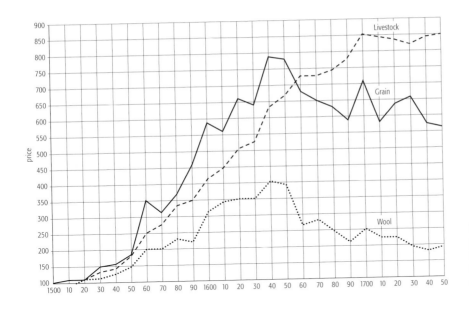

The prices of agricultural produce, 1500–1749
Source: Joan Thirsk (ed.), *The agrarian history of England and Wales*, Cambridge (1967)

Agriculture and industry

Agriculture

The seventeenth-century economy was predominantly agricultural. Farming was essentially subsistence in nature, producing for family needs, any surplus being sold at local markets. There was little commercial farming, though by the end of this period there was much more than there had been. The steady long-term growth in population made growing food to meet people's needs more profitable, if produce could be got to market. England responded to the pressure of population by developing commercial agriculture. It need not have done. The response of some European economies was to subdivide farms between the larger families into ever smaller plots, thus making farming less efficient. In England, the process went the other way. More land was brought together into larger units. Those farming these units often employed farm labourers who had little, if any, land themselves. The self-sufficient peasant economy was on the way out. These larger farms could adopt new methods. Most improvements were continuous throughout the era, for example the enclosure of open fields and improved rotation methods. However, there is one that can be linked with the early seventeenth century. This is the introduction of water meadows, whereby frequent flooding of pasture resulted in several crops of hay rather than just one. This illustrates the small-scale continual change that went on, helping to increase agricultural production. The amazing expansion of London at this time (see page 179) meant that the development of a market for food that had an impact nationwide. By 1660 agriculture, though still predominantly subsistence, was more commercial and more productive than it had been in 1603.

Industry

The industrial or manufacturing sector formed only a small part of the economy, probably less than 10 per cent. Furthermore, most English industries seemed inferior in technique and innovation to their counterparts in Europe, such as the Netherlands and northern Italy. Goods were produced locally, often in the home, by traditional methods, and sold locally. There was little reason to innovate and few resources to do so. Guilds, groups of craftsmen, usually based in London, tried to control the supply of goods. They succeeded to some extent but, across the country, craftsmen were producing versions of a guild-controlled product more cheaply for those who could not afford the real thing.

The leading industry, located primarily in East Anglia, was textiles. In particular, a heavy woollen cloth was produced in an unfinished form for export to the Netherlands. This was because the English lacked the techniques to produce the finished product. When, in 1585, this market was closed off, the manufacturers turned to producing 'new draperies', a lighter woollen cloth exported to the Mediterranean region. During the seventeenth century, textile production gradually became concentrated in East Anglia, the West Country, Yorkshire and Lancashire, each area specialising in a certain textile. The methods of production changed little, however. Some combined farming with some aspect of making textile goods; for others, textiles were the main form of employment, usually through the domestic or **putting-out system**.

The **putting-out system** was a system whereby some part of the textile process such as fulling, dyeing or finishing that could not be achieved within the domestic circle was passed on to other labourers.

The other products that formed the basis of the industrial revolution over a century later, coal and iron, were provided locally. Perhaps the main exception was the coal mining industry of north-east England. This produced more and more coal to meet the needs of the people of London, 300 miles to the south. The coal was transported by sea, which was a good deal quicker and cheaper than carrying it over land. However, coal production was limited by the inability to mine far below the surface. Until a pump was developed to stop mines from flooding, most mining was open cast, which restricted the amount that could be produced. The main use of coal was on domestic fires. Only occasionally did it have an industrial use.

Limitations of technology also held back the iron industry. By the seventeenth century, charcoal provided the best form of heat to convert the iron ore into cast iron but further heat was required to turn cast iron into wrought iron. The process was slow and expensive. Alternative materials to iron such as wood and leather were more accessible and cheaper. Only in the next century, with the newly discovered means of using coke as the furnace fuel, did iron production expand to meet demand.

This picture of localised production using traditional methods was true of another important industry of the time. As England began to develop an overseas empire, it needed a merchant fleet and a royal navy to provide transport and protection. Even the coal trade between the north-east and London suffered during the wars with the Dutch, the price of coal in London suddenly doubling. The English merchant fleet totalled some 100,000 tons in 1600 and grew threefold during the seventeenth century.

The economy of the early seventeenth century developed in ways which met immediate needs but did not lead to new products or new techniques. If anything, changes in agriculture, though limited, were more significant than those in industry, which still lagged behind the best in Europe. However, more important than either was the growth of external trade. This is the one part of economic life that did see some significant developments between 1600 and 1660.

In what ways did agriculture develop in the early part of the seventeenth century? What was the main industry at this time?

Trade and empire

The main British export has already been mentioned. Unfinished cloth, whether old or new, heavy or light, provided 80–90 per cent of English exports throughout the period. No product dominated imports in the same way. A wide range of specialist goods was imported. To build and equip ships, naval supplies came from the Baltic, and to improve the taste of food, spices were brought from the Far East. Trade expanded in the early years of the seventeenth century following the end of the war with Spain in 1604. This peace opened to English trade not just the Spanish Netherlands but also the Spanish empire in the Mediterranean. Not only did this latter trade expand but also English merchant ships proved the best defence against the many pirates in the area. Blake's expedition to the Mediterranean in 1654 merely reinforced a well-established English presence. The merchants got there first.

The various voyages of discovery of the early sixteenth century had introduced Europeans to a wide range of exotic goods. By the late sixteenth century, the English government was encouraging this trade by giving different companies the monopoly of trade with different parts of the world and by trying to establish colonies in the Americas. Only in the early seventeenth century did these attempts start to succeed.

During the reign of the early Stuarts, the English established colonies in different parts of North America and the Caribbean. There were two sets of colonies on the eastern seaboard of the continent, Virginia and Maryland to the south, New England to the north. The former became a major centre for growing tobacco, which was imported into England thereafter, despite its unpopularity with James I. The New England settlements were first established by the **Pilgrim Fathers**. They left England to escape the religious persecution of the time, though material motives were often just as important

The **Pilgrim Fathers** were a group of disaffected Puritans who left England in the *Mayflower* in September 1620. They settled at Plymouth, in New England, in December 1620, inaugurating one of the first English colonies.

to many of those who followed. The number of settlers grew rapidly in the 1630s as the result of Charles I's religious policies. They developed a more self-sufficient economy than the colonies to the south. A third set of colonies was established in various small islands of the West Indies, such as St Kitts, Barbados and Antigua. The first crops grown were tobacco but this was soon replaced by sugar cane, a much more profitable product. This was especially true as slaves, imported from West Africa, were used as labour.

Considered in this context, Cromwell's Western Design continues the policy of colonisation begun by the Stuarts. Cromwell's policy was both more ambitious and less successful but it was an attempt to develop a greater English presence in the Spanish empire of the New World. Jamaica, though no great acquisition at the time, was a much larger Caribbean island than any acquired beforehand. It, too, was soon producing sugar to meet the growing demand of the English market.

No colonies were established to the south in Africa or east in Asia. Trade with the latter did, however, expand following the establishment of the **East India Company** in 1600. In 1623 English traders clashed with the Dutch over control of the spice trade with the East Indies (now Indonesia). This was the first of many conflicts over trade between the Dutch and the English in the seventeenth century. The English had to withdraw from the area and so concentrated on developing trade with India. Its tea and coffee became very fashionable in England and trade with India grew, especially after 1660.

Bringing these various goods back to England was a lucrative trade. Dutch ships had the greater share of this business. The main aim of the 1651 Navigation Act was to ensure that this trade was carried in English ships. Enforcing this act and a similar one passed in 1660 was far from easy. However, these acts were to form the basis of British trading policy for the next century or more. They were one of the reforms of the Interregnum that did endure.

Thus the first 60 years of the seventeenth century saw the gradual establishment of a pattern of overseas settlement and trade that was to become the basis of the British empire of the eighteenth century. New commodities such as tea, coffee, sugar and tobacco were provided for both the British and European markets. A major feature of British trade was that many imports were re-exported to other countries. London, in particular, was to become a great *entrepôt*. Britain became a trading nation before it became the first industrial nation. This significant development of the time, often overlooked, was carried on by Englishmen, whether royalist or republican. There was a continuity of trading policy between the Stuart and Cromwellian periods that might seem surprising. The great battles being fought in England had only a limited effect on trading policies with the rest of the world.

The **East India Company** was a trading company, chartered by Elizabeth I in 1600, to challenge the Dutch–Portuguese monopoly of the spice trade. It established trading posts in the Bay of Bengal but, when its merchants were massacred by the Dutch in Amboina, in the Moluccas, in 1623, it concentrated on Indian trade and acquired a site near modern Madras in 1640.

An *entrepôt* is a centre, usually a seaport, through which imports and exports pass.

What did the 1651 Navigation Act stipulate?
What new commodities had England begun to trade in by the mid seventeenth century?

The Civil Wars and the economy

The impact of the Civil Wars on the slowly developing Stuart economy is hard to calculate. Information is scarce and the impact of the war is difficult to separate from other factors. Until recently the subject has also received little attention from historians. They have preferred to consider how economic factors caused the war rather than how the war affected the economy.

The war affected economic life in a number of important ways, including the costs of several years' campaigning, the seizure of lands, deaths and casualties, and general wartime destruction.

The cost of the war

The waging of effective war is an expensive business. Both sides obtained funds through a variety of means such as loans and fines but especially by instituting a weekly levy or assessment and an excise tax. In almost every respect, parliament was far more successful than the royalists. Indeed, parliament's collection process for the weekly (later monthly) assessment was so effective that, as early as 1643, it amounted to a parliamentary subsidy every fortnight. In contrast, the total number of subsidies granted by all the parliaments during the period 1603 to 1629 was 15. By 1645–46 Kent was paying more each month in assessments than it had for an entire year of ship money. It is not surprising that there was bitter hostility towards what was regarded as an illegal tax. This hostility turned into violent protest in the early part of 1648. Excise taxes were similarly resented, not least because they were levied on such vital goods as beer, meat and salt. Local studies show that not all communities suffered these taxes to the same extent, some villages being forced to pay money to both sides. In these cases, some people were left with debts, which were never made good. On the other hand, research into the financial demands of the war in north Somerset suggests that 'local people in general were able to absorb the costs of the war comfortably without permanent hardship or distress'.

The seizure of lands

Both sides also obtained resources through the sequestration of enemy estates. Again, parliament seems to have been the more efficient, commandeering the lands of nearly 5,000 Catholics and royalists in order to administer them for their own purposes. Where the yield from these lands proved disappointing certain **delinquents** were allowed to regain them by paying heavy fines and taking Oaths of Loyalty.

A **delinquent** was a royalist who was not considered to be a substantial threat to parliament.

The impact of casualties

It is extremely difficult to estimate the number who were either killed or maimed from fighting in the Civil Wars. Nevertheless, Charles Carlton has

This portrayal of the 'English–Irish soldier' who 'had rather eat than fight' demonstrates the reason why civilians were so fearful of soldiers: their desire for plunder.

calculated the total casualties as follows:

Casualties during the Civil Wars	
Direct deaths from combat	84,738
Indirect deaths (that is, from disease)	100,000
Accidents	300
Casualties from the Bishops' Wars	500
Total	185,538

What devices did both sides use in order to raise war finance? What percentage of the English population were casualties of the Civil Wars?

If this figure is rounded down to 180,000, Carlton points out that this would mean that, of England's population of around 5 million, 3.6 per cent perished as a consequence of the Civil Wars. Since 2.6 per cent of the population of the United Kingdom lost their lives as a result of the First World War and only 0.6 per cent as a result of the Second World War, Carlton argues that the Civil Wars of the seventeenth century were the bloodiest conflict in English history.

In his book *Destruction in the English Civil Wars* (1994), Stephen Porter has estimated that at least 150 towns and 50 villages sustained some destruction of property during the Civil Wars, many towns destroying dwellings outside their city walls in order to deny cover to a besieging force. For example, at York, the royalist garrison undertook a suburban clearance programme so that 'all the houses in some streets were burnt and broken down to the ground'. A close examination of the data suggests that 10,000 houses were

This print shows the effects of the parliamentarian storming of Colchester in the Second Civil War.

destroyed in cities and towns and 1,000 in villages, implying that 55,000 people (1 per cent of the population) were made homeless. Of course, some areas suffered far more than others did. Towns in the defensive ring around Oxford, such as Abingdon, Wallingford and Woodstock, for example, suffered much greater damage than did those away from the military corridors. Many fortified houses, such as Basing House, incurred extensive damage, often through fires ignited by bombardment. Castles were often sited to be untenable as a fortification. 'The evidence suggests', concludes Porter, 'that property destruction was one of the deleterious effects of the war which could temporarily check the prosperity of a well established industry, and do considerable, even fatal, harm to one which was already faltering.'

Summary questions

1 (a) Identify and explain any *two* causes of economic change in England from 1603 to 1660.

    (b) Compare the importance of at least *three* developments in producing the growth of England's prosperity during these years.

2 How significant was the impact of the Civil Wars upon the English economy?

16

London

Focus questions

◆ Why did London play an increasingly important part in national affairs?

◆ What part did London play in the English Civil Wars and Revolution?

Significant dates

1600   The population reaches 200,000.

1635   The corporation of London is fined over the Londonderry plantation.

1641   London presses for action against Strafford.

1642   The Five Members flee to the City, which refuses to hand them over to Charles.
Trained bands halt Charles I at Turnham Green.

1643   London trained bands help relieve the siege of Gloucester.

1646   The Leveller movement emerges in London.

1647   London Presbyterians prepare their own forces against the army.
The crowd enters parliament and the army moves into London.

1659   Londoners protest against second return of the Rump.

1660   The population reaches 400,000.
London welcomes Charles II.

Overview

London is of great significance to the history of early seventeenth-century England in two ways. Firstly, it played a leading part in the political events of the time. As the events of 1640–60 have been described, London has been mentioned on at least four occasions: 1641–42, 1643, 1647 and 1659–60. Each time, London's reaction to national developments helped influence those developments. In less dramatic ways, throughout the period from 1603 onwards, the attitude of key groups of Londoners often affected events. To take one example, London was home to many of the radical sects which became a significant political force in the late 1640s and 1650s. The outbreak and development of the English Civil Wars and Revolution cannot be fully understood without a proper appreciation of the role of London. As Macaulay wrote, in *The history of England* (1848), 'It is no exaggeration to say that, but for the hostility of the City, Charles I would never have been vanquished and that, without the help of the City, Charles II could never have been restored.'

Secondly, and more importantly, London was significant because it was the great centre of many different aspects of national life. Obviously it was the focus of government and politics but it was equally important in terms of trade, finance, culture and industry. It is hard to think of any other European city of the time that played as many different roles as did London. The nearest equivalent was, perhaps, Paris but it was not the centre of French trade. The reason for London's exceptional predominance over national life needs to be understood. Geography and history played their part but, by the seventeenth century, the main reason was demographic.

London, the largest city

The location of London, at the mouth of the Thames, was obviously important to its growth. Since Roman times, trade has been at the heart of London's development. In the eleventh century, Edward the Confessor decided to locate his government at Westminster, two miles up river from London, where he built an abbey and a palace. About 500 years later, the Tudors made the Whitehall Palace, on the east side of Westminster, their main royal residence. Thus, by 1600, London and Westminster – strictly speaking, the two should be kept separate – were the economic and political heart of the country.

The population of London in 1600 is estimated at around 200,000. Most historians accept that it doubled in size in the next 60 years, a phenomenal rate of growth. An increase on this scale was generated by people moving from the rest of England and often from Europe. London was larger than the next 50 English towns put together. Towns such as York, Bristol, Exeter, Newcastle and Norwich had populations of only 10,000 to 20,000 each.

The rapid growth of London, which had begun in the sixteenth century, was impossible to contain within the city walls. It spread along the river to the east and the west and over the river to the south. To the east, docks were built to facilitate the growth in trade and London's role as an *entrepôt*. To the west, the City expanded to become closer to Westminster. By 1600 the main road between the two, the Strand, had already been developed. To its north, the building of Soho was started in the 1630s. Moreover, across the river, Southwark, with 10 per cent of the London population, was expanding along the south bank of the river in both directions.

This rapid expansion alarmed both City and government authorities. The work people did in the new suburbs was beyond the control of the City guilds,

A print showing London before the Great Fire

whose economic power they were undermining. Government ministers feared that London would grow too large and impossible to control. It was already regarded as a centre for radical Puritanism. Clarendon called it 'the sink of all the ill humour of the kingdom'. If too many Puritans moved into the City, they might overwhelm the authorities. There was no police force at that time. Thus, the early Stuarts passed regulations to halt the expansion of the City by preventing the construction of new buildings. The controls failed. Charles I finished by using them as another revenue-raising device, allowing the buildings to go up and then fining their owners for breaking planning regulations. The buildings were needed because people were moving into London from all directions. They saw London as a place of wealth and opportunity.

> Identify factors that help to explain the growth of London during this period.

The importance of London

Trade

London, which had begun as a trading post, experienced a great growth in its trade in the first half of the seventeenth century (though not as great as the growth to come). The building of new docks down river was evidence of that growth. The goods were not just to and from the people of London. London was starting to develop as a distribution centre, taking goods from one part of the world and passing them on to another. This had been the case for some time; most of the woollen exports of East Anglia passed through London. However, with trading companies such as the East India Company based there and the growth of links with the Americas and Asia, London docks were soon distributing goods to and from all parts of the world.

Industry

London was an industrial centre in its own right. It produced a wide range of goods, primarily for its own large market. Since the Middle Ages, craftsmen had organised themselves into guilds, which aimed to control quality and production and thus the market. The leading guilds were the Grocers, Drapers, Haberdashers, Merchant Taylors and Mercers. Four of the five dealt with cloths and clothes of some kind or other, which suggests that conspicuous consumption was important even in early modern times. By the seventeenth century, the economic power of the guilds was on the wane as London expanded and the economy became larger and more diversified. Thus, the industrial element of London's economy probably became more important as cheaper goods could now be produced for the mass market of London.

Finance

Trade required other services to ensure its continued success, not least of which was the provision of credit and insurance. London companies developed the skill of providing loans or insurance, which were cheaper than their competitors and yet still made a profit. Business grew. London became a centre for finance as well as for trade and industry. The companies had surplus funds, which they could lend to a government in a tight spot. Usually they did so. When they did not, as in 1640, then the government was in serious trouble because, before 1650, there were neither English banks nor bankers.

Government

Not only was the crown's main residence in London but parliament was located there as well. The importance of parliament in the seventeenth century and the frequency with which it met focused national politics on London. If there was a political nation or elite, then most of them could be found in and around Westminster when parliament was in session.

This growing tendency to think of London or Westminster when thinking of national politics was reinforced by the centralised nature of English politics. Unlike seventeenth-century France, England had no regional centres of power. The sovereign body was king-in-parliament and the three parts of that secular trinity, king, Lords and Commons, were to be found in Westminster.

This focus on Westminster might seem to be weaker with regard to church government, as the spiritual leader of the church was the archbishop of Canterbury, not London or Westminster. In fact, the archbishop had an official residence in London, Lambeth Palace, just across the river from Westminster.

The law

The legal system was also based in London. Though the high courts travelled around the country, leading lawyers were found only in London. They resided in the eight Inns of Chancery during the four legal terms each year was divided into. Those wanting the best legal advice had to go to London. Many gentry needing legal help with issues of property or a marriage settlement would have to set time aside to visit their lawyer in London. There were also four Inns of Court which provided legal training for aspiring sons of the gentry – Lincoln's Inn, Gray's Inn, Middle Temple and Inner Temple. These were regarded by some as the third university of England after Oxford and Cambridge. All 12 Inns were located on the western edge of the City.

The royal court

In an age when monarchs saw themselves as gods, the royal court was the centre of national life. The Tudor court had developed spectacular ceremonies and buildings in order to project the image of the monarch, who travelled round from palace to palace (in part because of limited sanitation facilities). The Stuart court was identified much more closely with Whitehall which, in the 1630s, Charles I started to convert into a grandiose palace in the newest Classical style. In this large, rambling palace courtiers would occupy the time they had to spare between banquets, **masques** and other entertainments. During James I's reign they would have experienced a royal court which was dissolute and debauched, if open and informal. The court of Charles I was a complete contrast, being closed, formal and almost austere. Whatever the style, the gentry and nobility, if they wanted to see and be seen at the Stuart court and to gain the benefits of royal patronage, had to go to London.

Fashionable London

Such were the many needs which could be met by going to London that many gentry found themselves spending more time there. The crown, occasionally worried that the gentry might be neglecting their duties as county landowners and justices of the peace, encouraged them to return home. In 1616 James I knew who was responsible. In a speech in the Star Chamber, he asserted:

> One of the greatest causes of all Gentleness [the gentry's] desire . . . to dwell in London is apparently the pride of the women. If they be wives then their husbands, and if they be maids then their fathers must bring them up to London because the new fashion is to be nowhere but in

Masques were performances which involved a blend of dance, drama and fantasy.

In what ways was London important in terms of commerce, industry, law and politics?

Winter fashion during the First Civil War. It was necessary to dress to keep warm, since Newcastle, from where London drew its coal supplies, was in enemy hands.

London. Here, if they be unmarried, they mar their marriages and if they be married they lose their reputations and rob their husband's purses . . . all the country is gotten into London so [that] with time England will be only London and the whole country be left waste.

The gentry continued to come to London, staying for longer periods, usually renting fashionable accommodation in the West End between the City and Westminster. Theatres, amusement parks and an increasing number of shops and coffee houses kept the gentry entertained. The London season began to emerge, a round of social engagements during the winter months. In summer, the country was preferable. Lifestyle was an indication of status.

What entertainments did London offer the gentry?

Summary questions

1 (a) Identify and explain any *two* ways in which London was important during this period.

   (b) Compare the importance of at least *three* developments in bringing about the growth of London during this period.

2 How important is a knowledge of London to the historian of the early seventeenth century? Explain your answer.

17

The growth of radical sects

Focus questions

◆ Why was there a growth in radical religious and political groups after 1640?

◆ How important were these radical groups?

Significant dates

1641   The Star Chamber is abolished and press censorship ended.

1645   *September* *England's misery and remedy* is published.
       October *England's birthright justified* is published.

1646   *July* *Remonstrance of many thousand citizens* is published, following the imprisonment of Lilburne.
       November *London's liberty in chains* is published.

1647   *March* The Levellers' *Large Petition* appears.
       July *An appeal from the degenerate representative body* is published.
       October *The case of the army truly stated* appears.
       The first Agreement of the People is discussed in the Putney Debates.

1648   *September* The Leveller *Humble Petition* (sometimes also called the *Large Petition*) is published.
       December The second Agreement of the People is published and discussed in the Whitehall Debates.

1649   *February* *England's new chains* is published.
       March *The hunting of the foxes* is published.
       The Leveller leaders are arrested.
       April The Diggers establish communities at St George's Hill, Walton-on-Thames and Cobham.
       May The third Agreement of the People is drawn up.
       November Lilburne is acquitted of high treason by jury.
       The Ranters emerge.

1650   The Blasphemy Act is passed.
       The Quakers and the Fifth Monarchists emerge.

1653   Lilburne is brought to trial and kept in prison.

Overview

In the mid 1640s there emerged into public view a number of radical religious and political sects that challenged the arguments of even the parliamentarians opposed to the king. They grew in number and impact over the next five or six years before disappearing once more, making only the briefest of reappearances in 1659 to 1660. Of these groups, only the Quakers have survived to the present day and then in a different form from that of the 1650s.

Though marginal and marginalised at the time, the groups argued for ideas of which some anticipated reforms won only several centuries later. For example, the Levellers demanded a more democratic system of government. Thus, some historians argue that these groups, rather than the Independents and certainly not the Presbyterians, were the true revolutionaries of the time. They were important in another way. They were usually craftsmen or mechanics or landless labourers, from social groups that were 'lower' than the landed gentry, who dominated events of the time. Thus, they represent social classes whose views were rarely heard in the early modern period. In England, in the late 1640s and early 1650s, they were. We need to understand why.

The freedom of the presses

H. N. Brailsford, in his sympathetic account of the Leveller movement, *The Levellers and the English Revolution* (1961), dates precisely the origins of the movement, the first of the many sects of the next few years. He points to 7 July 1646 when the first pamphlet written on behalf of a group and not an individual was published. The main issues and argument of the pamphlet are summed up in the very long title. It was called:

> *A Remonstrance of many thousand citizens and other freeborn people to their own House of Commons, occasioned through the illegal and barbarous treatment of that famous and worthy sufferer for his country's freedoms, Lt-Colonel John Lilburne. Wherein their just demands on behalf of themselves and the whole kingdom concerning their public safety, peace and freedom are expressed, calling their commissioners in parliament to an account: how they (since the beginnings of their session to this present) have discharged their duties to the universality of the people, their sovereign lord, from whom their power and strength is derived and by whom it is continued.*

The title introduces the man who was to emerge as the leading Leveller, John Lilburne, currently in the Tower of London by order of the House of Lords for criticising the earl of Manchester. It introduces the main Leveller idea, the principle that the 'the universality of the people' is the 'sovereign lord' over parliament. The people are sovereign, not the king in parliament.

The means of publicising these arguments is also significant. A pamphlet was quick to write, quick to print and easy to distribute. The new technology of the printing press gave people a means of communication they had not had before. The government had tried to control the press in pre-war times. It licensed printers and it prosecuted those who published books, magazines and pamphlets that were deemed to be 'seditious, schismatical or offensive' in the Star Chamber or in church courts. How effective those controls were is a matter of dispute among historians. Christopher Hill, in *The world turned upside down* (1972), asserts that 'before 1640 . . . there was strict censorship'. Others doubt how strict that control was in practice. Kevin Sharpe, in *The Personal Rule of Charles I* (1992), argues that 'in general the licensing laws were frequently circumvented or ignored'. The abolition of the Court of Star Chamber in 1641 meant the end of regulation of the press, which helps explains the flood of pamphlets thereafter. (There were to be attempts by the Long and Rump Parliaments to reimpose controls in 1647 and 1650, with varying success.) However, the end of press censorship is not enough to explain the emergence of radical groups five or six years later. Other factors were more important.

What was the principal idea of the Levellers and by what means did they promote their message?

The Levellers

Origins

F. D. Dow, in *Radicalism in the English Revolution 1640–1660* (1985), provides a useful framework for understanding why the radical groups emerged in the mid and late 1640s. She identifies three sets of causes. The first is the grievances, whether long-term or short-term, which pushed people into joining the movement. Dow argues that long-term economic changes threatened the little man and that these threats were made worse by short-term economic and financial problems caused by the dislocations of civil war. These factors were especially important in London, the home of the radical groups. In addition, there were the uncertainties surrounding the religious and political settlement of the country. The second set of factors covers what Dow calls 'the intellectual heritage' of the leaders, the ideas of Calvinistic Puritanism, of the Renaissance-based idea of natural law and the traditions of English law, for example Magna Carta. The third cause was the personal experiences of the Leveller leaders and especially of John Lilburne, the man whom Derek Hirst, in *Authority and conflict in England 1603–1658* (1986), labels 'the genius of the Leveller movement' and goes on to describe as 'restless, irascible, and egocentric'.

Lilburne spent most of his adult life in prison or exile. He was first arrested in 1637, aged just 22, for smuggling 'schismatical' literature and for refusing to recognise the Court of Star Chamber. He was flogged the two miles from London to Westminster. He fought in the First Civil War and, in 1645 and 1646, was back in prison. In the Tower, in October 1646, he wrote *London's liberty in chains*, which attacked the undemocratic nature of both the City government and, more significantly, the Long Parliament. Lilburne was turning his specific grievances into a wider political attack upon the parliamentarians. The Leveller movement – though it was not given that name by its enemies until some months later – was starting to form.

What reasons explain the emergence of radical groups in the 1640s?

The Levellers advance, 1647–48

In March 1647 the Levellers drew up a set of proposals known as the *Large Petition*, a document Austin Woolrych calls, in *Soldiers and statesmen* (1987), 'an important stage in the formation of a comprehensive Leveller political programme'. It was addressed to the 'supreme authority of this nation, the Commons in Parliament assembled'. Two months later, the Commons rejected the petition. Another Leveller leader, Richard Overton, wrote *An appeal from the degenerate representative body to the free people of England*, in which he also appealed to the leader of the army, Fairfax. The army leadership was no more sympathetic to Leveller arguments than MPs were. The Levellers' best allies were the Agitators, who in the summer of 1647 were being chosen by the soldiers. An important link was formed between Levellers and Agitators. By the autumn, the Levellers and Agitators had published *The case of the army truly stated*, which attacked army officers and called for political and social reform. The officers agreed to debate this document but, instead, ended up discussing a revised version of it, the Agreement of the People, in the famous Putney Debates. The Agreement of the People was a Leveller-inspired draft of the constitution of England. In just six months, the Levellers had moved from the margins of English politics to its centre.

Though the grandees' defeat of the mutiny at Corkbush Field, near Ware, meant that Leveller contacts in the army had been weakened, during the winter of 1647–48 the Levellers built up their own organisation. In this way, the Leveller movement became an early version of a modern political party. Its main support was in London, though it did develop branches in other parts of the country, mainly in the home counties. The Levellers played little part in the events of the Second Civil War. In the autumn of 1648 they became important once more as England moved towards the final settlement of the problem of Charles I and the monarchy and the army. Independents needed all the allies they could get. In September 1648 the Levellers' *Humble Petition* (which Brailsford calls the '*Large Petition*' but is not to be confused with the *Large Petition* of March 1647) set out the case for abolishing the veto powers of the king and Lords and accepting the Agreement of the People. The

What role did the Agitators play in the emergence of the Leveller movement?

William Walwyn (1600–80) was an apprentice to a silk dealer who became a successful cloth merchant. From about 1641, he emerged as a champion of religious liberty. After his meeting with Lilburne in 1646, however, he became more involved in secular politics. Little is heard of him after 1649.

Commons ignored it. The grandees arranged more discussions with the Levellers about the Agreement of the People in the Whitehall Debates at the end of the year, while they tried Charles I.

The Levellers retreat, 1649

As the trial and execution of Charles took place, and even in the first weeks of the Rump Parliament, the Leveller leaders were untypically silent. Then, in late February, Lilburne published *England's new chains discovered*. Overton soon followed with *The hunting of the foxes*, an attack on army leadership. The leadership responded very quickly. Lilburne and Overton, together with **William Walwyn** and the party treasurer, were arrested. Lilburne overheard Cromwell arguing with the Council of State. He reported:

> Lt. Gen. Cromwell (I am sure of it) very loud, thumping his fist on the table, till it rang again, and Heard him speak in these very words or to this effect: I tell you, Sir, you have no other way to deal with these men but to break them in little pieces ... If you do not break them, they will break you.

All four were sent to the Tower. They could still write pamphlets and published a third and final version of the Agreement of the People. There were petitions for their release. There were petitons for political reform. One, in September 1649, claimed to have been signed by 98,000 people. However, the army leaders were in control. They took further action against army mutinies. They brought Lilburne to trial. The jury acquitted him. The people of London lit bonfires to celebrate.

Brailsford argues that 'from John Lilburne's triumph at the Guildhall dates the decline of the Leveller party'. He goes on: 'it was neither defeated nor suppressed. It faded out because it had nothing to do.' Lilburne himself settled with Cromwell and the Rump, which offered him lands to compensate for earlier wrongful arrest. He drifted away from the Leveller movement, as did Overton and Walwyn. The end of the Leveller movement in 1649 was something of an anti-climax.

Lilburne's life, however, remained far from quiet. He got involved in a personal quarrel with a leading member of the Rump, as a result of which he was fined and exiled. He came back to England after the Rump was dissolved only to be arrested and imprisoned once more. The year 1653 was almost a re-run of 1649. There were more petitions, another trial and Lilburne's acquittal. This time, however, he was not released. Eventually Cromwell exiled him to Jersey. He returned to prison in Dover Castle, where he became a Quaker and died, aged 42, in 1657.

The True Levellers

The Levellers always objected to the label they acquired around the time of the Putney Debates. They wanted liberty, not equality. Some think they did not want political equality, as they excluded alms-takers and servants from the franchise. They were certainly opposed to social equality if it meant giving property to those who had none. However, in 1649, there emerged a group that did believe in social and economic equality and that did try and put its beliefs into practice.

This group was the True Levellers or Diggers. They began by digging. In March 1649 a dozen True Levellers, led by William Everard, occupied waste land at St George's Hill and began to plant crops. They resisted attempts to move them off the land. One of their members, Gerrard Winstanley, wrote *The new law of true righteousness* to encourage others to follow their example. Some did so. The True Levellers were concerned more with achieving social and economic equality by means of local direct action than with achieving political goals through national bodies. They were taking immediate and – they hoped – effective action in response to the harsh economic conditions of 1648–49. In recent years, both communists and environmentalists have claimed them as their early ancestors. The group at St George's Hill kept going for about a year before the hostility of local landowners rather than action by the government caused them to give up the one-sided struggle. In 1652 Winstanley wrote his most significant work, *The law of freedom*, before disappearing into obscurity.

The True Levellers had a strong religious basis to their beliefs. Winstanley believed in the Digger cause as a result of a religious vision he had, when God told him what he needed to do. He believed that Christ was the 'true and faithful Leveller'. There was more of a religious element to the True Levellers than to the Levellers. In this respect, if in no other, the True Levellers had affinities with the other religious radicals of the time.

> In what ways did the True Levellers differ from the Levellers?

Seekers, Ranters, Quakers and Fifth Monarchists

There were a number of religious sects that believed that the thousand-year rule of the saints, which would precede the Second Coming of Christ, was about to happen, as predicted in the Book of Revelation. Though all were millenarians, they also differed one from the other in how they interpreted the expected arrival of the millennium. Among the more significant were the following sects.

Seekers

The Seekers were against any form of church organisation and did not engage in sectarian controversy. They thought that the arrival of the millennium was so close that they need do no more than wait. Their dislike of structure makes it difficult to assess the extent of their support or whether individuals were Seekers. Some argue that Cromwell could have been a Seeker; John Milton certainly was. The arguments of Seekers seem most prevalent in the late 1640s, after which other sects became more prominent.

Ranters

The Ranters believed in the inner spirit, in the presence of God in all humans. They rejected the importance of the Bible, they did not believe in Hell and they opposed the idea of imposed morality. If all humans contained the light of God, then they would and should decide what is right for them. The Levellers believed that the (limited) Levelling revolution would come by political action, the True Levellers by direct action, the Ranters by a God-given miracle. They could blaspheme and swear, get drunk and be sexually promiscuous and they would not necessarily be breaking any inner commandments. They subverted the social order and thus threatened the political and economic order. They appealed to the lower classes, especially in the towns. The movement suddenly emerged in 1649 and just as suddenly disappeared in 1651.

The Ranters have been the centre of an intense historical debate in recent years. J. C. Davis, in *Fear, myth and history* (1986), argued that the Ranters never existed as an organised movement, that it was an invention of other radical sects of the time. Modern historians, he believes, have been taken in by this invention. Christopher Hill, whose *The world turned upside down* (1972) provided much detail about the Ranters, has replied with the case for the defence in *A nation of change and novelty* (1993).

Quakers

No one doubts the existence of the Quakers; the Society of Friends still exists today. The first Quakers of the 1650s held different beliefs from the pacifism and quietism of modern-day Quakers. During the 1650s, the Quakers were often confused with the Ranters, whom they replaced in 1651. They were also subversive as they directly challenged traditional religious and social practices. They refused to take off their hats to their superiors, which was a very radical non-gesture at the time. Perhaps because they had more effective leaders in James Nayler and **George Fox**, who developed a structure of Quaker churches, the Quakers became a large and organised sect.

George Fox (1624–90), during the years 1643–47, wandered the country engaging in debate and studying his Bible. Having formulated the doctrine of the 'inner light', a conviction that the knowledge of truth comes from a belief within the soul, he founded the Society of Friends. They became known as 'Quakers' because they trembled when they felt the spirit of God touching them. He travelled widely in Britain but also visited Ireland, North America, the West Indies and Holland. He was imprisoned on eight occasions, amounting to a total of nearly six years in all. By the 1670s there were, perhaps, 50,000 Quakers in Britain.

The Fifth Monarchists

Unlike the Seekers, Ranters and Quakers, who all believed that salvation came to all, the Fifth Monarchists believed that only the chosen could be saved. They expected to form the Fifth Monarchy in which King Jesus would reign on earth for 1,000 years until the Day of Judgement (the other four monarchies were Babylon, Persia, Greece and Rome). They also took more of a political role than did the other three groups. They were the complete opposite to the Seekers in that they were not prepared to wait for the arrival of the millennium. They gained influence in the army and played a part in establishing the Nominated Assembly of 1653 and in the events of 1659–60.

Other groups

There were other radical religious groups. Particularly significant, in terms of numbers, were the Baptists. Not to be forgotten are the Muggletonians, who were the followers of Lodowick Muggleton, or the Grindletonians, named after Grindleton in Yorkshire. The disintegration of the political, religious and social order led to the rise of a wide range of radical groups, both political and religious. Once order was steadily restored in the 1650s and, after a brief hiatus, the 1660s, these groups disappeared. Only the Quakers survived as an organisation and only because they changed their ways. The Levellers' ideas eventually reappeared but only several centuries later.

Summary questions

1 (a) Identify and explain any *two* principles that were common to most of the radical groups of the 1640s and 1650s.

   (b) Compare the importance of at least *three* reasons for the emergence of radical groups in the 1640s and 1650s.

2 Account for the emergence of the Leveller movement and explain their ultimate demise.

18 Witchcraft

Focus questions

◆ Why were people persecuted for witchcraft?

◆ How prevalent was witchcraft in the early seventeenth century?

◆ Why did trials of witches die out after 1650?

Significant dates

1563   A Witchcraft Act is passed.

1597   *Demonologie* by James VI of Scotland is published.

1604   A second Witchcraft Act is passed.

1612   The trial of witches in Pendle, Lancashire, takes place.

1645   Matthew Hopkins is made witch-finder general.

1736   Legislation against witches is repealed.

Overview

Europe in the sixteenth and seventeenth century went in for witch-hunting on a scale never seen before or since. Historians estimate that between 50,000 and 100,000 were executed for being found guilty of witchcraft. The persecution on the continent lasted much longer, though with peaks and troughs, than in England. Here, there were two main periods of prosecutions of witches, the 1580s and 1590s and a brief period in the mid 1640s. Both persecutions and executions seem to have been on a lesser scale in England than on the continent. From the mid to late seventeenth century the phenomenon died out across Europe.

Historians need to explain why the persecution began in the first place, how extensive it was and why it died out. We also need to consider why the extent of persecution was less in England than elsewhere in Europe. Some find it puzzling that such practices, based entirely on superstition and ignorance, flourished at a time of growing rationalism and belief in science. In recent decades, there has been considerable debate about the origins of the widespread desire to persecute witches and extent of the trials and persecution. Before considering the arguments, we need to know more about the main features of witchcraft.

The main features of witchcraft

Definitions

In the seventeenth century, two different types of witchcraft came to be identified. The traditional, more popular idea was that a witch was a person who had the supernatural power to do wrong to others. A witch could interfere with nature, causing distress or death to farm animals and people. The so-called witches exercised this power, known as *maleficium*, in various ways. They could simply capture their victims with their gaze, a process known as 'fascination', make some form of physical contact, utter a curse on their victim or, less frequently, make a wax image of the victim into which the witch would stick pins.

The newer belief was that witches were in league with the Devil. This notion had been developed by the Roman Catholic Church in a treatise, *Malleus maleficarum*, written by two Dominican monks in 1486. More commonly accepted in countries other than England, this definition was nevertheless

Matthew Hopkins, the witch-finder-general, presiding over the Chelmsford trial of 1645. The scene shows witches and their familiar spirits or imps, among them a greyhound with a bull's head.

eventually adopted by English intellectuals and theologians. Thus, Sir Edward Coke, one of England's leading judges, argued that the defining feature of a witch was 'a person that hath conference with the Devil to consult with him or to do some act'. In 1655, in the supplement to the sixth edition of Thomas Wilson's *Complete Christian dictionary*, the definition of a witch was given as 'anyone that hath dealing with the Devil by any compact or confederacy whatsoever'. This redefinition of witchcraft in narrower, theological terms as heresy made it a more serious offence than the wrongdoing that had been the basis of prosecutions before 1604. Thus the 1604 act, the second of three Witchcraft Acts, defined witchcraft in terms of the compact with the Devil. The act stated that anyone who was to 'consult, covenant with, entertain, employ, feed, or reward any evil and wicked spirit to or for any intent or purpose' was guilty of witchcraft. Accusations of witchcraft now had serious religious connotations.

What was significant about the Witchcraft Act of 1604?

Persecution

It is difficult to estimate accurately the total number that were executed in England on a charge of witchcraft, nearly all by hanging. During the 100 years from 1570 to 1670, it seems that the figure is around 600. More than 80 per cent of this total were women. Those who seemed especially prone to accusation were old, poor women who suffered from physical abnormalities. John Gaule, writing in *Select causes of conscience touching witches* (1646), described a typical witch as having 'a wrinkled face, a furr'd brow, a hairy lip, a gobbler tooth, a squint eye, a squeaking voice, or a scolding tongue'.

Executions were preceded by a trial. Evidence about the rate of prosecutions is hard to come by; most court records have been lost. It is believed that not all those accused of witchcraft were taken to court. Indeed, it seems that pressure from local gentry, clergy and village officials resulted in many accusations being dropped. Alan Macfarlane has found that only one in three of those who thought that they had been bewitched actually initiated an indictment. Of those cases that did come to court, many could expect to be acquitted. Of the 291 persons accused in Essex during the whole of the witch-hunt period, more than half, 151, were acquitted.

The high acquittal rate was a function of the difficulties involved in procuring conclusive evidence that a person was indeed a witch. As Michael Dalton pointed out in the *Country justice*, first published in 1618, 'the justices of the peace may not always expect direct evidence, seeing all [witches'] works are the works of darkness and [there are] no witnesses present to accuse them'. Consequently, various tests were employed to determine whether someone was a witch. The most important of these, according to Dalton, was whether there was, in the presence of the accused, a familiar, 'as in the shape of a man, woman, boy, dog, cat, foal, fowl, hare, rat, toad &c,' and whether the witch bore the Devil's mark, some sort of blemish, perhaps a mole, which did not bleed when pricked. A suspect might also be obliged to repeat the Lord's Prayer or a passage of scripture. If she hesitated or stumbled it was concluded that she was demonstrating a sympathy for the Devil.

Perhaps the most infamous of these tests, though it never enjoyed any formal legal status, was the so-called trial by water. James Sharpe, in his book *Instruments of darkness, witchcraft in England 1550–1750* (1997), has described it in the following way:

> The standard method was to strip suspects to their shirts and tie their left thumb to their right big toe and their right thumb to their left. A rope would be placed to run under the suspects' armpits, each end to be held by a strong man. Suspects were then cast into a pond or river. If they sank they were thought to be innocent of witchcraft, and the hope was that the men on either end of the rope would pull them out before they drowned. If they floated the assumption was that they were witches. The underlying rationale was probably that water, as a 'pure' element, would reject the tainted agent of the devil.

There is some evidence that people occasionally took the law into their own hands, to act against those they believed had inflicted harm. However, formal witch trials were not always witch-hunts, as the term is often understood, when people are accused and prosecuted on the flimsiest of evidence, nor were they always show trials, a travesty of justice. The rules of evidence seem to have been upheld.

Witches and witch-finding, 1603–60

What sorts of people were labelled as witches? Firstly, they were predominantly – but not entirely – women. Women made up all but a handful of those executed. However, it seems likely that more men were charged with being a witch without reaching the gallows. Contemporaries, always male, explained the preponderance of women as a result of their being the weaker sex and therefore unable to resist the temptations of the Devil. James I estimated that there were 20 female witches to every one male. Secondly, they were poor. The vast majority came from the lowest social class and were often beggars. Thirdly, they were old. They were often widows relying on charity, whether public or private. Fourthly, they had got involved in a row with their neighbour, often another woman. Most witches were known to those who accused them of witchcraft. They had argued and the so-called witch had hurled abuse at the neighbour. Probably she had gone on to lose her temper and appeal to

A print showing the 'swimming' of Mary Sutton in a mill dam in 1612. 'If she swim, you may build upon it that she is a witch.' The black sow has caused the wheel to break off the cart and the sacks of corn to fall to the ground.

the Devil to attack her assailant. Finally, most came from small communities, villages rather than towns. The phrase 'neighbour from Hell' might sum up a modern parallel with some unintended ironies.

If most accusations of witchcraft were a result of local disputes it follows that there would be few examples of co-ordinated campaigns against witches. In fact, there were only two major incidents of organised witch-finding in this period. The lesser of these two incidents occurred in 1612, in Pendle, Lancashire. On this occasion, ten witches were executed along with one of their associates in Yorkshire, one suffered the lesser punishment of prison and the pillory and five were acquitted. The greater incident occurred in Essex and East Anglia in 1645–47 as a result of the efforts of Matthew Hopkins, a professional witch-finder, and his team of two. For a fee, he detected witches and extracted their confessions. He turned local grievances into more formal complaints under the terms of the 1604 act. There is some evidence that he used torture in the form of sleep deprivation to do so. The incomplete court records suggest that, as a result of his efforts, 250 'witches' were brought to trial, of whom around 100 were executed. This means that the activities of this one man in one part of the country in just three years accounted for some 15 per cent of all the executions for witchcraft in England over a period of 100 years. After these few years, Hopkins's efforts, in the words of one historian, 'just petered out'.

Hopkins's work is the only example we have of someone going on a professional witch-hunt. Virtually all the other prosecutions scattered across the years from 1570 to 1670 were brought by local people, usually on the lesser charge of wrongdoing rather than the graver charge of compact with the Devil.

What were the main characteristics of someone labelled as a witch?

Why were people persecuted for witchcraft?

The subject is a fascinating one and the evidence incomplete and often unreliable. This has resulted in the development of a range of theories, some influenced by the social science of anthropology.

The fact that the majority of those who were executed for witchcraft were women indicates to some that the witch-hunt was a terrible manifestation of the patriarchalism that was such a feature of the early modern period. In other words, as recently argued by Marianne Hester, witchcraft accusations were one aspect of the male domination of women. Feminist historians have shown that *Malleus maleficarum* is misogynistic. They assert that this treatise was responsible for shaping educated clerical beliefs about witchcraft. However, it is possible to doubt the influence of the *Malleus maleficarum*. Although read by intellectuals from the time it first appeared, there was no English translation of the *Malleus* until modern times. 'By contrast', observes Keith Thomas, 'it was issued sixteen times in Germany before 1700 and eleven times in France.' Moreover, detailed research has revealed that women were not only victims of the witch-hunt but also acted as searchers for the Devil's mark, witnesses and complainants. One of Matthew Hopkins's assistants was a woman. Male domination might help explain the persecution of witches but it is not a complete explanation.

How might the untypical Hopkins-led persecution of 1645–47 be explained? The date might be significant, the end of the First Civil War, a time of dislocation and confusion. The witch-finders were able to employ methods of torture such as sleep deprivation because the war's end resulted in the temporary absence of the circuit judges from the Essex **assizes**. Why, however, in Essex and East Anglia? The region was prosperous and Puritan. By comparison, Pendle in 1612 was poorer and more pro-Catholic.

The **assizes** were courts held twice yearly in each county by royal judges, travelling in pairs, on circuit around England.

Identifying either religious or economic causation common to the two regions seems impossible. Local factors must be significant, factors about which we have insufficient knowledge almost 400 years later.

A more convincing explanation for the majority of the prosecutions of witches seems to have been disputes over charity. In an age before the creation of the welfare state, the old and the poor, significant numbers of whom were women who had outlived their husbands, were forced to rely upon their neighbours for alms. The identification and subsequent prosecution of a witch would invariably take place after the victim had refused to give charity that had been asked for, the old woman muttering a curse as she left empty handed. In 1602 a 14-year-old maid, called Mary Glover, reported to her mistress that Elizabeth Jackson, the old charwoman who had recently been begging at the door, reprimanded her and wished 'an evil death to light upon her'. When the girl died shortly afterwards, Elizabeth Jackson was prosecuted for witchcraft, her 'prophesying threatenings, ever taking effect, which Judge Anderson observed as a notable property of a witch'. Witches helped to explain otherwise inexplicable misfortunes – the death of a child, the failure of a crop, an inability to produce children or just general bad luck. If a person believed himself to be bewitched, then it was generally held that a cure could best be provided by the execution of the witch. This social explanation seems to be especially compelling when it is realised that growth in population, prices and commercial values – all significant features of this period – acted collectively to threaten the traditional community.

Religious changes also contribute to the explanation of the persecution of witches. As Keith Thomas has pointed out, a consequence of the Reformation was the prohibition of what he calls 'protective ecclesiastical magic', for example the power of exorcism. The removal of such practices meant that people felt more vulnerable to *maleficium*. If they could no longer turn to the priest for help, then they would turn to the courts.

However, these various factors do not fully account for the growth of witch-hunts. For instance, the economic problems which some see as a cause of the witch-hunts were not wholly peculiar to that time. Why were there no witch-hunts in similar periods of economic distress? It is not possible to demonstrate any correlation between upheavals such as plague and famine and the numbers charged with being a witch. Moreover, some other countries that had witnessed a Reformation had also persecuted witches before that event. 'No Puritan writer on witchcraft ever did more than echo the opinions of the Catholic demonologists,' observes Keith Thomas. Indeed, it is difficult to detect any significant variation in the prosecutions for witchcraft in Catholic and Protestant states, although, after 1600, some Catholic states were more vigorous in prosecuting witches.

Some argue that the changing attitudes and values of the political nation help explain the growth in persecutions. Intellectuals and theologians seem increasingly to have absorbed continental theories of Devil-worship, in particular the belief that a witch was a person who had made a pact with the Devil. If proved, this was technically sufficient to secure the charge of felony, even if there was no evidence of the alleged witch having harmed anyone. As Christina Larner has argued, in *Enemies of God: the witch-hunt in Scotland*

(1981), the new type of Christianity promoted by the Reformation introduced 'validating ideologies'. In other words, an essential purpose of the church was henceforth to extol the virtues of moral purity. It follows that any campaign for moral purity identifies, perhaps even creates, deviants. In the sixteenth and seventeenth centuries, these deviants came to be known as witches. The new religious values help to explain the growing concern with witchcraft.

When those values changed yet again, the concern with witchcraft declined. Religious enthusiasm gave way to rational scepticism in the late seventeenth and early eighteenth centuries. The new beliefs, linked with the scientific revolution, accepted that there were natural causes for such things as the Devil's mark and human illness. Thus, the number of prosecutions declined. The last person hanged for witchcraft in England was Alice Molland in 1685; the last to be condemned but later reprieved was Jane Wenham in 1712. Eventually, in 1736, parliament repealed the act of 1604. The legal witch-hunt was over. There is evidence, however, that occasional, illegal witch-hunts continued in some rural areas until well into the nineteenth century. Even in the twenty-first century, the belief in and practice of witchcraft have not entirely disappeared.

> Identify, in brief terms, the main arguments that have been put forward to explain the persecution of witches.

Summary question

1 (a) Identify and explain any *two* characteristics of someone charged with being a witch.

   (b) Compare the importance of at least *three* explanations for the persecution of witches.

Document study
The English Civil Wars, 1637–49

Focus questions

◆ Why did civil war break out in 1642?

◆ Why did the royalists lose the First Civil War?

◆ Why was the king executed in 1649?

Introduction

The following documents have been selected to help you to answer the three focus questions set out above. These are the questions most often asked by historians of the 1640s. Since some of them expect you to display a contextual knowledge of the 1640s, you should refer to Chapters 6, 7 and 8.

How to deal with questions on sources

Questions dealing with usefulness

When dealing with this type of question, make certain that your response deals directly with the notion of 'useful for what', usually identified in the question. Look closely at the content of the source. Does it offer any purely factual material, such as names, dates or statistics? Is this information supported or contradicted by the details given in other sources? Examine carefully the written style of the source. It may well be biased and, if so, it will probably be useful *as an example* of a piece of invective or propaganda produced at the time. On an even more basic level, it will be useful *as an example* of its type, such as a formal parliamentary record or a radical pamphlet.

Questions dealing with reliability

The first thing to do is to examine the provenance of the source and identify who has produced it and decide whom it has been written for. If written for a private audience, then the historian will assess its reliability in a different way than if it has been written for a public audience. Is the author a contemporary of the events he is describing? If so, where is it likely that he obtained his information? Does the author himself give any clues? Is it possible to deduce, from the style and the words chosen, the reason why the author has bothered to record his views? Is the account balanced? Look out, in particular, for individual words or phrases which illustrate a biased opinion. Finally, check the content with the other sources in the collection. Does the detail of this source support or contradict that of the others?

Questions requesting a comparison of sources

In this type of question, you do not have to evaluate the sources, simply compare. Ensure that your answer covers all parts of the question. An answer that compares should illustrate differences as well as similarities.

Questions which ask for consideration of an historical problem in relation to the sources and your own knowledge

This type of question demands that you refer to both the sources and your own knowledge. You are probably best advised to blend these two elements *as your answer develops* rather than to have two effectively separate parts to your response. When dealing with the sources, you should provide some quotations or line references. However, a quotation on its own will not win marks. You must demonstrate that you have understood the meaning of the quotation – usually by paraphrasing – and then relate it to the question. Quite often, this style of question will ask you to form a judgement, indicated by the phrase 'how far'. A useful device to indicate you have recognised this request is to employ in your answer the phrases 'on the one hand' . . . 'on the other hand'.

Why did civil war break out in 1642?

Religious differences, 1640–42

1.1 The Root and Branch Petition presented to parliament on 11 December 1640

The Humble Petition of many of His Majesty's subjects in and about the City of London, and several counties of the Kingdom . . . That whereas the government of archbishops and lord bishops . . . have proved prejudicial and very dangerous both to the Church and Commonwealth . . . We therefore most humbly pray, and beseech this honourable assembly . . . that the said government, with all its dependencies, roots and branches, may be abolished.

Source: John Rushworth (ed.), *Historical collections of printed passages of state*, 8 vols., 1659–1701, vol. 5, London, pp. 93–96

1.2 Charles I's speech to parliament, 25 January 1641

Now I must clearly tell you, that I make a great difference between reformation and alteration of government . . . If you shall show me that bishops have some temporal authority inconvenient to the state . . . I shall not be unwilling to persuade them to lay it down; yet, by this, you must not understand that I can consent for the taking away of their voice in parliament, which they have so anciently enjoyed, under so many of my predecessors, even before the Conquest, and ever since; and which I conceive I am bound to maintain, as one of the fundamental institutions of this kingdom.

Source: *Lords' Journals*, vol. 4, p. 142

1.3 Lord Digby's speech to the House of Commons concerning bishops, 9 February 1641

I do not think that any people hath ever been more provoked than the generality of England of late years by the insolence and exorbitances of the prelates . . . Do not be led on by passion to popular and vulgar errors . . . We all agree upon this: that a reformation of Church government is most necessary . . . but [not] to strike at the root, to attempt a total alteration . . . I am confident that instead of every bishop we put down in a diocese, we shall set up a Pope in every parish.

Source: John Rushworth (ed.), *Historical collections*, abridged edn, 6 vols., 1708, vol. 3, pp. 356–59

1.4 The Remonstrance and Petition of the county of Huntingdon, 1642

Divers petitions from several counties and other places within this kingdom . . . have been carried about to most places against the present form and frame of church government . . . and the hands of many persons of ordinary quality solicited to the same with pretence to be presented to this honourable assembly in parliament . . . which we conceive and fear not so much to aim at the taking away of the said innovations, and reformation of abuses, as tending to an absolute innovation of church government. Out of a tender and zealous regard hereunto, we have thought it our duty not only to disavow all such petitions, but also to manifest our public affections and desires to continue the form of divine service, and common prayers, and the present government of the Church.

Source: *Thomason Tracts*, E. 131/5

Document-study questions

1 Use 1.2 and your own knowledge to explain the reference to 'the taking away of their [the bishops'] voice in parliament, which they have so anciently enjoyed'.

2 How useful is 1.3. for the historian researching the extent of religious division in the period immediately prior to the Civil Wars?

3 How do 1.1 and 1.4 differ? How might these differences be reconciled?

4 Using the sources and your own knowledge, assess to what extent the English Civil Wars broke out because of arguments over religion.

A crisis of counsel?

1.5 Clarendon's *History of the Rebellion and Civil Wars in England*, written 1646–74

Edward Hyde, made earl of Clarendon in 1661, was an MP in the Long Parliament. He emerged as a constitutional royalist and joined the king at York in 1642. He was a leading councillor to Charles I during the First Civil War and rose to prominence as adviser to Charles II during the latter's exile in the 1650s. He wrote his history over a number of years from 1646 to 1674.

If [before the meeting of the Long Parliament] Mr Pym, Mr Hampden and Mr Holles had then been preferred with Mr St John, before they were desperately embarked in their desperate designs, and had innocence enough about them to trust the King and be trusted by him, having yet contracted no personal animosities against him, it is very possible that they might either have been made instruments to have done good service, or at least been restrained from endeavouring to subvert the royal building, for supporting whereof they were placed as principal pillars.

Source: Edward Hyde, *The history of the Rebellion and Civil Wars in England*, W. Dunn Macray (ed.), vol. 6, Oxford, 1888, pp. 222–23

1.6 Parliament's Nineteen Propositions, 24 June 1641

Third Head, about his Majesty's Counsels: That his Majesty may be humbly petitioned to remove such evil counsellors against whom there shall be any just exceptions, and for the committing of his own business, and the affairs of the kingdom, to such counsellors and officers as the parliament may have cause to confide in.

Source: *Lords' Journals*, vol. 4, pp. 285–87

1.7 The Grand Remonstrance, presented to the king on 1 December 1641

The duty which we owe to your Majesty and our country cannot but make us very sensible and apprehensive, that the multiplicity, sharpness and malignity of those evils under which we have now many years suffered, are fomented and cherished by a corrupt and ill-affected party, who amongst others their mischievous devices for the alteration of religion and government, have sought by many false scandals and imputations, cunningly insinuated and dispersed amongst the people to blemish and disgrace our proceedings in this Parliament, and to get themselves a party and a faction amongst your subjects, for the better strengthening themselves in their wicked courses, and hindering those provisions and remedies which might, by the wisdom of your Majesty and counsel of Parliament, be opposed against them.

Source: John Rushworth (ed.), *Historical collections of printed passages of state*, 8 vols., 1659–1701, vol. 4, London, pp. 437–51

[Those responsible for all our troubles are] a faction of Malignant, Schismatical and Ambitious persons, whose design is, and always has been, to alter the frame of the Government both of Church and State, and to subject both King and People to their own lawless arbitrary power and Government.

Source: From R. Ellis, *People, power and politics: was there a mid seventeenth-century English Revolution? – a study in depth*, Cheltenham, 1992, p. 103

Document-study questions

1 Use 1.5 and your own knowledge to explain why it was important for the king to obtain the support of Pym, Hampden, Holles and St John.
2 How useful is 1.7 for the historian researching into the methods of opposition MPs in the Long Parliament?
3 Paying particular attention to the language employed, compare the explanations given in 1.7 and 1.8 for the country's 'evils' and 'arbitrary government'.
4 'The inevitable consequence of each side believing that the other was being driven forward by a "malignant faction"'. Referring to all the sources and your own knowledge, assess to what extent this is a sufficient explanation for the outbreak of the English Civil Wars.

The attempt on the Five Members, 4 January 1642

1.9 Clarendon's *History of the Rebellion and Civil Wars in England*, written 1646–74

The next day in the afternoon, the King, attended only by his own guard and some few gentlemen . . . came to the House of Commons. Commanding all his attendants to wait at the door and to give offence to no man, himself with his nephew, the prince elector [Charles Louis], went into the House, to the great amazement of all. The Speaker left the chair [whereupon] the King went into it and told the House 'he was sorry for that occasion of coming to them . . . He declared to them that no King of England had ever been, or should be, more careful to maintain their privileges than he would be, but that in cases of treason no man had privilege and therefore he came to see if any of those persons whom he had accused were there . . . Looking then about, and asking the Speaker whether they were in the House, and he making no answer, [Charles] said he perceived the birds were all flown.

Source: Edward Hyde, *The history of the Rebellion and Civil Wars in England*, W. Dunn Macray (ed.), vol. 6, Oxford, 1888, pp. 222–23

1.10 From the journal of an MP, Sir Simonds D'Ewes

About three of the clock we had notice that his Majesty was coming . . . to Westminster with a great company of armed men, but it proved otherwise in the issue [event] that there were only some of the officers who served in His Majesty's late army and some other loose persons to the number of about some 400 . . . His Majesty came into the House with Charles, Prince Elector Palatine. [His Majesty] went to the Speaker's chair on the left hand of it, coming up close by the place where I sat . . . He first spoke to the Speaker, saying 'Mr Speaker, I must for a time make bold with your chair' . . . When he asked for Mr Pym . . . there followed a general silence . . . [Therefore] he pressed the Speaker to tell him [but the Speaker said] that he could neither see nor speak but by the Command of the House.

Source: W. H. Coate (ed.), *The journal of Sir Simonds D'Ewes*, Yale, 1970

1.11 A declaration of the House of Commons touching a late breach of their privileges, 17 January 1642

The next day His Majesty in his royal person came to the House, attended with a great multitude of men armed in a warlike manner with halberds, swords and pistols, who came up to the very door of the House . . . and His Majesty, having placed himself in the Speaker's chair demanded of them the persons of the said members to be delivered unto him, which is a high breach of the rights and privileges of Parliament, and inconsistent with the liberties and freedoms thereof . . . Many soldiers, Papists and others, to the number of about five hundred, came with his Majesty . . . armed with swords, pistols and other weapons, and divers of them pressed to the door of the House, thrust away the door-keepers . . . some holding up their pistols ready cocked near the said door and saying 'I am a good marksman; I can hit right, I warrant you' . . . If the word had been given, they should have fallen upon the House of Commons and [would] have cut all their throats.

Source: John Rushworth (ed.), *Historical collections of printed passages of state*, 8 vols., 1659–1701, vol. 4, London, p. 484

Document-study questions

1 Using 1.9, explain why the king's appearance in the Commons met with 'the great amazement of all'.
2 Who was Charles referring to in 1.9 when he spoke of the 'birds' having flown and what were the circumstances of their flight?
3 How reliable is 1.11 as an account of the events of 4 January 1642?
4 Identify the similarities and differences between the two accounts of the king's attempt on the Five Members in 1.9 and 1.10. How might a historian reconcile their differences?

Difficulties in the First Civil War

2.1 From the notebook of Sir John Oglander, a committed royalist, who was arrested for his attachment to the king's cause in 1643 and 1651

Truly all, or the greatest part, of the King's commanders were so debased by drinking, whoring and swearing that no man could expect God's blessing on their actions . . . They imputed their failures to want of money . . . not caring how they burdened the country, thereby making of their friends their enemies . . . [On the other hand] the Parliament took all course possible to civilise their soldiers and therefore chose preaching commanders, no drunkards or swearers, kept their army in outward show very civil [and] duly paid them to avoid discontenting the country.

Source: Francis Bamford (ed.), *A royalist's notebook: the commonplace book of Sir John Oglander, Kt*, London, 1936, pp. 117–19

2.2 An account by Bulstrode Whitelocke, a parliamentarian lawyer, of some royalist troops staying at his home in November 1642

There was no insolence or outrage usually committed by common soldiers on a reputed enemy which was omitted by these brutish fellows at my house. They had their whores with them, they spent and consumed a £200 load of corn and hay, littered their horses with sheaves of good wheat and gave them all sorts of corn in the straw. Divers writing[s] of consequence and books which were left in my study, some of them they tore in pieces, others were burnt to light their tobacco, and some they carried away with them.

Source: Bulstrode Whitelocke, *Memorials of English affairs*, 1853, vol. 1, pp. 188–89

2.3 Clarendon's *History of the Rebellion and Civil Wars in England*, written 1646–74

[In Cheshire, the parliamentarians] had no other . . . difficulties to struggle with than what proceeded from their enemy, being always supplied with money to pay their soldiers; . . . whereby it was in their power not to grieve and oppress the people; and thereby the common people were more devoted to them . . . Whereas they who were entrusted to govern the King's affairs had intolerable difficulties to pass through, being to raise men without money . . . and to keep them together without pay; so that the country was both to feed and clothe the soldier, which quickly inclined them to remember only the burden and forget the quarrel.

Source: Edward Hyde, *The history of the Rebellion and Civil Wars in England*, W. Dunn Macray (ed.), vol. 6, Oxford, 1888, pp. 222–23

2.4 A description of the sacking of Birmingham by a royalist force in 1643

That night few or none of [the royalists] went to bed, but stayed up revelling, robbing and tyrannising over poor afrighted women and prisoners, drinking [until] drunk [and even] drinking healths to Prince Rupert's dog.

Source: *Thomason Tracts*, E. 100/8

Document-study questions

1 Read 2.1. Explain how parliament was able to mobilise resources so that its army was 'duly paid'.
2 How reliable do you consider 2.2 as an account of the nature of the fighting during the First Civil War?
3 To what extent, and in what ways, is document 2.1's account of the difficulties of the king supported by 2.3?
4 Using all the sources and your own knowledge assess how far the judgement on royalist soldiers that they were 'poorly led, badly paid and ill-disciplined' explains why Charles I lost the First Civil War.

The background to the formation of the New Model Army

2.5 *The memoirs of the life of Colonel Hutchinson* by his wife, Lucy Hutchinson, written 1664–71

Colonel Hutchinson signed the king's death warrant.

It was too apparent how much the whole parliament cause had been often hazarded, how many opportunities of finishing the war had been overslipped by the Earl of Essex's army; and it was believed that he himself with his commanders rather endeavoured to become arbiters of war and peace than conquerors for the parliament . . . Wherefore those in the parliament who were grieved at the prejudice of the public interest . . . devised to new model the army, and an ordinance was made called the Self-Denying Ordinance whereby all members of parliament of both Houses were discharged of their commands in the army. Cromwell had a particular exception, when Essex, Manchester and Denbigh surrendered their commissions and Sir Thomas Fairfax was made general of the new modelled army.

Source: Lucy Hutchinson, *The memoirs of the life of Colonel Hutchinson*, London, 1995, p. 162

2.6 Clarendon's *History of the Rebellion and Civil Wars in England*, written 1646–74

[The Independents] had been long unsatisfied with the Earl of Essex, and he was as much with them; both being more solicitous to suppress the other than to destroy the King. [The Independents] bore the loss and dishonour

[Essex] sustained in Cornwall very well, and would have been glad [should] both he and his army had been quite cut off, instead of being dissolved, for all of his officers and soldiers were corrupted in their affections towards them and desired nothing but peace.

Source: Edward Hyde, *The history of the Rebellion and Civil Wars in England*, W. Dunn Macray (ed.), vol. 6, Oxford, 1888, pp. 222–23

2.7 Cromwell's deposition to the House of Commons, 25 November 1644

The said Earl [Manchester] hath always been indisposed and backward to engagements, and the ending of the war by the sword . . . Since the taking of York, as if the Parliament had now advantage fully enough, he hath declined whatsoever tended to farther advantage upon the enemy. [He] hath neglected and studiously shifted off opportunities to that purpose, as if he thought the King too low, and the Parliament too high.

Source: *The letters and speeches of Oliver Cromwell*, vol. 1, introduced by Thomas Carlyle, 1904, pp. 184–85

2.8 Deposition of Sir Arthur Haselrig, 6 December 1644

Haselrig was one of the Five Members impeached by Charles I in 1642. He emerged as a leading Independent after the passing of the Self-Denying Ordinance.

The Earl of Manchester said that . . . 'if we beat the King ninety and nine times yet he is King still, and so will his posterity be after him, but if the King beat us once we shall be all hanged, and our posterity made slaves'. These were the very words as this examinant remembers . . . Whereupon Lieutenant-General Cromwell replied, 'My Lord, if this be so, why did we take up arms at first? This is against fighting hereafter; if so, let us make peace, be it never so base.'

Source: Public Record Office, SP 16/503/56. IX

Document-study questions

1 Explain the reference to the Self-Denying Ordinance in 2.5.
2 How useful is 2.5 as evidence about the origins and nature of the New Model Army?
3 To what extent is Cromwell's opinion as expressed in 2.7 supported by 2.8?
4 How far is it true that parliament's commanders were 'indisposed and backward to engagements' during the First Civil War and to what extent does this explain parliament's failure to win the First Civil War before 1645? Refer to all the sources and your own knowledge in explaining your answer.

The background to the trial of the king

3.1 An account of the army prayer meeting at Windsor, 28–30 April 1648

This was written 11 years after the event by the Agitator William Allen.

Lieutenant General Cromwell did press very earnestly on all there present to a thorough consideration of our actions as an army . . . [The Lord] did direct our steps, and presently we were led and helped to a clear agreement amongst ourselves, not any dissenting, that it was our duty of our day, with the forces we had, to go out and fight against those potent enemies, which that year [1648] in all places appeared against us, with a humble confidence in the name of the Lord only, that we should destroy them; also enabling us then after seriously seeking his face, to come to a very clear and joint resolution . . . that it was our duty, if ever the Lord brought us back again in peace, to call Charles Stuart, that man of blood, to an account for that blood he had shed, and mischief he had done to his utmost against the Lord's cause and people in these poor nations.

Source: William Allen, 'A faithful memorial of that remarkable meeting of many officers of the army', London, 1659, reprinted in John Baron Somers, *A collection of scarce and valuable tracts*, Sir Walter Scott (ed.), vol. 6, London, 1811

3.2 Cromwell to the speaker of the Commons, 20 August 1648

Surely, Sir, this [the Battle of Preston] is nothing but the hand of God, and wherever anything in this world is exalted, or exalts itself, God will pull it down, for this is the day wherein He alone will be exalted. It is not fit for me to give advice . . . more than to pray you, and all that acknowledge God, that they would exalt Him, and not hate His people . . . for whom even Kings are reproved; and that you would take courage to do the work of the Lord, in fulfilling the end of your magistracy.

Source: *The letters and speeches of Oliver Cromwell*, vol. 1, introduced by Thomas Carlyle, 1904

3.3 From a record by Clement Walker, a Presbyterian MP, of a speech to the House of Commons by Cromwell on 26 December 1648

When it was first moved in the House of Commons to proceed capitally against the King, Cromwell stood up and told them, that if any man moved this upon design, he should think him the greatest traitor in the world, but since providence and necessity had cast them upon it, he should pray God to bless their counsels.

Source: W. C. Abbott, *The writings and speeches of Oliver Cromwell*, 4 vols., Oxford, 1937–49, 1988, p. 719

3.4 *The memoirs of the life of Colonel Hutchinson* by his wife, Lucy Hutchinson, written 1664–71

The Presbyterian party [was] so prevalent there [in parliament] that the victories obtained by the army displeased them, and so hot they grew in the zeal of their faction that they from thenceforth resolved and endeavoured to close with the common enemy [the king], that they might thereby compass the destruction of their Independent antagonists . . . The commissioners that [had] treated with the King had been cajoled and biased with promises of great honours and offices to every one of them, and so they brought back their treaty [Newport] to be confirmed by the Houses.

Source: Lucy Hutchinson, *The memoirs of the life of Colonel Hutchinson*, London, 1995, pp. 230–31

Document-study questions

1   Explain the reference in 3.1 to 'those potent enemies, which in that year [1648] in all places appeared against us'.
2   How reliable do you consider 3.3 as evidence of Cromwell's attitude towards the killing of the king?
3   Compare the impressions of Cromwell given by 3.2 and 3.3.
4   'Providence and necessity had cast them upon it.' Use all the sources and your own knowledge to assess to what extent this remark offers an explanation for the army's support for the killing of the king.

The trial of Charles I

3.5 Bishop Gilbert Burnet, *History of my own times*, published in 1723

Burnet lived from 1643 to 1715.

Cromwell was in some suspense about the King's death. Ireton was the man who drove it on and found out Cook and Bradshaw, two local lawyers to manage it. [Ireton] . . . stuck at nothing that might have turned England into a Commonwealth. Fairfax was much distracted in mind, and changed purpose every day. The Presbyterians and the body of the City were utterly against it, and were everywhere fasting and praying for the King's preservation.

Source: Bishop Gilbert Burnet, *History of my own times*, Thomas Stackhouse (abridged), London, 1906, pp.14–15

3.6 Clarendon's *History of the Rebellion and Civil Wars in England*, written 1646–74

The next day [28 January 1649] after the horrid sentence was pronounced [Ingoldsby went to the Painted Chamber where he saw Cromwell and others] assembled to sign the warrant for his Majesty's death. As soon as Cromwell's eyes were upon him, he ran to him, and taking him by the hand, drew him by force to the table and said . . . he should now sign that paper as well as they, which [Ingoldsby], seeing what it was, refused with great passion . . . But Cromwell and others held him by violence; and Cromwell, with a loud laughter, taking his hand in his, and putting the pen between his fingers, with his own hand wrote Richard Ingoldsby, he making all the resistance he could.

Source: Edward Hyde, *The history of the Rebellion and Civil Wars in England*, W. Dunn Macray (ed.), vol. 6, Oxford, 1888, pp. 222–23

3.7 *The memoirs of the life of Colonel Hutchinson* by his wife, Lucy Hutchinson

Some [of the regicides] afterwards, for excuse, belied themselves, and said they were under the awe of the army, and overpersuaded by Cromwell and the like. But it is certain that all men herein were left to their free liberty of acting, neither persuaded nor compelled . . . In 1660, when it came to Ingoldsby's turn, he, with many tears, professed his repentance for that murder, and told a false tale how Cromwell held his hand and forced him to subscribe the sentence.

Source: Lucy Hutchinson, *The memoirs of the life of Colonel Hutchinson*, London, 1995, p. 279

Document-study questions

1. Look carefully at the illustration on page 114. What evidence is there that the artist was a supporter of Charles I?
2. How reliable do you consider 3.6 for the historian researching the role of Cromwell during the trial of Charles I?
3. Compare the accounts of the trial offered by 3.6 and 3.7.
4. 'An action for which there seems to have been generally very little support'. Use all the sources and your own knowledge to discuss this remark about the execution of Charles I.

Further reading

Document collections

J. P. Kenyon, *The Stuart constitution, documents and commentary*, Cambridge, 2nd edn, 1986, offers an extremely comprehensive selection of documents and excellent commentary. Students may like to supplement their reading of Kenyon with the following, all of which provide a useful collection of extracts and observations: Irene Carrier (ed.), *James VI and I, king of Great Britain*, Cambridge, 1998; Christopher W. Daniels and John Morrill (eds), *Charles I*, Cambridge, 1988; and David. L. Smith (ed.), *Oliver Cromwell: politics and religion in the English Revolution, 1640–1658*, Cambridge, 1991. Those wishing to get a real feel for the period ought to read some Clarendon, probably most readily available in Richard Ollard (ed.), *Clarendon and his friends*, Oxford, 1988.

General surveys

Angela Anderson, *The Civil Wars 1640–1649*, London, 1995, provides a very good, readable account of the Civil War period and offers helpful note-making sections and essay questions; G. E. Aylmer, *Rebellion or revolution?: England 1640–1660*, Oxford, 1986, gives an excellent overview of the period; Toby Barnard, *The English republic*, Harlow, 1982, is a splendid, short account of the 1650s; Katherine Brice, *The early Stuarts 1603–1640*, London, 1994, is a useful account of these years; Barry Coward, *The Stuart age*, London, 2nd edn, 1994, provides an excellent survey of the period; Derek Hirst, *England in conflict 1603–1660: kingdom, community, commonwealth*, London, 1999, is a challenging book which should, perhaps, only be read once the student is broadly familiar with events; Ann Hughes, *The causes of the English Civil War*, London, 2nd edn, 1998, considers events in their European context and comments upon the current state of the historiographical debate; Ronald Hutton, *The British republic, 1649–1660*, London, 1990, is a very useful survey of events at national and local level in the 1650s; D. E. Kennedy, *The English Revolution 1642–1649*, London, 2000, contains a detailed summary of this period and its historiography; Roger Lockyer, *The early Stuarts: a political history of England 1603–1642*, Harlow, 1989, provides a thorough overview of the period; Michael Lynch, *The Interregnum 1649–1660*, London, 1994, provides a helpful outline on the Interregnum along with useful summary diagrams, note-making aids and essay questions; and John Morrill, *Revolt in the provinces: the people of England and the tragedies of war 1630–1648*, Harlow, 2nd edn, 1999, is a famous book, rather broader in content than its title suggests, and is required reading. Ivan Roots, *The Great Rebellion, 1642–1660*, Stroud, 2nd edn, 1995, is essential reading for any student of this period; Alan G. R. Smith, *The emergence of a nation state: the commonwealth of England 1529–1660*, Harlow, 1984, is a book offering short chapters which provide first-rate summaries of all the main topics; and David L. Smith, *A history of the modern British Isles 1603–1707*, Oxford, 1998, is well organised and readable. It offers chronologies and a compendium of pertinent information and is an indispensable handbook for all students of this period.

Specialist texts

Conrad Russell, *The causes of the English Civil War*, Oxford, 1990, is demanding but full of exciting observations and insights and offers an excellent character sketch of Charles I; and John Morrill (ed.), *The nature of the English Revolution*, Harlow, 1993, is a collection of essays which range over a number of topics.

Biographies

Christopher Durston, *James I*, London, 1993, provides a very useful, concise introduction to the reign of James I; S. J. Houston, *James I*, Harlow, 2nd edn, 1995 gives a helpful summary of the reign of James I. Angela Anderson, *Charles I*, Harlow, 1998, is an excellent, accessible introduction to Charles I. Christopher Durston, *Charles I*, London, 1998, provides a very useful, concise survey of the reign of Charles I; Charles Carlton, *Charles I, the personal monarch*, London, 2nd edn, 1995, is extremely readable and rewarding – in it Carlton offers a psychological analysis of his subject; Michael B. Young, *Charles I*, London, 1997, is essential reading for those who wish to master the historiographical debates of the period; Kevin Sharpe, *The personal rule of Charles I*, London, 1992, is a very long book, highly favourable towards its subject. It contains a large amount of very useful detail. Hugh Kearney, *Strafford in Ireland, 1633–1641: a study in absolutism*, Cambridge, 2nd edn, 1989, is a difficult and detailed book but essential reading for anyone really wanting to come to terms with the career of Wentworth; C. V. Wedgwood, *Thomas Wentworth, first Earl of Strafford*, London, 1961, is a highly readable account and offers a full, if a little dated, view of Wentworth; Peter Gaunt, *Oliver Cromwell*, Oxford, 1996, provides one of the best recent studies; and Barry Coward, *Oliver Cromwell*, Harlow, 1991, is organised thematically, argues a case throughout and is a book to read once the chronology of events has been mastered. Christopher Hill, *God's Englishman*, Harmondsworth, 1972, provides a thought-provoking thematic analysis of Cromwell; Charles Carlton, *William Laud*, London, 1987, is a very good survey of Laud's life and times; and Roger Lockyer, *Buckingham: the life and political career of George Villiers, first duke of Buckingham 1592–1628*, Harlow, 1981, is a very favourable and detailed interpretation of Buckingham.

Books on religion

Andrew Foster, *The Church of England, 1570–1640*, Harlow, 1994, provides a very helpful summary of the key features and problems of the early modern church; Alan

Dures, *English Catholicism 1558–1642*, Harlow, 1983, is an excellent summary of Catholicism in the early modern period; R. J. Acheson, *Radical Puritans in England, 1550–1660*, Harlow, 1990 provides an accessible overview of Puritans; and Kenneth Fincham (ed.), *The early Stuart church, 1603–1642*, London, 1993, offers a range of challenging essays on religion in the early part of the seventeenth century.

Books on the Civil Wars and radicals

Martyn Bennet, *The English Civil War*, Harlow, 1999, offers an excellent, short summary of the Civil War period; and J. P. Kenyon, *The Civil Wars of England*, London, 1989, is a very good narrative account that combines political and military events; J. P. Kenyon and J. Ohlmeyer (eds.), *The Civil Wars: a military history of England, Scotland and Ireland*, Oxford, 1998, provides a comprehensive review of all military aspects of the Civil Wars. The chapters are accessible, with lots of detail and excellent illustrations. Graham E. Seel, *The English Wars and republic, 1637–1660*, London, 1999, provides a useful collection of document questions and offers answers to typical examination questions; F. D. Dow, *Radicalism in the English Revolution 1640–1660*, Oxford, 1985, is perhaps rather difficult but well organised and contains lots of useful detail; H. N. Brailsford, *The Levellers and the English Revolution*, London, 2nd edn, 1983, is a long and detailed book but important reading for those wanting more information on the Levellers; and Christopher Hill, *The world turned upside down*, Harmondsworth, 1972, is a book that breaks new ground discussing the appearance of the radical groups of the 1640s and 1650s in Marxist terms.

Foreign policy

J. R. Jones, *Britain and Europe in the seventeenth century*, London, 1966, gives a short and lucid introduction to foreign policy in the period; and Timothy Venning, *Cromwellian foreign policy*, London, 1995, while full of detail, is a difficult book but will service well those who need to know more about Cromwell's foreign policy.

Social history

Keith Wrightson, *English society 1580–1680*, London, 1982, provides a readable survey of the main events and developments; J. A. Sharpe, *Early modern England: social history 1550–1760*, London, 1987, provides a helpful introduction to the social history of this period; and J. A. Sharpe, *Instruments of darkness: witchcraft in England 1550–1750*, Harmondsworth, 1997, offers an explanation for the witchcraft phenomenon in England. Keith Thomas, *Religion and the decline of magic*, Harmondsworth, 1991, is a fascinating book, carefully argued with lots of examples.

Index

coal mining industry, 172, 173
Cockayne project (1614), 18
Commission of Array, 81, 89, 101
common law, 6, 41
Commonwealthsmen, 137, 142, 144, 147;
 and the Restoration, 157, 160
communion, and Laud's anti-Calvinist
 reforms, 57, 60, 61
Convention parliament, 159, 162
Cottington, Sir Francis, 54, 64
Council of the Marches, 77
Council of the North, 50, 77
council of state, 123–4, 130
county committees, 112
Court of High Commission, 77
Coventry, Lord, 49
Cranfield (lord treasurer), 15, 17–18
Cromwell, Henry, 147
Cromwell, Oliver, 2, 91, 190; and the
 Agreement of the People, 110, 111; aim
 of 'just and righteous reformation', 135;
 aim to 'heal and settle' the nation,
 134–5, 144–5, 146, 162; assessment of,
 143–6; death of, 143; and the
 dissolution of the Rump Parliament,
 123, 128–9, 144; and the Fifth
 Monarchists, 144–5; and the First Civil
 War, 91, 93, 97, 98, 99, 104; foreign
 policy, 137, 148–55, 165; and the
 Humble Petition and Advice (1657),
 133, 140–3, 163, 164; in Ireland, 125;
 and Lilburne, 188; and the Nominated
 Assembly, 129, 130, 131; and
 parliament, 144; and Penruddock's
 Rising (1655), 137, 155; and Pride's
 Purge, 119; and the Protectorate,
 133–46, 164–5; and the Restoration,
 161; and the Scots, 108, 125–6; and the
 trial and execution of Charles I, 114,
 116, 117, 120, 209, 210, 211
Cromwell, Richard, 133, 141, 146–7, 157,
 164, 165
the crown: and the government of
 England, 4, 5, 6; and parliament, 9,
 10–11

decimation tax, 138–9, 144, 164
Denmark, and Cromwell's foreign policy,
 151
Desborough, John, 137
Diggers, 124, 189
Digges, Sir Dudley, 41
divine right of kings, 11, 35
Dunbar, battle of (1650), 125, 129, 143,
 158
Dunkirk, English acquisition of (1658),
 152, 153, 154

East India Company, 174, 181
economic change, 168–77; agriculture,
 171; and the Civil Wars, 169, 175–7;
 industry, 172–3, 181; population,

169–70, 171; prices, 169, 170, 171;
 recessions, 4, 14, 50, 51; trade and
 empire, 173–4
Edgehill, battle of (1642), 34, 91, 92, 100
ejectors, 135, 136, 143
Eliot, Sir John, 35, 43, 49
Elizabeth (daughter of James I), 26, 28, 34,
 36, 38, 44
Elizabeth I, Queen, 2–4; death of, 2, 7;
 Essex and the revolt in Ireland, 3–4;
 foreign policy, 149; and parliament, 4, 9,
 10, 11; and religion, 2, 6–7, 19, 20; and
 royal finances, 16, 17, 45; and war with
 Spain, 3, 16, 24, 44, 45
episcopalianism, and the Church of
 England, 7, 21
Erastian Presbytery, 107
Essex, Robert Devereux, 2nd Earl, 2, 4,
 17
Essex, Robert Devereux, 3rd Earl, 90–1,
 92, 93, 94–5, 97, 99, 102
Etcetera Oath, 62, 73
Everard, William, 189

Fairfax, Ferdinando, 93
Fairfax, Sir Thomas, 93, 95, 99, 101, 120,
 124, 164, 187
Felton, John, 38, 39, 42
Feoffes of Impropriations, 60–1
Ferdinand, Holy Roman Emperor, 28
Fifth Monarchists, 123, 124, 136, 144–5,
 157, 191
finances, see royal finances; taxation
First Civil War, 88–104; allies and
 divisions, 95–8; armies, 90–1; and the
 Clubmen movement, 101;
 consequences of the, 104; geographical
 divisions in the, 89–90, 101, 102; and
 Ireland, 95–6, 101; and the Nineteen
 Propositions (1642), 81–2, 91–2, 107,
 203; and the persecution of witches,
 197; reasons for royalist loss, 100–4,
 206–7; royalist ascendancy (1642–43),
 92–5; and the Self-Denying Ordinance,
 99, 101–2, 104, 120, 208; and social
 class, 83, 90
Five Knights' Case, 41–2
Fleetwood, Charles, 141, 147, 158
Form of Apology and Satisfaction (1604),
 12
Fortescue, Sir John, 12
Foulis, Sir David, 55
Fox, George, 190
France: and James I's foreign policy, 25;
 Charles I and war with, 36, 37–40, 41,
 44, 49; and Cromwell's foreign policy,
 149, 150, 151, 152, 153, 154–5; and the
 First Civil War in England, 101
franchise, and the agreement of the
 people, 110–11
Frederick V, elector of the Palatinate and
 king of Bohemia, 26, 28, 34, 36, 38, 40

Geddes, Jenny, 69
gentry: and the Civil War, 83, 89, 90; and
 London, 182–3; and the Protectorate,
 136, 141
Goodwin, Sir Francis, 12
government of England, 4–6, 181–2
The Graces, 53
Grand Remonstrance (1641), 79, 84, 85,
 87, 203
Great Contract (1610), 13, 19
Gunpowder Plot (1605), 13, 22, 30

Habeas corpus, 41
Habsburg empire, anti-Habsburg alliance
 in Europe, 25, 28, 38
Hale commission on law reform, 127, 128
Hamilton, James, 1st duke of Hamilton,
 78, 112
Hampden, John, 55–6, 80
Hampton Court Conference (1604), 20–2
Harrison, Thomas, 123, 129–30, 136
Haselrig, Sir Arthur, 90, 97, 137, 142, 147,
 157, 158, 160, 208
Heads of the Proposals (1647), 110, 119,
 129
Henrietta Maria, Queen, 33, 34; and
 Catholicism, 37, 38, 64; and the Civil
 War, 34, 81, 101; and factional politics,
 49; and the Histriomastix, 65; marriage
 to Charles I, 30, 34, 37, 38; and
 Wentworth, 72
Henry VIII, King, 6, 7, 19
Histriomastix, 65
Holland, Henry Rich, Lord, 48, 49
Holles, Denzil, 43, 49, 80, 97, 109
honours, sale of, 18
Hopton, Sir Ralph, 94
Huguenots, and Charles I's war with
 France, 38
Humble Petition and Advice (1657), 133,
 140–3, 145, 163, 164
Hyde, Edward, see Clarendon, Edward
 Hyde, earl of

iconoclasm, 79
impropriated tithes, 131
industry, 172–3, 181
Instrument of Government, 133–4, 136,
 137, 141, 143, 144
Interregnum, see Protectorate; Rump
 Parliament
Ireland: and the Civil War, 95–6, 101, 119;
 Essex and the revolt in, 3–4; native Irish,
 53; New English, 52, 53; and the
 Nominated Assembly (1653), 130; Old
 English, 52–3; opposition to the Rump
 Parliament, 123, 125; policy of
 Thorough in, 51–4; Rebellion (1641),
 53–4, 79, 80, 81, 85, 86; and the
 Restoration, 158, 161; Ulster, 4, 53, 79
Ireton, Henry, 110–11, 116–17, 119–20,
 125, 129

Italy, and Cromwell's foreign policy, 151

James VI and I, King, 8–31; accession of, 2, 7, 8; achievements of, 30–1; attempts to create a political union between England and Scotland, 12–13; *Book of sports*, 24; and the civil war, 2, 8–9; death of, 30; and divine right of kings, 11; foreign policy, 24–30, 44, 149; and London, 182–3; and parliament, 5, 9, 10, 11–15, 44; and the Privy Council, 4; religious policies, 19–24, 46, 58; and the royal court, 182; and royal finances, 13, 14, 15–19, 31, 46; on witches, 195
Jesuits, 38, 59
Jews, and Cromwell, 145, 150
justices of the peace, 5, 6, 182, 194; and the Books of Orders, 50, 51
Juxon, William, 54, 61

Lambert, John, 129, 133, 140, 158, 159
land seizure, and the Civil Wars, 175
Lansdown, battle of (1643), 94
Laud, William, archbishop of Canterbury, 2, 42, 49, 50; character and beliefs, 58–9; impeachment and execution of, 76; and religious policies, 56–65; and the Scottish Covenanters, 70
law: and government, 6; London and the legal system, 182; and parliament, 10
Levellers, 62, 185, 186–9, 190; and the Agreement of the People (1647), 110–11, 116, 124, 144, 187–8; and the Rump Parliament, 123, 124–5, 188
Lilburne, John, 62, 124, 136, 185, 186–7, 188
local government, 5, 6; and the Books of Orders, 50
Lockyer, Robert, 124
London, 80, 81, 178–83; and the agricultural economy, 171; as an *entrepôt*, 174, 179; and the Civil Wars, 87, 92, 94–5, 100, 102, 178–9; fashionable, 182–3; finance, 181; and government, 181–2; growth of, 179–80; and the Protectorate, 136, 155; and the Restoration, 159, 160, 178, 179; and the royal court, 182; trade and industry, 180–1; and Wentworth's government of Ireland, 53
Long Parliament, 55, 64, 74, 75–82, 86, 187; attempt on the Five Members (1642), 80, 204–5; and the Civil Wars, 88–9, 91–2, 96–8, 99, 101–4, 175; failure to negotiate a settlement with Charles I (1646–47), 111–12; and the New Model Army, 107; and the Newcastle Propositions (1646), 106–7, 110, 111; and the Nineteen Propositions (1642), 81–2, 91, 107, 203; Political Independents, 97, 104, 108, 109, 118; Political Presbyterians, 43, 97, 104, 108,

109, 113; and press censorship, 186; purge by the army, 109, 113, 115–17, 123, 128; restoration of the (1660), 159; and the Scots, 96, 102, 107; and the Solemn League and Covenant (1643), 96, 102, 107, 160; and the trial and execution of Charles I, 114
lords lieutenant and deputy lieutenants, 5, 51, 71; and the Militia Ordinance, 81
Lords Spiritual and Temporal, 9–10
Louis XIII, king of France, 25, 30, 37, 38
Ludlow, Edward, 137
Lunsford, Colonel, 80

Magna Carta, 6, 186
Manchester, earl of, 90, 97, 98, 99, 104, 185, 208
Marston Moor, battle of (1644), 34, 93, 97, 98, 102
Marten, Henry, 115, 137
Marxist historians, and the Civil Wars, 83, 89, 90
Maurice, Prince, 94
Maximilian of Bavaria, 28
Michell, Sir Francis, 14
middle classes, and the Civil Wars, 83
Millenary Petition (1603), 20
Mompesson, Sir Giles, 14
Monck, George, 149, 158, 159, 160, 161, 163
Montagu, Richard, 23, 40–1, 42
Montagu, Walter, 64–5
Montrose, Marquis of, 97, 99
Mugggletonians, 124, 191

Nantwich, battle of (1644), 95, 158
Naseby, battle of (1645), 34, 91, 99, 100, 102, 104
Navigation Act (1651), 127, 153, 154, 174
navy, 25, 36, 93, 102, 155
Nayler, James, 139–40, 142, 145
Neile, Richard, archbishop of York, 56, 57, 58, 62
Netherlands: Anglo-Dutch wars, 127, 149–51, 158, 173; and Cromwell's foreign policy, 152–3, 154, 155; and Spain, 3, 25, 37, 40, 44; and trade, 173, 174
Newbury, First Battle of (1643), 91, 95
Newbury, Second Battle of (1644), 98, 99
Newcastle Propositions (1646), 106–7, 110, 111
Newcastle, William Cavendish, marquis of, 93, 97, 101
Nominated Assembly (1653), 129–31, 134, 136, 143, 144

Oath of Engagement (1650), 124, 136
ordinances, and the Civil War, 89
Overbury, Sir Thomas, 16
Overton, Richard, 124, 144, 187
Oxford, Treaty of (1643), 92

the Palatinate, 14, 28–30, 36, 38, 44
parliament, 9–11; Cavalier, 162, 164; and Charles I's foreign wars, 25, 33, 36, 39; and Charles I's Personal Rule, 48–9; Charles I's relations with, 32–3, 40–3; Convention, 159, 162; elections to, 10, 11–15; and Elizabeth I, 4, 9, 10, 11; and the government of England, 4, 5, 6; House of Commons, 5, 9, 10, 13; House of Lords, 5, 9, 13, 123; and impeachment, 14; Irish, 52; and James I, 5, 9, 10, 11–15, 44; and London, 181; MPs, 6, 10, 13, 14, 19; and the Nominated Assembly (1653), 129–31; and the Protectorate (1653–59), 133–4, 136–7, 139–43, 144, 147; and the Restoration, 161, 162; and the right to free speech, 10–11, 14; and royal finances, 10, 13, 14, 18; Short Parliament (1640), 62, 64, 72, 73, 75; *see also* Long Parliament; Rump Parliament
patronage, royal, 6
Penruddock's Rising (1655), 137, 155, 161
Petition of Right (1628), 35, 39, 41, 42, 45, 78, 101
Pilgrim Fathers, 173
Poor Laws, 4
population growth, 169–70, 171, 179
Portugal, England's trade treaty with, 151, 154
post-revisionist historians, on the origins of the Civil Wars, 83–4
predestination, doctrine of, 23–4, 56–7, 119
Presbyterians, 7, 185; and James I, 19, 20–1; Political, 43, 97, 104, 108, 109, 113; Scots call for Presbyterian Church in England, 107, 108, 111, 112, 119, 125
presses, freedom of the, 185–6
Pride's Purge (1648), 113, 119, 123, 128, 159
privy council, 4, 5, 34–5, 36, 62; and the Books of Orders, 50, 51
Protectorate (1653–59), 132–47, 163–5; and the army, 163, 164–5; collapse of the, 147, 156, 160, 165; and finance, 136, 142–3, 165; and the Instrument of Government, 133–4, 136, 137, 141, 144; and the Nayler case, 139–40; and parliament, 133–4, 136–7, 139–43, 144, 147; and religious policies, 134, 135, 136, 138–9, 140, 142, 143, 145, 146, 164; and Richard Cromwell, 146–7; rule by the major-generals (1655–56), 133, 137–9, 140, 143, 164; rule by ordinance (1654), 135–6; *see also* Cromwell, Oliver
Protestant Union, 25–6
Protestantism: and Cromwell's foreign policy, 152–4; and Cromwell's religious reforms, 136; and the Elizabethan Church of England, 6, 7; Huguenots and Charles I's war with France, 38;